GREAT
BRITONS

Other Books by Anglotopia

101 Budget Britain Travel Tips
101 London Travel Tips
101 UK Culture Tips
Anglotopia's Guide to British Slang

Other Books by Jonathan Thomas
Adventures in Anglotopia
Anglophile Vignettes

GREAT BRITONS
TOP 50 GREATEST BRITS WHO EVER LIVED

By
Anglotopia

Copyright © 2021 by Anglotopia LLC
Cover Design by Anglotopia LLC
Cover Copyright © 2021 Anglotopia LLC

Anglotopia LLC supports the right to free expression and the value of copyright. The purpose of copyright is to encourage writers and artists to produce the creative works that enrich our culture.

The scanning, uploading, and distribution of this book without permission is a theft of the author's intellectual property. If you would like permission to use material from the book (other than for review purposes), please contact info@anglotopia.net. Thank you for your support of the author's rights.

Anglotopia Press - An Imprint of Anglotopia LLC
www.anglotopia.press

Printed in the United States of America

1st US Edition: May 2021

Published by Anglotopia Press, an imprint of Anglotopia LLC.
The Anglotopia Press Name and Logo is a trademark of Anglotopia LLC.

Print Book interior design by Jonathan Thomas, all fonts used with license.

All location photographs © Jonathan Thomas
All photos and art used in this book are in the public domain in the USA except for the following licensed images:
Image of Grace Darling © Colin Waters / Alamy Stock Photo
Image of J.R.R Tolkien © INTERFOTO / Alamy Stock Photo
Image of John Constable © V&A Images / Alamy Stock Photo
Image of Octavia Hill © Album / Alamy Stock Photo
Image of Agatha Christie © World History Archive / Alamy Stock Photo
Image of Elizabeth Fry © National Portrait Gallery, London
Image of Mary Seacole © National Portrait Gallery, London
Image of Nancy Mitford © National Portrait Gallery, London
Image of Beatrix Potter © National Portrait Gallery, London

ISBN: 978-1-955273-02-2

TABLE OF CONTENTS

INTRODUCTION..1
HORATIO NELSON..5
ADA LOVELACE..11
THOMAS HARDY...17
NELL GWYN...23
CECIL RHODES..29
AGATHA CHRISTIE...35
1ST DUKE OF WELLINGTON.............................41
BEATRIX POTTER...47
ALAN TURING...53
BESS OF HARDWICK..59
BENJAMIN DISRAELI.......................................65
BOADICEA..71
CAPTAIN JAMES COOK....................................79
ELIZABETH FRY...85
ISAAC NEWTON..91
EMMELINE PANKHURST..................................97
ISAMBARD KINGDOM BRUNEL......................103
JANE AUSTEN..109
WILLIAM BLIGH...115
FLORENCE NIGHTINGALE..............................121
OLIVER CROMWELL.......................................127
GEORGIANA CAVENDISH..............................133
ROBERT WALPOLE..141
CARTIMANDUA...147
SIR WALTER RALEIGH...................................153
EMMA HAMILTON..159
1ST DUKE OF MARLBOROUGH......................167

MARY SEACOLE...173
WILLIAM WILBERFORCE....................................179
THE BRONTE SISTERS..187
CHARLES DARWIN...193
OCTAVIA HILL...199
JOHN CONSTABLE...205
LADY MONTAGU..211
CHARLES DICKENS..217
GRACE DARLING...223
ROBBIE BURNS...231
MRS BEETON..237
SIR CHRISTOPHER WREN......................................243
MARIE STOPES...249
RUDYARD KIPLING..255
NANCY ASTOR...261
WILLIAM SHAKESPEARE...267
NANCY MITFORD..273
WILLIAM TYNDALE..279
VIRGINIA WOOLF..285
JMW TURNER..293
MARGARET THATCHER...299
JRR TOLKIEN..307
PRINCESS DIANA...315
SIR WINSTON CHURCHILL...................................323

INTRODUCTION

Twenty-five women. Twenty-five men. The greatest Britons who ever lived. A few years ago we started a regular column on Anglotopia called 'Great Britons' which was intended to be an ongoing survey of great British historical figures. Almost 100 articles later, it's been one of my favorite columns to publish. We've learned so much over the years, and learned about so many historical figures you don't simply learn about in a typical American education.

We have sought to create the first guide to great British historical figures, evenly split down the middle between women and men. There are so many important women in British history, that have been brushed out of it. But we're rediscovering more every day. You may not have heard of a lot of the women we've chosen to include, and that's a good thing! As a corollary to that, whittling down to just 25 men was a challenge as well. I've leaned on my own interests in historical figures and who are widely considered the 'most' important. So, Tolkien is in while someone like William Morris is out (though he was fascinating!).

Growing up in America and going through an American centered education, I encountered a major problem as an Anglophile watching hours and house of British TV: I was actually very unfamiliar with a lot of the major figures in British history. I simply didn't know who they were or why they were important. I knew all about the Founding Fathers, our great and terrible presidents, and other American historical figures. But very little about who Nelson was or why he was 'great.' This book is for those like me, who simply didn't know who a lot of these people are.

First, I need to define by what we mean by 'great.' It does not mean they were amazing people, it means they had a massive or important impact on British history. Their greatness derives from their importance. So, you will find less then savory characters in here - like Cecil Rhodes or Margaret Thatcher or Cromwell (and their terribleness is up for lots of debate which is not what this book is). When we initially published these articles on our website, the internet commentariat had a lot of problems with this definition of 'great.' Hopefully it makes more sense in book form.

Who is a 'Briton' exactly? Technically, anyone born on the Island of Great Britain. But this is too narrow of a definition because several great figures in British history were born in Ireland or in Britain's empire. So, we define a 'Briton' as anyone who played a role in overall British history - locally and globally. An example is someone like Mary Seacole, a Jamaican who was a very important person in British nursing history. Someone like Nancy Astor is an American, but she became part of the British aristocracy and was the first woman to take her seat in the British Parliament - a major achievement.

With the exception of a few Roman era queens, we've deliberately left monarchs out of this selection. They'll get their own book like this in time. There are a few important aristocrats, however, and we've included Princess Diana for the effect she had on Britain when she lived and when she died.

Undoubtedly some will think that we've left someone important out. And they would be right. It's not possible to include all of them in a reasonably sized book. But it is possible to give a good overview of the most important ones so you know what they're talking about when watching British TV documentaries or British films. If you want an encyclopedia of all the most important Brits who have ever lived, I highly recommend browsing the Oxford Dictionary of National Biography (heavily consulted in the writing of these articles I might add!).

We have made every effort to ensure that each article is accurate and true. Each article was fact-checked before they were initially published and now before publication in this book. Inevitably some mistakes will slip through. We're not trained historians, we're enthusiastic amateurs with a passion for British history, doing our best to break down these great figures for a non-British audience. We have done our best.

Each entry is meant to be a survey of the person's life and impact. They're not exhaustive biographies but rather springboards for your own further research - which is why each one has a list of books, dramas, documentaries etc where you can learn a lot more.

Finally, Sir Winston Churchill is included as a 'bonus' chapter, considered by most historians to be the 'Greatest Briton' who ever lived, he deserves the last spot in the book along with an extended essay that covers his whole complicated and fascinating life.

What you will find in this book are people who have shaped Britain into what it is today, whether you think that is a good thing or not. We've tried to stick to the facts, and keep our opinions to a minimum. We hope you enjoy this guide to the Greatest Britons.

HORATIO NELSON
The Victor of the Battle of Trafalgar

Key Facts

- Born 29 September 1758. Died 21 October 1805
- Established British naval power around the world
- Defeated Napoleon at the Battle of Trafalgar, where he died

In the 18th century the European powers were caught up in a global power struggle for control of the various foreign territories they had seized during the earlier era of exploration. Shipping, territorial claims, the control of the various trade routes and trading agreements were vital national interests for each country. The main method of settling the inevitable disputes that arose was by engaging in naval battles, seizing each other's ships and fighting for the control of coastal trading ports. Although bloody, these battles in distant seas had an heroic quality that had not yet been diminished by the mass slaughter characteristic of the wars of the 19th century and which culminated in the two world wars of the 20th.

Horatio Nelson was born into this environment on 29 September 1758, in Norfolk, England. He was one of 11 children of a clergyman. In an age before adolescence had been invented, by the age of 12 he had entered naval service on a boat commanded by his mother's brother – Captain Maurice Suckling. He was quickly made a midshipman and began to be trained as an officer. He also quickly discovered that he suffered from seasickness, which persisted throughout his career but never seemed to hamper his success.

When he heard of a naval expedition to the Arctic he persuaded his uncle to transfer him to it and the expedition came close enough to the North Pole for Nelson to try without success to kill a polar bear to give the skin to his father.

Shortly after turning fifteen Nelson went on the HMS Seahorse to the East Indies (today's India and south-east Asia) to assist the East India Company enforce its trading monopoly with India and keep out the French. His ship spent most of its time protecting trading vessels, but he also experienced his first battle in February 1775. A short time later he contracted malaria and was sent back to England.

Following his recovery his now highly-placed uncle found him a position as an acting lieutenant on a ship sailing to the British colony of Gibraltar. After he became a full lieutenant – his uncle made up one-third of the examination board – in 1777 he sailed to the Caribbean. France had by this time allied with the American Revolutionaries, so most of Nelson's time was spent catching and looting French trading and naval vessels, a practice referred to as 'taking prizes'.

After a peace was made Nelson returned to England and indeed spent some time in France, where he attempted to learn the language.

Britain had a number of restrictive laws on trading – the Navigation Acts – designed to give her an advantage which the new independent Americans did not like. So by 1784 Nelson was back in the Caribbean. After seizing several American ships under dubious circumstances he was for a time in danger of being imprisoned for illegal seizure, but the courts ruled in his favor.

At this time too he met Frances "Fanny" Nisbet, a young widow from the British island of Nevis. They quickly married and when Nelson returned to England Fanny followed him.

Nelson spent the next five years on half-pay without a commission, which frustrated him very much. However in 1793 Britain was again at war with Revolutionary France on the side of the remaining royalists and moderates. His fleet sailed to Toulon, on the French Mediterranean to protect the royalists who still held the city. After several encounters the British fleet captured the French island of Corsica with the intention of using it as a naval base.

However during the final battle for the town of Calvi Nelson had an eye damaged when a shell hit a sand-bag and exploded sand and gravel in his face. It is widely believed that Nelson wore an eye-patch to cover the wound, but in fact this is not true – he had no need for a patch as the eye appeared normal – only the vision had gone.

In 1795 the French attempted to re-capture Corsica, but following an extend battle near the Italian city of Genoa, the French lost several ships

Emma Hamilton

and were forced to retreat. But by the end of 1796 a new alliance between Genoa and France made the British activities in the Mediterranean impossible so Nelson and his fleet set off for England. However they had not even left the Mediterranean when they began fighting with Spanish ships, capturing several.

This war with Spain continued for several years during which Nelson developed a reputation not only for bravery bordering on bravado, but for disobeying orders that he did not agree with. Nelson became a successful leader because he treated those under him with respect and concern, compared with the standard way of leading sailors at that time, which was mostly floggings and executions. As his career developed he gained more and more loyalty and even love from his officers and crews.

In 1797 at the battle of Santa Cruz de Tenerife, Nelson was shot and his right arm was amputated. While being helped to board his ship he refused, saying "Let me alone, I have got my legs left and one arm!"

In 1798, Napoleon Bonaparte, on his way to becoming Emperor of France, took an army to Egypt and seized the country in the name of France. This outraged the British and Nelson was sent to Egypt to confront Napoleon's fleet. At the Battle of the Nile he destroyed or seized a good part on Napoleon's fleet and stranded his army, who were forced

The Battle of Trafalgar by JMW Turner

to battle their way north. France's ambitions were severely set back. However Napoleon was seen by the people as a hero and this enabled him to seize power in France.

Nelson went to recover from the campaign at the home of an old friend, Sir William Hamilton the British consul in Naples. Hamilton was married to woman half his age, the model Emma Hart, now Emma Hamilton. Emma was an artist's model and had been mistress to several powerful Englishmen. She had briefly met Nelson some years earlier but this time he and her, both very famous for very different reasons, began a passionate affair. Sir William did not seem to object. This quite public affair became notorious but Nelson's fame was so great it did not damage his military reputation. Nelson needed constant praise and Emma seems to have provided that.

Over the next few years Nelson and the British fleets continued to fight the French as Napoleon rose to greater power as Emperor. In 1805 Nelson took an opportunity presented him to attack the French fleet in the Mediterranean and the Battle of Trafalgar began. This decisive battle destroyed the French fleet and Napoleon's power, but in the battle Nelson was shot and died on the 21st of October, 1805.

He received a hero's funeral back in England – Emma was not allowed to attend.

His Legacy

Nelson was a complex person. A brilliant leader and battle strategist, he was independent and often defiant of authority. He was also brave to the point of bravado and desperate for approval – which he certainly received. Some of his military actions, including the execution of prisoners, might today be seen as war-crimes, yet he was considerate, kind and interested in those under him.

His affair with Emma Thompson and the abandonment of his wife was considered a scandal, but the public and many powerful people adored him.

Today he is remembered as a British hero, who defeated Napoleon and established Britain as the supreme naval power.

Sites to Visit

- There are numerous statues of Nelson, the most famous being Nelson's Column, in Trafalgar Square, London. Others can be seen in Portsmouth, Edinburgh, Liverpool, Birmingham, Glasgow, Montreal (Canada) and Bridgetown (Barbados).
- Museums to visit are: Royal Navy Museum, Portsmouth; National Maritime Museum, Greenwich; Lloyd's Building, Lime Street, London.

Further Research

- A TV mini-series called "I Remember Nelson" (1982)
- A film "Emma Hamilton"(Le calde notti di Lady Hamilton) (1968)
- A documentary "Leaders in Battle: Lord Admiral Horatio Nelson"(2007)
- Of the numerous biographies the best are "Nelson: a Dream of Glory" and "Nelson: The Sword of Albion", both by John Sugden

ADA LOVELACE
Mathematician

Key Facts

- Born 1815, died 1852
- Mathematician and early developer, with Charles Babbage, of proto-computers
- Rare female scientist of the 19th century
- Daughter of the poet Lord Byron

Ada Lovelace was a daughter of the poet Lord Bryon and a member of the British aristocracy. She was part of the group of British amateur scientists that made significant discoveries in the 19th century and laid the foundations for modern science. She worked with Charles Babbage on the development of his Difference Engine and Analytical Engine, precursors of the computer. She was the first person to appreciate and describe the advantages of a machine capable of accurately and quickly carrying out any manner of calculation, no matter how complex.

The poet Lord Byron had a reputation for amorality and agnosticism. So, it is not surprising that although he had numerous children with several partners, he only had one legitimate child, which to his disappointment was a girl. Bryon had married her mother, Anne Isabella Milbanke, the previous year, following a protracted pursuit of this strict and moral woman by the dissolute Byron. Ada was born on the 10th of December 1815.

The marriage was brief, and early in 1816, Anne left their home in London with Ada, largely to avoid the erratic and unpredictable behavior of her husband. Under the law at that time, Byron could have taken full custody of the baby, but he made no attempt to do so. A few days after signing the official separation he left England for good. He died in 1824 fighting in the Greek War of Independence against the Ottoman Empire.

If Byron had little interest in Ada, her mother had hardly any more. Although she strove to keep custody, Ada was brought up by her maternal grandmother, Judith, Lady Milbanke. Around the time of her father's death, Ada suffered from a bout of severe headaches that caused temporary blindness, followed by a case of measles for which she was treated with a year in bed. Not surprisingly, she needed crutches when she was finally allowed up.

To avoid the contamination of poetry, Ada's mother had her daughter taught mathematics and music. The mathematics came in handy when Ada was 12, and she decided she wanted to fly. She set about the project in a thorough fashion. She researched the structure of birds to determine the appropriate wingspan, researched various choices for materials and wrote a book – Flyology – with her own plates and summaries of her findings. It doesn't seem that she used her research in any actual flight attempts.

Scientific pursuits, such as botany and geology, were acceptable pastimes for men of wealth in the elite circles that Ada moved in. It was in those circles that she met Charles Babbage, Professor of Mathematics at Cambridge, when she was 17. They entered into a long and voluminous correspondence on mathematics, logic and all things scientific. She also was acquainted with other natural philosophers, including Michael Faraday and Charles Wheatstone, as well as lesser-known 'gentleman scientists' such as Andrew Crosse and Sir David Brewster. At that time, science as a profession was not known. Indeed the term 'scientist' was not coined until 1836.

Following her separation, Ada's mother had devoted herself to exposing Byron's amoral behaviors and she also had friends watching Ada during her teenage years for signs of morally deviant behavior. The first signs did indeed seem to emerge, when Ada, just 18, had an affair with one of her tutors and then tried to elope with him. She was returned to her mother by the tutor's relatives.

Two years later Ada was married to William King, a noble ten years older than her, which was not uncommon in those times. King inherited his family title in 1838, and the couple became the Earl and Countess of Lovelace. The marriage did not, however, free Ada from the grip of her mother, who continued to control and direct the family, meeting little resistance from King. They lived at Ockham Park, in Surrey, where Ada had three children, two boys, and a girl, between 1836 and 1839. Her oldest son was called Byron.

Keen to prevent the moral decay of the children, Ada's mother appointed William Benjamin Carpenter as a tutor for them. Carpenter was a doctor and zoologist who is remembered mostly for devising the concept of the unconscious, but with Ada, he fell in love and tried to begin an affair with her, an offer she rejected. Generally, her relationships with men were not within the appropriate framework for her class and time, and there were numerous rumors of affairs. A notable one was with John Crosse, the son of the amateur scientist in electricity, Andrew Crosse. The exact nature and extent of their relationship is unknown since John destroyed all their correspondence after Ada died.

Throughout her life, she continued to study mathematics. This was a period in the history of science when many things that are considered unscientific were blended with real research. A hundred years earlier, Newton had been an alchemist as well as a mathematician and Ada was also a believer in metaphysics, which treated speculation as a valid tool for making scientific discoveries. Fashionable beliefs with no factual basis were widespread, and Ada believed in phrenology – reading character from the bumps on the head – and animal magnetism, the precursor of hypnosis, which was believed to offer cures for a variety of diseases. She was interested in developing mathematical models for the workings of the brain and in the then mysterious properties of electricity and magnetism.

Her most famous work was with Charles Babbage. He had designed a Difference Engine, which was effectively an early mechanical computer to produce error-free tables for astronomy, navigation, and mathematics. Although funded by the British government, the engine was never completed, but Babbage put forward plans for a new machine, the Analytical Engine. This was based on work by an Italian mathematician, Luigi Federico Menebrea. Since his work was in French, Babbage recruited Ada Lovelace to translate it, and between 1842 and 1843 she did so, adding a set of Notes of her own analysis. In these Notes, she was the first person to realize the potential for a general-purpose calculating device that could work with any function, regardless of how general and complex – a pretty good definition of a computer. She also dismissed the idea that a calculator could ever constitute an artificial intelligence.

Like other early mathematicians, she also turned her skills to the problems of probability and gambling. In 1851 she formed a secret syndicate with a group of men-friends, but her calculations failed, and she ended up owing the syndicate thousands of pounds, which she had to reveal to her husband in order to settle the debts.

In 1852, she died of a combination of uterine cancer and the bloodletting, which was standard medical practice at the time. During her last months, she was entirely controlled by her mother, who excluded all her friends and worked on her moral salvation. She succeeded in having

Ada repent her sins and also became the executor of her estate.

After a mysterious confession to her husband, he abandoned her, and she died without him or her friends on the 27th of November, 1852. She was the same age as her father had been when he died – just 36.

Her Legacy

Despite the exclusion of women from the roots of science in the 19th century, Ada Lovelace showed that there was no inherent inferiority in the mathematical abilities of women. With skills equal to the greatest men of the time she was the first to see the potential for the development of computers from the primitive beginnings she witnessed. The place of women in science is today assured, but that would have been a more difficult achievement without Ada Lovelace demonstrating their abilities and capacity to make an equal contribution.

Sites to Visit

- Ada Lovelace is buried in the Byron family vault, alongside most of the Byron family, in the churchyard of the Church of St. Mary Magdalene in Hucknall, Nottinghamshire.
- Ockham Park, in Ockham, near Guilford, Surrey, is today a listed building, partly converted into flats. It has been extensively re-modeled since Ada lived there.
- Worthy Manor, known in her time as Ashley Combe, was another Lovelace property in Porlock Weir, Somerset. Although the house was destroyed during World War II, ruins and the grounds can still be visited. Babbage and Lovelace would walk on the Philosopher's Terrace, discussing mathematics.
- Babbage never completed his Difference Engine, but in the 1980's one was built using his original plans and technology that would have been available to him at the time. It worked perfectly. A second model can be seen at the Computer History Museum, Mountain View, California.

Further Research

There are several biographies available, including:

- Ada's Algorithm: How Lord Byron's Daughter Ada Lovelace Launched the Digital Age, by James Essinger (2012)
- The Thrilling Adventures of Lovelace and Babbage: The (Mostly) True Story of the First Computer, by Sydney Padua (2015)
- Ada Lovelace: The Computer Wizard of Victorian England, by Lucy Lethbridge (2001)
- Ada, the Enchantress of Numbers: Poetical Science, by Dr. Betty Alexandra Toole (2010)
- The Bride of Science: Romance, Reason, and Byron's Daughter, by Benjamin Woolley (2015)

THOMAS HARDY
Writer and Romantic

Key Facts

- Born 1840, died 1928
- Lived around Dorchester his whole life
- Wrote some of the greatest novels of the 19th century
- Acclaimed during his life as a literary giant

Thomas Hardy was a 19th-century novelist who led a relatively uneventful life and produced 14 novels, 40 short stories, 900 poems and two plays. He lived almost his whole life in a small area around the Dorset town of Dorchester and set all his novels in that area. His works caused some outrage for their outspoken depiction of ordinary lives.

"Kiss me, Hardy!" legend tells us, were the dying words of Horatio Nelson at the Battle of Trafalgar in 1805. Sir Thomas Masterman Hardy was Nelson's aide and close friend, who died himself in 1839. A year later his cousin, Thomas Hardy, was born on the 2nd of June, 1840, in the small village of Bockhampton, a little west of Dorchester, the county capital of Dorset.

The Hardy family had noble roots on the Isle of Jersey, going back to the 15th century, but by the time young Thomas was born the family fortunes had fallen. His father, another Thomas, was a respectable local builder and stone-mason and although his mother came from a poor family and had been a maid and cook, she was self-educated, loved to read and taught Thomas to read and write before he was four. In this close-knit rural community, she knew many local stories and histories which she taught her son. When not working his father was a keen violinist and

chorister, so between his two parents, Thomas had a strong literary and artistic upbringing for such humble beginnings.

He at first attended the local school run by the Church of England, but when he was ten, his mother transferred him to the rival system of the time, the so-called 'British' not attached to the Church of England. Hardy remained there until he was 16. He was a 'bookish' child who preferred solitude and his books, and he became very proficient in Greek, Latin, and French. He read mostly romances, such as the novels of Sir Walter Scott and Alexander Dumas.

Since his family was poor, further education at a University was out of the question for Hardy, so like many other children of those times, he was apprenticed to learn a trade. In 1856 he went to work in Dorchester for a local architect who specialized in church restoration, John Hicks. He spent four years with Hicks, during which time he traveled extensively in the surrounding area, learning more of the local towns and unconsciously collecting material that would later re-appear in his works. He also met a local schoolteacher and poet called William Barnes, who is believed to have been the inspiration for Hardy to become a writer.

Like many a boy with his head in a book, Hardy was unsuccessful at courtship, and after rejection by what seems to have been at least his third frustrated attempt at romance, he set out for London to perhaps make a fresh start. He became assistant architect to Arthur Blomfield, another church restorer and had a successful if brief career. He won prizes from both the Royal Institute of British Architects and the Architectural Association and worked on several projects with Blomfield.

London was a revelation for Hardy. He attended a lecture by Charles Dickens as well as plays and operas at London's famous theaters. He visited museums and art galleries. He was influenced by important writers of the time, from John Stuart Mills to Charles Darwin and John Ruskin and he abandoned the established Church. He also developed an interest in poetry, reading Swinburne and Browning but his own efforts were rejected for publication. His first published work seems to have been a short humorous piece called How I Built Myself a House, which was published in 1865 and won Hardy a prize.

Although he earnestly studied literary technique, he seems to have remained an outsider in London society and after five years there and no literary career in sight he returned to Dorchester in 1867 and resumed working for John Hicks. Back home his love-life took a turn for the better and although himself by now 28; he developed a passionate relationship with a sixteen-year-old cousin, Tryphena Sparks. Relationships with cousins have always been perfectly acceptable in English society, and the age difference was by no means unusual for the period. Hardy also began a novel, strongly influenced by the psychological style of George Meredith, who was exploring the emotions of his characters and using his own life for inspiration. Hardy's first novel was called The Poor Man and the Lady, a reflection of Hardy's own struggles with social class and his sense of loss in the decline of his family fortunes.

He submitted the novel to the publishing company Macmillan, who rejected it but urged him to continue writing. He did, and eventually had several of his early novels published in serial form, rather in the manner of Dickens' works. His fourth novel, Far from the Madding Crowd, published in 1874, finally brought him recognition and some financial success and was followed in 1878 by The Return of the Native, another success.

His career now more assured and his fortunes looking up, in 1874 Hardy married Emma Lavinia Gifford, the daughter-in-law of the rector of a church in Cornwall Hardy had been restoring and who had become an important encouragement of his writing. In 1885, now successful in every way, Hardy designed and had built a villa house he called Max Gate outside Dorchester, where Hardy would spend the rest of his life.

Following the publication of his last two (and greatest) novels, Tess of the d'Urbervilles in 1891 and Jude the Obscure in 1895, there was a public outcry about their 'immoral' plots, a view apparently also shared by his wife. Shocked and hurt Hardy announced his withdrawal from novel writing and returned to his first love, poetry. His career as a poet proved as successful as his career as a novelist and his Napoleonic epic The Dynasts proved a great success. He received honorary degrees from Cambridge and the University of Aberdeen, the Order of Merit from King George V and a gold medal from the Royal Society of Literature.

In 1912 Emma suddenly died and although the marriage had long before become unhappy, Hardy was struck with grief. However, his grief seems to have been short-lived, for in 1914 he married his niece, Florence Dugdale, almost 40 years his junior. One of the causes of his estrangement from Emma had been his interest in young literary women and Florence was also of that type. However, his introverted habits and solitude in his study seem to have quickly soured things for Florence. She did, however, help him with his autobiography, which was completed shortly before his death. She also gave away or sold most of his manuscripts and destroyed many of his papers.

Max Gate became a place of pilgrimage for younger writers and Hardy continued to have an active involvement in literary society although rarely leaving his home. He even managed one last infatuation with a young actress when he was eighty. Becoming more reclusive and now staying entirely at Max Gate, Hardy died on the 11th of January, 1928, at the age of eighty-seven.

His Legacy

The middle of the 19th century was a time of great social upheaval in England, with the traditional rural society being displaced by industrialization and with many rural people migrating to the cities to work in factories. Hardy felt a great love of the old ways which was always reflected in his writing, so when it comes to depictions of life in 19th century England, few if any writers can rival Thomas Hardy in capturing the real sense of what it was like to live at those times.

He writes about the lives of ordinary people and his detailed descriptions, realistic characters and moving plots still speak to us today of the human condition and the courage of existence. Unlike some other writers, Hardy led a relatively quiet, introverted life but he had a rich internal one that produced some of the greatest novels in the English language.

Sites to Visit

- Hardy was buried twice. His body was cremated and his ashes interred at Poet's Corner, Westminster Abbey, in an official funeral. At the same time, his heart was buried next to Emma, in the churchyard of Stinsford Parish Church, Dorchester, where his father and grandfather had both sung in the choir.
- There is a statue of Hardy in Dorchester, Dorset.
- His childhood home in the cottage where he also wrote his first novels is a National Trust property, in the village of Higher Bockhampton, outside Dorchester.
- His home, Max Gate, Dorchester, is also a National Trust property. Unfortunately, the house contains very few artifacts directly related to Hardy as his possessions were dispersed before and immediately after his death. However, his dog, Wessex*, has a headstone in the Pet's Cemetery on the grounds of the house.
- Wessex was the Anglo-Saxon name for the part of England that Dorchester is in and was the fictional name for the area that he used in all his novels.

Further Research

Almost all Hardy's works are still in print, and they can also be accessed online.

Biographies of Hardy include:

- Thomas Hardy: The Time-Torn Man, by Claire Tomalin (2007)
- Thomas Hardy, by Robert Gittings (2001)
- Thomas Hardy: A Biography Revisited, Michael Millgate (2004)
- Thomas Hardy: His Life and Work, by F.E. Halliday (2001)
- Oxford Reader's Companion to Hardy, edited by Norman Page (2001)

NELL GWYN
The Actress Who Charmed a King

Key Facts

- Born 1650 – died 1687
- Rose from the slums to become a famous actress
- Mistress to King Charles II for 17 years
- Established a line of peers, through her son by the king

Most famous as an actress and the mistress of Charles II, who she had two sons with, Nell Gwyn, or Gwynne, had an unlikely start in life serving drinks in her mother's brothel while still a child. When the Restoration of the Monarchy in 1660 re-legalized theatre and allowed women to act on stage for the first time, she became famous for her portrayals of flirtatious girls. She caught the eye of the new monarch, Charles II, already known for his multiple mistresses, and became his most famous one, continuing until his death in 1685. She persuaded him to make a Lord of their eldest son, establishing a lineage that continues to this day. She died young, perhaps only 37, probably from complications of venereal disease. She has frequently been portrayed as the essence of the bawdiness and excess of the Restoration period, which followed the strict puritanism of the Cromwell years.

It is a measure of how obscure the origins of one of the best-known women in English history were when it is not at all clear exactly who her mother or father were. We don't even know for certain if she was born in the Covent Garden district of London, but that is the most likely possibility. Even her birth date is uncertain since the one usually given – the 2nd of February, 1650 – is derived from a horoscope done later in her life. 1642 has been suggested as a perhaps more plausible year. It does

seem she grew up in Covent Garden, probably on Coal Yard Alley, a slum area near Drury Lane. It seems that her father was not part of her life, perhaps having died in Oxford when she was very young. We do know that the young Nell, whose baptismal name was Eleanor, worked in Old Ma Gwyn's 'bawdy house,' that is to say a brothel, from an early age. It is pure conjecture whether she worked solely as a serving girl, bringing drinks to the guests, or whether she was a child prostitute, but in either case, she would have been very worldly from an early age. When she was twelve, she was supported for about two years by a lover called Duncan, who housed her in a tavern, and it was while with him that she became an actress.

After the English Civil War, the Puritans had banned theatre, but when Charles II was restored to the throne he not only re-opened the theaters, but he legalized acting by women and created two companies of actors. One, the King's Company, opened The Theatre in Bridges Street, which later became the Theatre Royal, on Drury Lane, still open today. Nell and her sister Rose were hired by an ex-prostitute called Mary Meggs, or "Orange Moll," to help sell oranges in the theatre, not dissimilar to the cigarette girls who used to be found in movie theatres not so many decades ago. For tips the girls would also carry messages from men in the audience to the actresses backstage, arranging liaisons. Since the King and his court regularly attended the theatre, in this way Nell became known to a higher level of society.

Within a year Nell had joined the King's Company as an actress, being perhaps 14 at the time. Thomas Killigrew, the head of the Company, had created a school for young actors, and Nell entered it, quickly beginning an affair with Charles Hart, the drama teacher and one of the major actors of the time. There was a temporary delay in her career during the Great Plague of London, which began in the summer of 1665. The Royal Court, and many other people, including Nell and her mother, retreated to Oxford. Perhaps 100,000 people died, about a quarter of the population, and just as the plague was retreating the Great Fire of London occurred, delaying the return of the Court until late in 1666.

Upon her return Nell had her first opportunity to tread the boards in March 1667 (or 1665?), appearing in The Indian Emperour, a drama by John Dryden loosely based on the Spanish conquest of the New World. Nell played Cydaria, the Inca Emperor Montezuma's daughter, who Cortez falls in love with. Since Cortez was played by Charles Hart, perhaps not too much acting was involved. Samuel Pepys attended a performance, and although a later admirer of Nell, found her performance poor.

Drama was clearly not her thing, and she had much more success a little later in a comedy called All Mistaken, or the Mad Couple, by the Royalist playwright James Howard, again playing opposite Charles Hart. Between them, they established a new theatrical trope, the 'Gay Couple,' which was widely used by them and others in numerous Restoration Comedies. At that time productions ran for only a short period, since the audience was limited, so Nell had the opportunity to appear with Hart in a number of plays, culminating in their greatest performance in Secret Love, or The Maiden Queen. Pepys saw the play three times and was effusive in his praise for Nell.

It was difficult for theatrical companies to keep good actresses since they were swept off the stage to become the mistresses of nobles. This was the fate of Nell too, when she became the mistress of the poet, courtier, and rake Charles Sackville, Earl of Dorset. She also caught the eye of Charles II, although he passed her by on the first occasion when through the intermediary of the Duke of Buckingham she asked for too much money. He relented in 1668 when he found himself in an adjacent box at a theatre in Lincoln's Inn Fields. The story is that she ended up paying for the supper he invited her to when he discovered he had no money with him. She returned to the King's Company, where her notoriety as Charles' mistress ensured packed houses. However, as she became a more permanent feature in the King's life, her appearances reduced considerably.

In 1670 she gave birth to her first son, and the King's seventh, by five different mistresses. The King's wife, the Portuguese Catherine of Braganza, had failed to provide him with an heir, so she had to accept the semi-official status of his string of mistresses. In 1671 Nell was installed in a fine house at 79 Pall Mall, but only as a leaseholder. Always one thinking of her own best interests, she pressured for the property to be given to her outright, which was eventually done.

At the end of 1671, she gave birth to a second son, James, who was sent to Paris to be brought up. However, he died there six years later, perhaps of blood poisoning. Her first son, who she named Charles, remained with her, and she pressured the King to legitimize him. One version is that she called him 'you little bastard' in front of the King, saying she had nothing else to call him, at which point the King relented. Another is that she held the baby out of a window and threatened to drop him, but in either case, the King made little Charles Beauclerc Earl of Burford and Baron of Heddington and granted him a house outside Windsor. He also gave Nell Bagnigge House, a country house with healthy spring water at 61-63 Kings Cross Road.

In 1685 the king died, leaving instructions to his heir, James II, to "not let poor Nelly starve." James did not, giving her a pension of £1,500 a year, roughly equivalent to at least a quarter million pounds today. She did not have long to enjoy her retirement from whoredom, however, as she suffered a series of strokes and seizures, probably the consequences of syphilis, and died on the 14th of November, 1687, less than three years after the death of the king.

Her Legacy

Although Nell openly and regularly referred to herself as a whore, it would seem from her pleading with the king to legitimize their son, that she did not truly enjoy her situation. Her image as the archetypal woman who sells her body to improve her situation underestimates the privations of life for the poor of the time, and how eagerly almost anyone would grasp at a chance to survive. She was undoubtedly a lot smarter than she might appear, given her ability to stay in the King's favor for 17 years, acquire several properties and establish her son as a man of privilege. There is today still an Earl of Burford, Charles Francis Topham de Vere Beauclerk, a member of the House of Lords and famous for defending the rights of hereditary peers. He has some of his ancestor's genes, having married a pop star.

Sites to Visit

- Nell Gwyn's grave is St Martin-in-the-Fields Churchyard, Westminster.
- There are blue plaques at 79 Pall Mall, the house Charles II gave Nell to live in, and at the site of Bagnigge House, 61-63 Kings Cross Road. In the 18th century, the house became a popular spa, before giving way to development.

Further Research

Plays:

- In Good King Charles's Golden Days, by Bernard Shaw (1939)
- Our Nell, a musical, by Harold Fraser-Simson and Ivor Novello (1924)
- Nell Gwynn, by Jessica Swale (2015)

Films:

- Mistress Nell, starring Mary Pickford (1915)
- Love, Life and Laughter, starring Gracie Fields (1934)
- Stage Beauty, starring Zoe Tapper (2004)

Novels:

- The King's Favorite, by Susan Holloway Scott (2008)
- Exit the Actress, by Priya Parmar (2011) (uses contemporary documents to show the larger political and social context)
- The Darling Strumpet: A Novel of Nell Gwynn, Who Captured the Heart of England and King Charles, by Gillian Bagwell (2011)

Biographies of Nell Gwyn include:

- Nell Gwynn, by Jessica Swale
- Nell Gwyn: Mistress to a King, by Charles Beauclerk
- Nell Gwynn (Life of a Harlot), by Jenny Stone
- House of Nell Gwynn: Fortunes of the Beauclerk Family, 1670-1974, by Peter Beauclerk Dewar and Donald Adamson

CECIL RHODES
Businessman, Politician, Imperialist

Key Facts

- Born 1853 – died 1902
- Businessman and founder of De Beers diamond mines
- Carried out extensive imperial purchases and seizures of African lands
- Established the Rhodes Scholarship to Oxford University after his death

Cecil Rhodes was a businessman and politician who made his fortune in the late 19th-century Scramble for Africa by the European powers. After cornering diamond production in South Africa and forming De Beers Consolidated mines to maintain high diamond prices, he moved into politics and served as Prime Minister in the colony from 1890-1896. He then undertook a commercial and political land-grab of the countries of the eastern part of Africa, almost succeeding in bringing a continuous strip from the Cape to Cairo under British control. His attitude to Africans led to him being described as the father of apartheid. After his death, his considerable personal fortune created the Rhodes Scholarship, which brought overseas students to Oxford University and began the careers of many prominent people.

Cecil John Rhodes first set foot in South Africa when he was 17, having been sent there for his health by his Church of England clergyman father. Cecil was asthmatic and so sickly he had been taken out of Grammar School, in Bishop's Stortford, Hertfordshire, where he was born on the 5th of July, 1853.

Rhodes landed in the Colony of Natal, which had been annexed by the British is 1843, joining the formerly independent Boer province to the larger Cape Colony. Rhodes brother Herbert had set up a cotton farm in

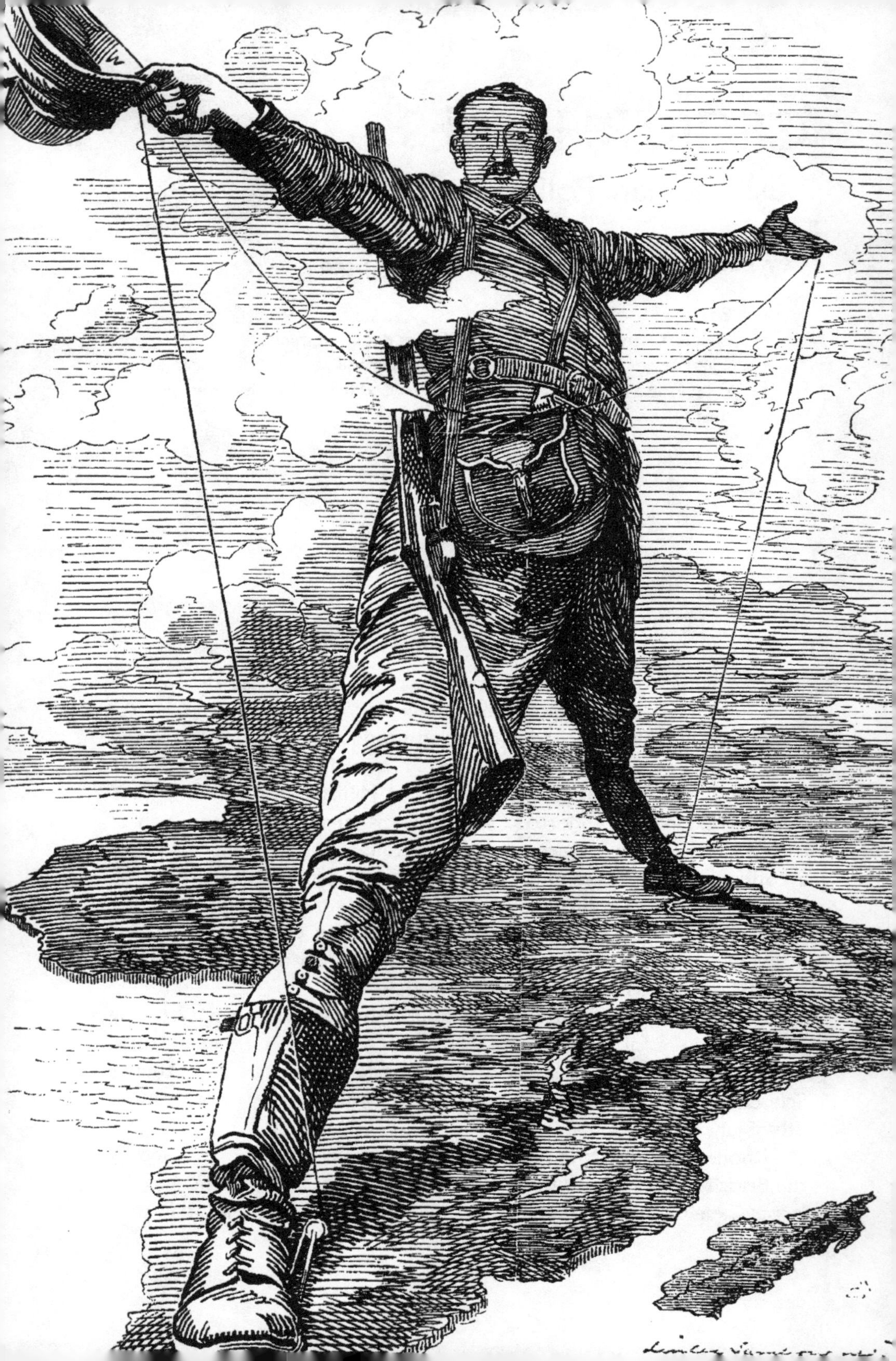

Natal, and Cecil joined him. The venture failed as the climate and soil were not suitable for cotton. A diamond rush had just begun at Kimberley in the Cape Colony, and the brothers went there to try their luck. At first, he rented water pumps to miners, but he used the profits of this enterprise to start buying small diamond mine claims, helped by the financial backing of the London banking family Rothschild.

Cecil did return for a term at Oxford in 1873 but quickly returned to Kimberley, where he continued to expand his operations. In 1876 he returned to Oxford for a second term, and it was there that he attended a lecture by the polymath John Ruskin, who presented an idealized view of the British Empire as a force for good, lifting up the 'lower races' and spreading peace and prosperity across the Earth. This inspired Rhodes to adopt the cause of British Imperialism and take the view that Britain, through its excellence, had a right to rule. At the same time he joined the Freemasons, and in his first will, written in 1877, he left money for a secret society with but one object – the furtherance of the British Empire and the bringing of the whole uncivilized world under British rule, (and) for the recovery of the United States ...

Back in the Cape, his chief partner was John Rudd, another young Englishman seeking his fortune. They found a rival in Barney Barnato, a Cockney Jew, who had seized control of the diamond market and was manipulating prices. Rhodes and Barnato were both racing to consolidate all the tiny mines into a large company, and after complex financial maneuverings they combined forming De Beers Consolidated Mines, which at one point controlled 90% of the world's diamonds. By being able to control production and keep supply close to demand, Rhodes was able to maintain an artificially high price for diamonds, and create a large fortune for Rothschild Bank, Barnato, De Beers, and of course himself.

In 1880 Rhodes entered the Cape Parliament, and within ten years he was Prime Minister of the Cape Colony. His first task was to remove black Africans from land required for industrial development and, in his words, show them that in future nine-tenths of them will have to spend their lives in manual labor, and the sooner that is brought home to them the better. By setting limits on the amount of land black people could own, and setting the level for the right to vote above that limit, he succeeded in preventing them from developing as a political force, arguing that the native is to be treated as a child and denied the franchise. He also attempted to overthrow the neighboring Boer Republic of Transvaal, launching, with the approval of the British government, the Jameson Raid over the New Year weekend of 1895–96. The purpose was to send a small force to encourage an uprising by British settlers in the Transvaal, but it failed completely, forcing Rhodes to resign as Prime Minister. A brother, Frank Rhodes was jailed and nearly executed in Transvaal for treason, and the raid was a factor in the outbreak of the Second Boer War.

Driven by his belief in the right of the superior British race to rule, and by a desire to increase his fortune, Rhodes now began to purchase mining concessions from local chiefs and simultaneously expand the control of the British government over the areas he purchased. By covering the costs of administration and having his companies administer the areas thus occupied, he prevented the perhaps more benevolent direct rule form Britain that distressed missionaries and others wanted while keeping these territories legally British. This gave him the security and legality needed to sell shares in his mining operations to investors. In this way, he was instrumental in keeping Britain dominant in the so-called Scramble for Africa with other European countries, especially in the eastern half of the continent. Many of his tactics were secretive and technically illegal, but a blind-eye was often turned by the British government. Rhodesia (now Zimbabwe and Zambia) were the jewel in Rhodes' Cape to Cairo Red Line, a reference to the desire to have red, the traditional color on maps of British territories, run the length of Africa. By 1914 only the German colony of Tanzania broke the continuity, and that country also fell into the hands of Britain via the WWI peace treaties. The railway line Rhodes dreamed of, from the Cape to Cairo, was never completed.

Rhodes never married, arguing that he didn't have time, but it has been suggested, without any definitive evidence, that he was gay. Rhodes kept no diaries and wrote very few personal letters, so his private life remains largely concealed. His name has been associated with several potential lovers, the last of which was Leander Starr Jameson, who had led the Jameson Raid. Jameson was with Rhodes during his final illness, was the residual beneficiary of his will, giving him Rhodes' mansion, and although Jameson died in England, in 1920 his body was re-interred in Rhodesia beside Rhodes.

In the end Rhodes life-long ill health kept him regularly ill after he turned 40 and he died of heart failure on the 26th of March, 1902, just 48 years of age. His body was carried on a funeral train from the seaside cottage on the Cape where he died to a hilltop in Rhodesia called 'World's View,' where his grave remains today. Tribal chiefs attended his internment there.

His Legacy

Rhodes greatest legacy was the Rhodes Scholarship, established by Nathan Rothschild, the administrator of his estate, in compliance with the terms of Rhodes' will. This was the world's first international study program and allows students from any current or ex-British colony to study at Oxford. Important recipients include J. William Fulbright, Dean Rusk, and President Bill Clinton.

With the collapse of the Empire and the de-colonization that followed WWII, Rhodes reputation began to decline, and today it has reached a veritable nadir, with recent attempts to remove his statue from Oxford University. His racist views are widely considered to make him the father of the apartheid system that blighted South Africa, but he should perhaps be seen as being a product, as much as a maker, of his times.

Sites to Visit

- His grave is part of Matobo National Park, Zimbabwe.
- There is a statue of Rhodes on the façade of Oriel College, Oxford University.
- His birthplace is now the Rhodes Arts Complex & Bishop's Stortford Museum, containing records and artifacts of his life. It is at 1-3 South Road, Bishop's Stortford, Hertfordshire, and is open Monday to Saturday from 10 am to 4 pm.

Further Research

Biographies include:

- Cecil Rhodes: Man and Empire-Maker (1918), by Princess Catherine Radziwill, is still available. The princess was infatuated with Rhodes, and when he refused to marry her, she engineered a court-case for fraud based on false allegations she made. Although she lost the case, she went on to write this contemporary biography.
- The Founder: Cecil Rhodes and the Pursuit of Power (1988), by Robert I. Rotberg.
- Cecil Rhodes and His Time (2012), by Apollon Davidson
- Cecil Rhodes, His Private Life (2013), by Philip Jourdan

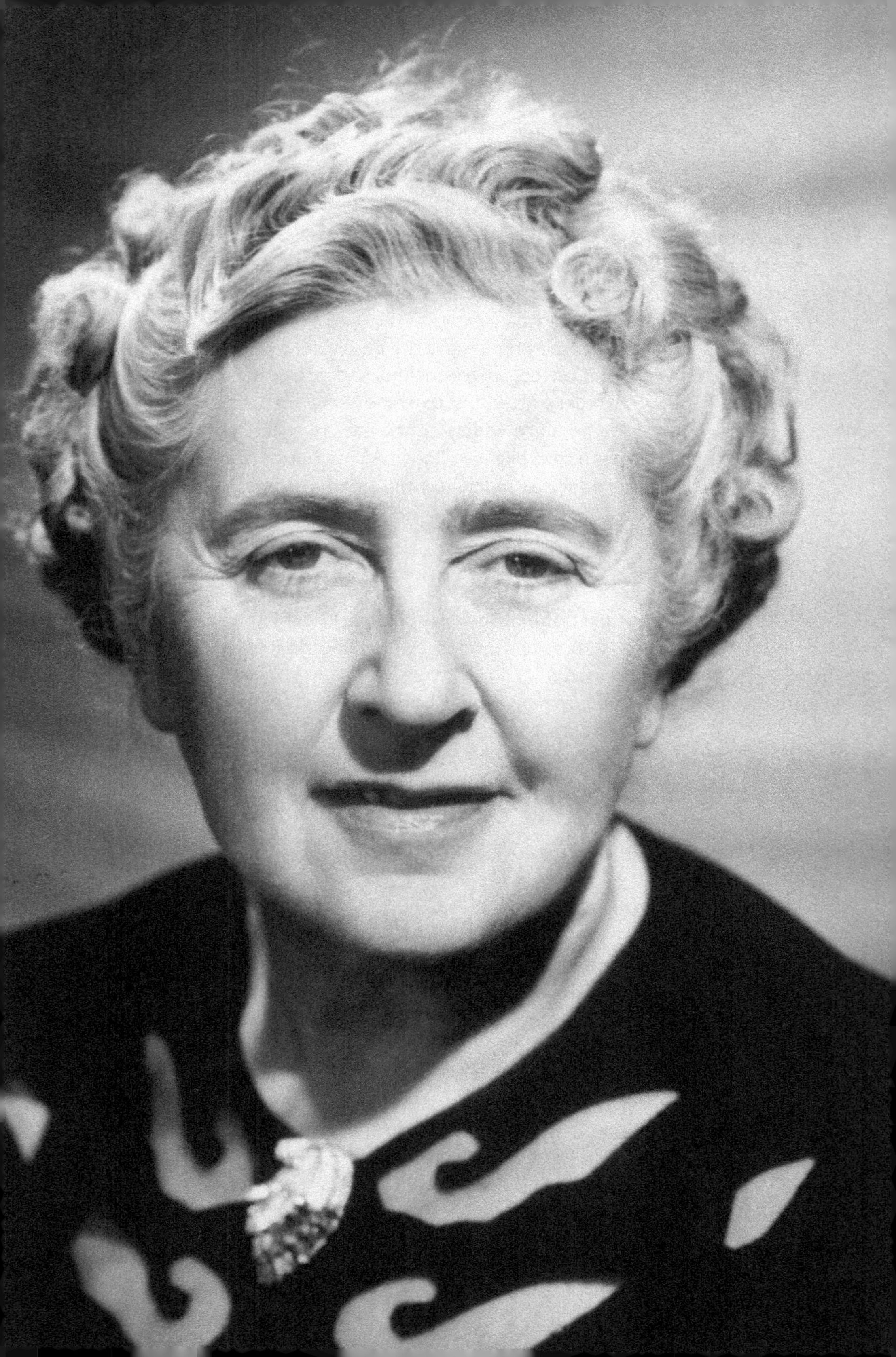

AGATHA CHRISTIE
The Queen of Mystery

Key Facts

- Born 1890, died 1976
- The world's best-selling novelist
- Led a varied life with interests in spiritualism and archaeology
- Widely traveled and incorporated her travels into her writing

Agatha Mary Clarissa Miller was born in Torquay, Devon, on September 15th, 1890 into a comfortably well-off middle-class family. She was the daughter of an American stockbroker and an English mother. Although she had an older brother and sister, they were ten and eleven years older than her, so the age difference was so great that she was effectively an only child and seemed to have led a lonely but happy childhood. Although her family were nominally Christian, esoteric and spiritualist beliefs were common in Britain at that time, and her family was not immune to them. The children all believed that their mother was a psychic with the gift of second sight.

Her mother loved to read stories to her children and tried to delay Agatha's learning to read until she was eight. However, the defiant Agatha taught herself before she was five. Her mother also did not want to her go to school, so taught her at home, where she learned the three R's, along with the piano and mandolin. She was a voracious reader of all the standard children's books of the period, from Edith Nesbit to Edward Lear and Lewis Carroll.

She spent her time alternating between Torquay, the West London home of her step-grandmother and, in common with other wealthy Britons, various parts of southern Europe where her family spent the winter months. When she was five, the family rented out their Devon home and spent an extended time in the South of France. As a young, not yet successful writer, she was to return there and live for a time in the French-Italian border town of Menton.

However, her happy life suddenly fell apart when at the age of eleven, her still-young father died of a heart attack. Christie was to later describe this event as the 'end of her childhood', but despite the family's reduced income, they continued to live in Torquay. The next year, in 1902, she was sent to boarding school but found the transition difficult. She was then sent to various 'finishing schools' in Paris, no doubt aided by the French she had acquired from the family trips to Europe. When, now aged 20, she returned to England and found her mother ill, they decided to move to Cairo, which was a popular destination for wealthy Britons. There she spent her time husband-hunting, and although she did visit the Pyramids, she did not yet show the interest in archaeology that she would later in her life.

In 1912 she met Archie Christie, a pilot in the embryonic British air-force, the Royal Flying Corps. After a whirlwind romance, they were married on Christmas Eve, 1914, just after the outbreak of WWI. Archie rose through the ranks during the war and ended it as a Colonel in the War Ministry.

At the end of the war, the couple settled in a terrace house in fashionable St. John's Wood, London. In 1919 she gave birth to a daughter, Rosalind.

Since the age of 18, Agatha had been writing short stories and plays, often expressing her interesting in spiritualism. These were uniformly rejected for publication, and even with the help of a successful writer and family friend, Eden Philpotts, who introduced her to his literary agent, the rejections continued. A breakthrough occurred when she was inspired by her reading of Sherlock Holmes and Wilkie Collins to write a detective novel, The Mysterious Affair at Styles featuring a character called Hercule Poirot. She based Poirot, a Belgian living in exile from German-occupied Belgium, on her real-life experiences with exiled Belgians she had met in Torquay. After agreeing to change the ending and accepting a contract she later described as 'exploitive', the book was published by The Bodley Head. It was followed by further novels and short stories.

At the end of 1926, after an argument with her adulterous husband, Christie disappeared for eleven days, leaving her car and clothes by a lake. Following a national manhunt, she was discovered staying at a Spa Hotel in Yorkshire. Although doctors diagnosed amnesia, the public saw this as an attempt to frame her husband for murder, or at least a publicity stunt.

Later evidence suggests she wanted to cause her husband embarrassment and was surprised at the uproar. They were divorced in 1928.

Christie developed an interest in archaeology and took the Orient Express to Baghdad, then under British control, to visit the excavations of the city of Ur. It was there that she met archaeologist Max Mallowan, who became her second husband. The married in 1930 and remained happily married until Christie's death. They established a routine of digs in Iraq, summers at her family home in Torquay and time divided between their London homes and their country houses, first at Wallingford, outside Oxford and later at the Greenway Estate in Devon.

They also often stayed at Abney Hall in Cheshire, a home run in a grand manner by her brother-in-law, which become the model for the various country homes featured in many of her books.

The Second World War interrupted their regulated life, but Christie learned some useful things about poisons volunteering at the pharmacy of the University College Hospital, London. She was also briefly investigated as a potential spy for her use of the name 'Bletchley' for a character since Bletchley Park was a top-secret code-breaking center.

Following the war, she resumed her life of travel and writing, but by the 1970's she began to decline, possibly with Alzheimer's disease. She continued to write until 1975. She died on January 12th, 1976 aged 85, at another of her homes, Winterbrook House in Oxfordshire.

Her Legacy

Agatha Christie is one of the biggest-selling authors in history. Her total book sales have only been eclipsed by Shakespeare and the Bible. And Then There Were None has sold 100 million copies, one of the biggest-selling books in history and The Murder of Peter Ackroyd was voted the best crime novel ever by the Crime Writers' Association. She is also the world's most translated author and is read in 103 languages.

Her play The Mousetrap has been running continuously in the West End since 1952, making it the longest-running play ever, with well over 25,000 performances.

Her characters, such as Hercule Poirot and Miss Marple, have become part of popular culture. Her persona as a successful and independent-minded woman has been important as a role model for modern women.

Sites to Visit

- Her Greenway Estate home in Devon now belongs to the National Trust and is open to the public.
- The Pera Palace Hotel in Istanbul, Turkey maintains Christie's room where she wrote parts of Murder on the Orient Express as a memorial to her.
- The house at 5 Northwick Terrace, St. John's Wood, London is still standing. She also lived in Chelsea, first at 22 Cresswell Place and later at 58 Sheffield Terrace. Both properties are now marked by blue plaques.

Further Research

- Her life in her own words is told in Agatha Christie: An Autobiography and in The Grand Tour: Around the World with the Queen of Mystery.
- Recent biographies include: Duchess of Death: The Unauthorized Biography of Agatha Christie by Richard Hack (2009) and Agatha Christie: A Biography by Janet Morgan (1985).
- The semi-biographical film Agatha focuses on her 11-day disappearance in 1926, as does the TV movie, Agatha: a Life in Pictures. There is an episode on her in the TV series 'Biography'.
- Almost all of her many works are still in print in numerous languages, and many have also been made into full-length films and television series.

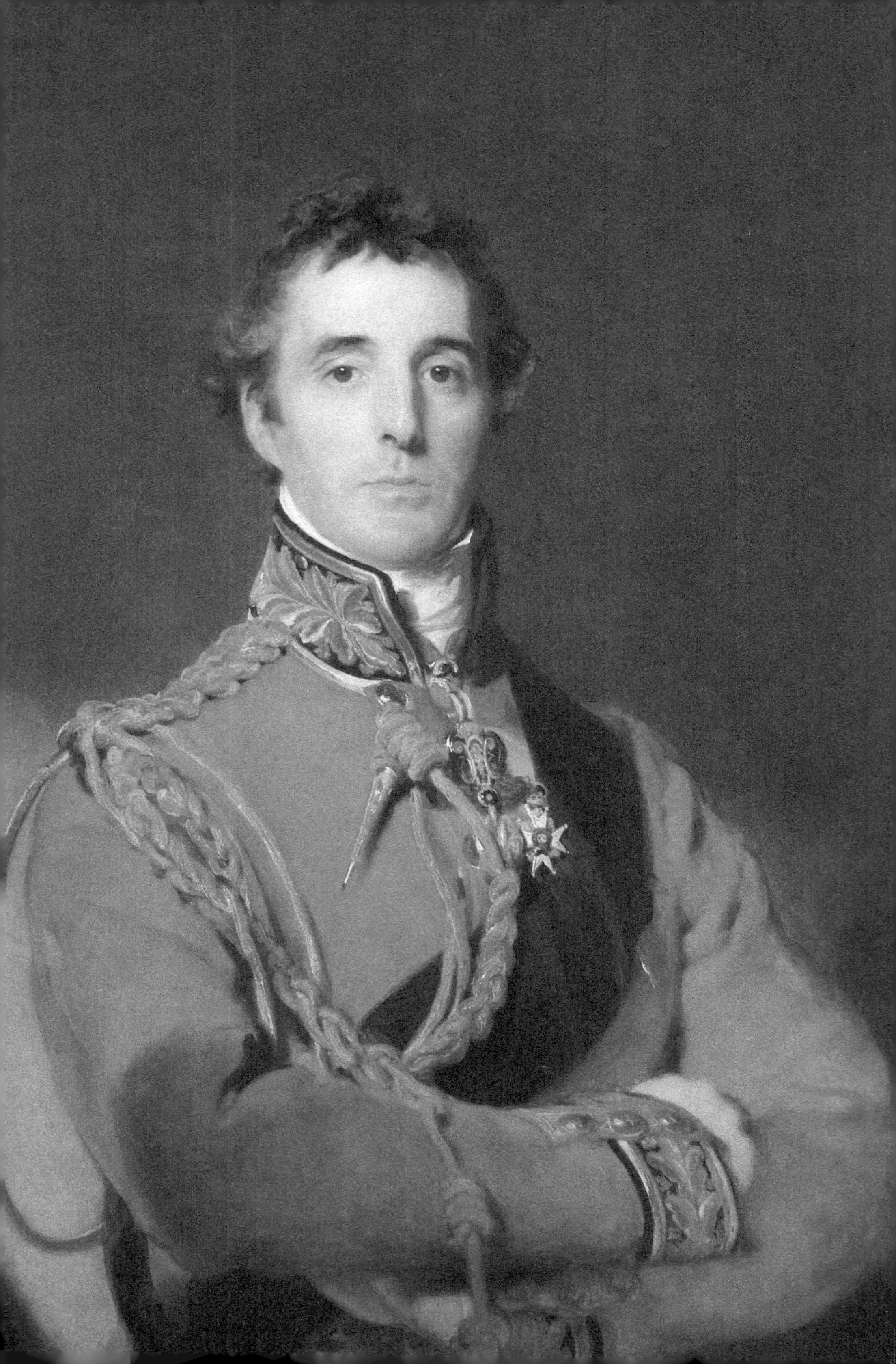

1ST DUKE OF WELLINGTON

Napoleon's Menace

Key Facts

- Born 1769, died 1852
- One of the greatest generals in English history
- Defeated Napoleon at Waterloo
- Combined a military career with a political career

Arthur Wellesley, the 1st Duke of Wellington, was a military leader and politician who fought in India and is best remembered for defeating Napoleon at the Battle of Waterloo. He also served as Prime Minister for several years.

As Britain gradually grasped control of Ireland during the 16th and 17th centuries, the ownership of lands seized from Irish landowners passed to English Protestants who became the ruling class in Ireland until the 20th century. They were usually referred to as the Protestant Ascendancy, and when around the 1st of May, 1769 the Honourable Arthur Wesley was born in Dublin, he entered that Anglo-Irish upper class. His parents, the Earl and Countess of Mornington had a grand home in Dublin as well as the estate of Dangan Castle in County Meath, and young Arthur grew up dividing his time between these two properties.

Despite spending four years at Eton School, he had a lack-lustre childhood and seemed headed for idleness until he enrolled in a French aristocratic academy and learned to ride and to speak French. When he returned to see his mother, who was now living in Brussels following the death of her husband, the change in him astonished her.

Looking for a career and with contacts provided by his brother, Arthur joined the British Army and quickly became a lieutenant in the

76th Regiment in his old home town of Dublin. He also took a seat in the gerrymandered Irish Parliament for two years, but when he was refused the hand of the woman he loved because of his poor prospects Arthur decided to establish a career in the Army and proceeded to buy commissions – a standard practice at the time – until he reached the rank of lieutenant-colonel in the 33rd Regiment in 1793, at the ripe age of 24.

1793 was also the year he saw his first battle experience when the 33rd went to Flanders with the Duke of York with the intention of invading France. The French Revolution was at its height at this time, with the Reign of Terror just beginning. The Duke's invasion plans failed, and Wesley was later to say that his time on that campaign taught him the valuable lesson of what not to do in a war.

By 1796 he was a full colonel, and his Regiment was sent to Calcutta, where Britain was engaged in extending the rule of the British East India Company over the territory of India. There he was successful in leading his men to victory over the Army of the rebellious Sultan of Mysore.

Following the death of the Sultan and the capture of his fortress at Seringapatam, Colonel Wellesley (he had changed the spelling of his name by this time) remained behind as Governor of Seringapatam and Mysore, taking up residence in the Sultan's palace.

Over the next years, Wellesley engaged with the Maratha Empire, Hindus who had controlled most of India since defeating the Islamic Mogul Empire. Although when he left India, the Marathas were still in control of considerable territory, his victories in battles at Assaye, Argaum and Gawilghur set the stage for a third and final war, which by 1818 saw Britain in full control of India.

In 1805 Wellesley, weakened by a series of illnesses, returned to England. He had amassed a significant fortune in prize-money for his victories and been knighted. He had also adopted the dress he is usually seen in, with white trousers, tall boots and a cocked hat.

On his return to England, a hero and now wealthy, he found that the woman whose hand he had been denied was now his. On the 10th of April, 1806, he and Kitty Pakenham were married in Dublin. Having waited so long, and done so much to secure her, it must have been a great disappointment to Wellesley that the marriage did not turn out well and they spent years at a time apart. In the beginning, however, he gave up his military career and turned again to politics, securing a seat in Parliament, becoming Chief Secretary for Ireland and a Privy Counsellor as well.

However after hardly more than a year Wellesley was back in the military, fighting in Denmark and Portugal and next in Spain, where England was fighting France, and the Spanish were fighting for their independence.

He was by now a seasoned and skilled military strategist, but the Peninsula War dragged on from 1808 to 1813, with numerous battles, many casualties and no decisive victory on either side. Britain had allied with Spain to defeat the French, but victory was elusive until 1813 when Wellesley captured San Sebastian and reached as far into France as Toulouse. The Emperor Napoleon was meanwhile facing defeat in the north after his ruinous Russian campaign and losses in Prussia. Paris had been captured by the Coalition of European powers and the French Senate, realizing that it was Napoleon and not France that the Coalition opposed, deposed the Emperor in 1814 and exiled him to the island of Elba.

Wellesley returned to England a hero – for his dress and style as much as for his military victories. The title 'Duke of Wellington' was created for him and this hereditary title continues with his descendants to the present time. Because the title was created specifically for him, Arthur Wellesley was, therefore, the first Duke of Wellington.

Napoleon, however, had not given up and the following year he escaped from Elba, landed in the south of France and gathering an army as he went, he marched on Paris and seized power. The Coalition countries pledged to raise an army to defeat him and Napoleon, seeking to take the offensive, invaded what is today Belgium and was then part of the Netherlands. Wellington arrived at the head of a combined British, German and Dutch army, alongside the Prussian forces. After preliminary skirmishes, Wellington confronted Napoleon at the Battle of Waterloo on the 18th of June, 1815 and was victorious. Napoleon surrendered to the British to avoid capture by the Prussians and was exiled to the island of Saint Helena in the middle of the Atlantic Ocean, where he died in 1821.

Returning again as a hero, Wellington went back into politics where he occupied a variety of powerful positions, and by 1827 he was the Commander-in-Chief of the British Army. In 1828 he became Prime Minister at the head of a Tory government. His major contribution was to pass, against great opposition, the Catholic Relief Act of 1829 which gave full civil rights to Catholics. His sympathy with Irish causes such as this made him hugely unpopular in England, and his house was attacked several times by mobs. There was almost a revolution when the Tories refused to extend voting rights, and Wellington resigned as Prime Minister in 1830. He remained opposed to the reforms which were eventually passed amidst severe political turmoil. Control of the Tories gradually fell to Robert Peel and the party transformed into the Conservative Party. Wellington served several Cabinet posts in Peel's governments.

In 1846 he retired from active politics although he retained several honorary titles. He died on the 14th of September, 1852 after a series of strokes. He was honored with a State Funeral which drew enormous crowds - his popularity had been restored by that time.

His Legacy

Wellington secured Britain's hold on India and established the Empire. He prevented the conquest of Europe by Napoleon and the spread of the French Revolution. His conservative politics and resistance to democratic reforms contributed to the tensions and unrest which characterize much of the 19th century.

Sites to Visit

- Wellington's tomb is in the crypt of St Paul's Cathedral, in London. There is a large monument showing him on his horse in the main body of the Church.
- The Wellington Monument, erected shortly after the Napoleonic Wars, is at the south end of Park Lane, London.
- There are numerous other statues and monuments across

England and Ireland. These include a statue of Wellington outside the Royal Exchange in the City of London, and the Wellington Monument in Dublin. Others can be seen in Edinburgh, Glasgow, Leeds, Manchester and Liverpool.
- There is a large collection of memorabilia, including his funeral carriage made from melted-down French cannons from the Battle of Waterloo at Stratfield Saye House, Hampshire, the estate given to Wellington by the country at his investiture. His horse, Copenhagen, has a monument over its grave on the grounds.

Further Research

Biographies of the Duke of Wellington include:

- The Life of Arthur Duke of Wellington, by G.R. Gleig (2014)
- Wellington: The Iron Duke, by Richard Holmes (2003)
- Wellington: A Personal History, by Christopher Hibbert (1999)
- Wellington the Beau: The life and loves of the Duke of Wellington, by Patrick Delaforce (2014)

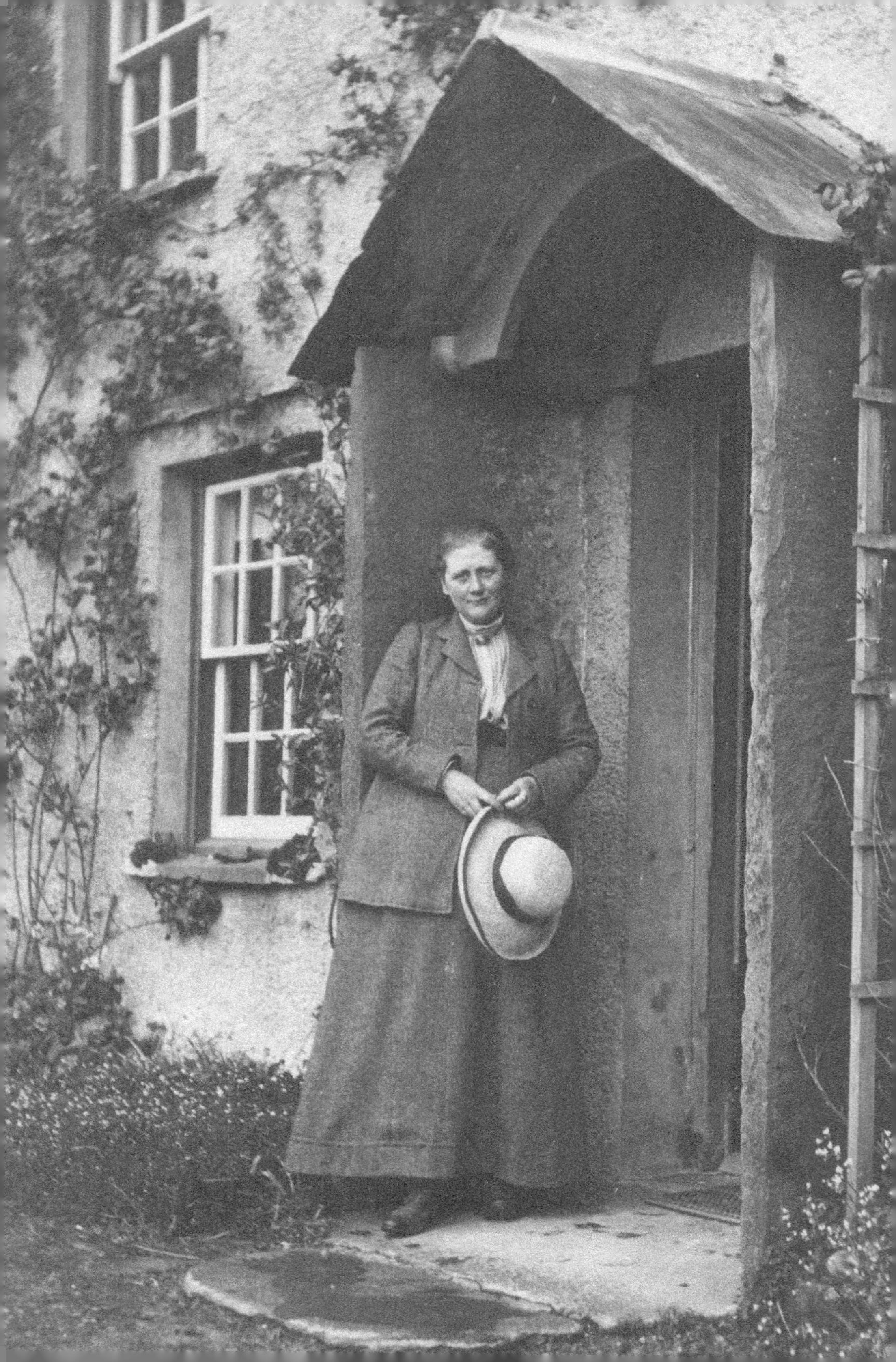

BEATRIX POTTER
Writer and Naturalist

Key Facts

- July 28, 1866 – December 22, 1943
- Author of the much loved 'Peter Rabbit' books
- Also a naturalist, mycologist and early conservationist
- Strongly associated with the Lake District, England

Beatrix Potter was born at her family home in South Kensington, London, in the summer of 1866. Her father, Rupert, was a lawyer and investor who by the time Beatrix was an adult had become extremely wealthy. Her mother also came from a wealthy family. Her younger brother, Walter Bertram Potter, was born in 1872 and completed the small family.

Both her parents had artistic talents, and her father was a keen amateur photographer at a time when that was still a complex and relatively uncommon hobby.

Since the family belonged to a dissenting protestant group, the Unitarians, which would have put them at odds which many of their class, they decided to have Beatrix raised by private tutors. This was anyway not an unusual choice for the wealthy at that time, particularly for the education of girls.

Beatrix seems to have been fortunate in that her tutors were all talented, particularly her last one, Annie Moore, who being only three years older than Beatrix was more of an older sister than a tutor. They remained life-long friends, and in fact, it was Annie who first suggested to Beatrix that she publish the illustrated letters she regularly wrote to Annie's eight children.

Beatrix also received private lessons in art and developed a distinctive style of watercolor painting which is where much of the charm of her books lies.

Her family regularly visited the Lake District (now the county of Cumbria) for summer holidays. In this beautiful region with its lakes and hills, she fell in love with nature and made many paintings of plants, insects, fossils and especially fungi.

In 1892, while on holiday in Scotland she met Charles McIntosh, a skilled amateur naturalist and expert on fungi.

Natural Science at that time still relied on the activities of amateurs, who were often the most knowledgeable experts in specific areas. Natural history enjoyed great popularity among all social classes in Victorian England and bridged class barriers, so it is not so surprising that Beatrix started corresponding regularly with McIntosh, who was the local postman in his village.

McIntosh would mail Beatrix specimens, which she would paint, while he taught her taxonomy and how to make her illustrations more scientifically accurate. Beatrix became interested in the still-unresolved question of the time as to how fungi reproduced. In 1897 she submitted a paper on this subject to the Linnean Society – a famous biological society. However, her theories did not agree with those of the time (although she would later be proved to be right) and pressure because she was a woman forced her to withdraw the paper. In 1997 the Linnean Society issued a public apology for their sexist treatment of Beatrix. So good were her drawings that they were included in a major work on fungi in 1967.

Beatrix and her young brother kept many small pets, such as kittens, rabbits, guinea pigs and mice in their school-room. These formed the inspiration for the illustrations she began at a very early age to draw for her favorite stories.

Rebuffed as a scientist and easily bored, Beatrix began to sell some of these drawings to local publishers for greetings cards and in 1890 Benjamin Bunny, one of her enduring characters, made his first appearance to illustrate poems by the prolific song-writer, Frederic Weatherley. She continued to sell illustrations throughout the 1890s.

Then in 1900 she wrote and illustrated a story about four rabbits. At first unable to find a publisher, she self-published the book and sent it to family and friends. One friend, Canon Hardwicke Rawnsley, took her book to several publishers.

In late 1902 the book was published as The Tale of Peter Rabbit.

There was at that time a new growing market for small children's books and Potter's was a great success, in part, it has been suggested, because it lacked the moral message usually so obvious in Victorian children's literature.

Over the next decade, Beatrix wrote and published around two books a year, all very successful, until the outbreak of World War I seems to have suspended her work. There were to be other works published in the 1920s, but that ten years period was the time of her major creative activity when all the most popular of her books were published.

Both Beatrix and her publisher, Frederick Warne & Co. made immense amounts of money from Peter Rabbit. Besides the books, they realized the value of spin-off merchandise and marketed a Peter Rabbit doll in 1903, immediately after the first book. This was followed by wallpapers, china sets, games, figurines, blankets and other merchandise – a market that continues today.

In 1905 Beatrix became informally engaged to Norman Warne, the son of her publisher. Her family objected to his low-class status as a 'tradesman', but before the matter could be resolved Norman died of leukaemia. They were in the process of buying a property – Hill Top Farm – in the Lake District and after Norman's death Beatrix finalized the purchase and over the following years bought a number of surrounding farms as well, developing a large landholding.

She visited the area as often as she could, and it figured increasingly in her books. Through her land purchases, she met a local solicitor, William Heelis and in 1915 they married. As her father had died the year before and Beatrix had inherited a large fortune, she moved to live with Heelis in Hill Top Farm and moved her elderly mother to a nearby property. She continued her land purchases and quickly became a major, prize-winning farmer of the local Herdwick sheep.

Her old friend Canon Rawnsley had founded the National Trust for Places of Historic Interest or Natural Beauty, in 1895. This evolved into the National Trust, a major holder of historic properties in the UK. Beatrix sold some of her properties to the Trust and left the balance when she died to them, creating the nucleus of the Lake District National Park.

Beatrix continued to write and draw but published little. She spent her later life farming and working to preserve the unique life of the Lake District. She and William lived happily together. They had no children, but Beatrix involved herself in the large Heelis family until her death from pneumonia in 1943.

Her Legacy

Beatrix Potter remains a strong favorite with small children who grow up with her books, dishes, wallpaper and toys. Her simple stories emphasize the virtues of kindness and co-operation, coupled with a love of nature and other creatures.

Her scientific work has come under scrutiny and been valued and vindicated.

Both the preservation of the beautiful Lake District and its success as a tourist destination owe much to the visionary work of Potter and Canon Rawnsley.

Sites to Visit

- Hill Top Farm, Sawrey, Cumbria, England is a National Trust property preserved as it was when Beatrix lived there.
- The Beatrix Potter Gallery, Hawkshead, Cumbria, was the office of William Heelis and now houses a collection of her drawings and illustrations.
- There is a museum/exhibition, The World of Beatrix Potter, in Bowness-on-Windermere Cumbria.
- The Birnam Institute, Exhibition Centre and Garden, Birnam, Perthshire, Scotland, emphasizes her naturalist's relationship with McIntosh.
- Her archives at the Victoria and Albert Museum, London can

- be viewed by appointment.
- The Perth Museum, Perth, Scotland has a collection of her scientific drawings.

Further Research

- A biography that emphasizes her scientific work is Beatrix Potter: A Life in Nature, 2007; Beatrix Potter: The Extraordinary Life of a Victorian Genius by Linda Lear, 2008. A good general biography is Beatrix Potter - Artist, Storyteller and Countrywoman by Judy Taylor, (1996).
- There is a large collection of her writings and illustrations at the Victoria and Albert Museum, London, and smaller collections in the US at the Free Library of Philadelphia and the Children's Library at Princeton University.
- There are two dramatizations of her life—The Tale of Beatrix Potter (BBC, 1982) and Miss Potter (2006).
- There is a ballet of her works — The Tales of Beatrix Potter, choreographed by Sir Frederic Ashton, choreography for the Royal Ballet — filmed in 1971 and performed regularly by many ballet companies around the world.
- Exhibitions of both her scientific and book illustrations are given from time to time.

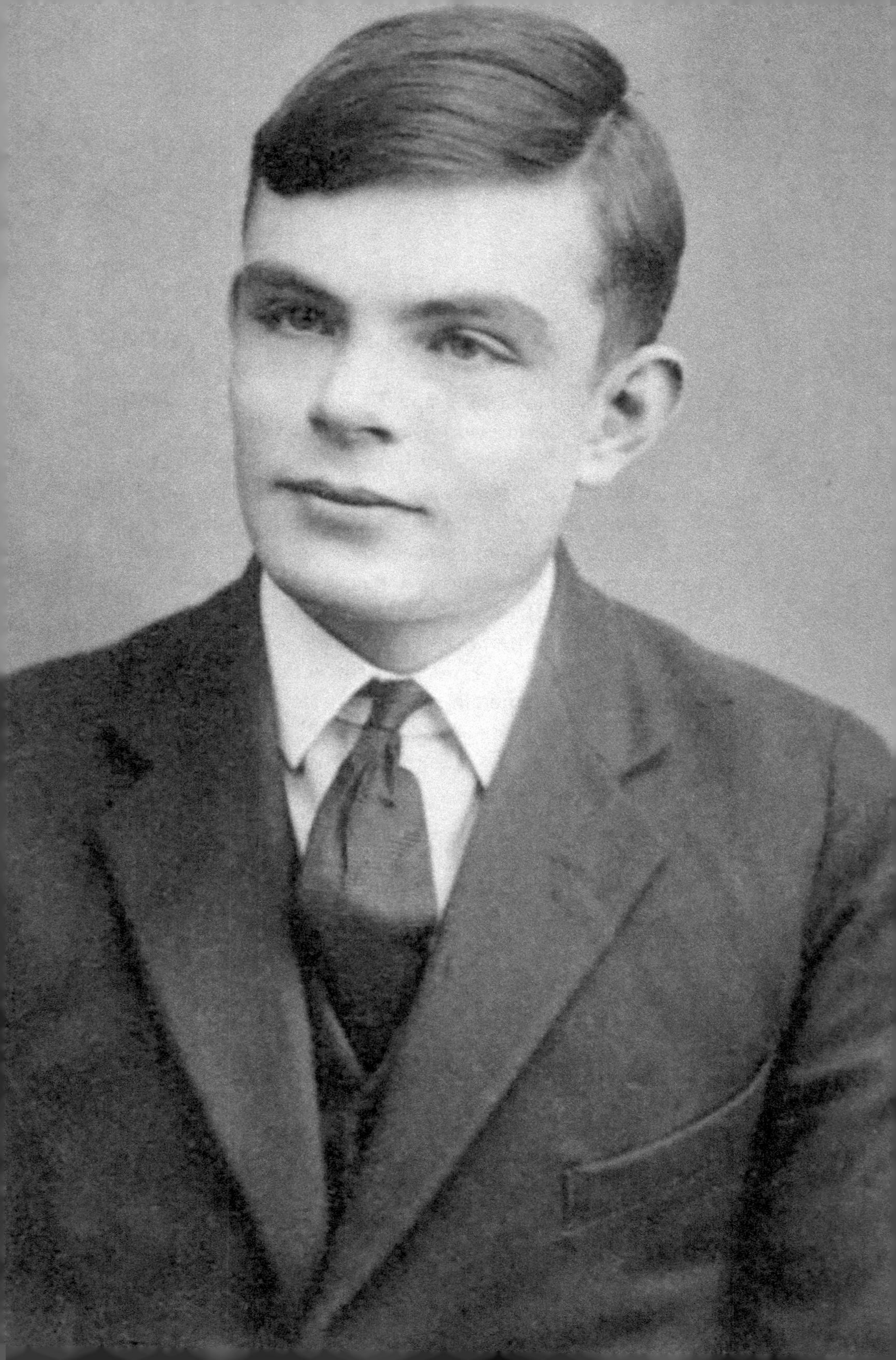

ALAN TURING
Codebreaker and Computer Genius

Key Facts

- Born 1912 – died 1954
- Instrumental in breaking the German Enigma codes in World War II
- Father of the computer
- Convicted as a homosexual and subsequently committed suicide

Alan Turing is widely seen as the father of computing and artificial intelligence. His work in WWII on breaking the German Enigma codes saved many ships and lives and was instrumental in the allied victory. His theories and early programs were ground-breaking in the development of the modern computer. His prosecution for homosexuality and his suicide have made him a cause célèbre for the gay-rights movement.

Born in Maida Vale, London, on 23 June 1912, Alan Turing was the son of a British civil servant in India who was a member of the protestant Anglo-Irish gentry, Julius Mathison Turing. Wanting his son to be brought up in England, his parents had returned there for the birth. Since his father continued to work in India, Alan and his older brother John were largely brought up by a retired couple in Hastings. When he was 15, his parents bought a house in Guildford, where the boys spent their school holidays.

His early education was at a day-school in Hastings, but at 13 he was sent to Sherborne School in Dorset, where he excelled in mathematics and science, fields not highly regarded by the classics-steeped teachers of the English public school system. He formed a close relationship with a fellow pupil, Christopher Morcom, who died in 1930, causing Turing considerable grief. In 1934, he graduated with first-class honors in mathematics from King's College, Cambridge and the following year became a Fellow at that College. It was while here that he developed a variety of mathematical models for early computers, showing that universal machines could do endless calculations of all kinds, using algorithms.

By 1938 he had received a PhD from Princeton University for his work on computing, studying under Alonzo Church, who developed the basis for theoretical computer science that Turing extended.

On his return to England, he began to work for the Government Code and Cypher School, at Bletchley Park, Buckinghamshire, which was to evolve into the Government Communications Headquarters (GCHQ), now in Cheltenham.

With the outbreak of World War II, he began to work with the Chief Cryptographer at Bletchley Park, Alfred Dillwyn (Dilly) Knox, on breaking the codes of the German Enigma Machine. The Enigma Machine was an elaborate electrical 'typewriter' that could produce coded messages using constantly-changing codes. It had been developed by a German engineer, Arthur Scherbius, toward the end of World War I, then further developed and adopted by Nazi Germany to transmit wartime messages. The first successful breaking of Enigma codes was done by Polish cryptographers, who Dilly Knox brought to Bletchley Park to explain their work to his team. Turing developed a dramatic improvement over their work with his Bombe, an electrical and mechanical device for systematically discovering the daily settings used by the Germans for their Enigma machines.

As the war went on, Turing, despite considerable successes in saving shipping by decoding U-boat messages, was frustrated with the lack of resources and manpower at Bletchley Park. In October of 1941, in violation of all chains-of-command, Turing and his team wrote a letter directly to Winston Churchill, who immediately ordered that they be given all the resources they needed. By the end of the war, they had 200 working Bombes breaking codes.

In his private life, Turing had a reputation for eccentricity, riding everywhere on a bicycle and sometimes wearing a gas-mask to reduce his pollen allergies. In 1941, he proposed to a fellow mathematician and friend at Bletchley Park, Joan Clarke, although he was an active homosexual, a criminal activity at that time, but widely accepted among academic and intellectual circles. Even when he revealed his inclinations to Joan, she was still happy to marry him, but in the end, he broke off the engagement.

At the end of 1942, he traveled to America to see their cryptography work on Enigma but was less than impressed. While there he worked at Bell Laboratories on devices for transmitting secure spoken messages. Back in England, he developed a machine called Delilah for encrypting spoken messages, but it was never adopted.

Immediately after the war, he moved to the National Physical Laboratory at Bushy Park, in Teddington, London, where he worked on the design of the Automatic Computing Engine (ACE), which was to be the first computer containing stored programs. However, by 1947 he was unhappy with the slow progress of the project and returned to Cambridge. The following year he was appointed Reader in the Mathematics Department at the University of Manchester. It was there that he proposed the famous Turing Test, designed to detect artificial intelligence by seeing if a person questioning a machine could tell it from a human being. He also wrote early computer programs, including a chess program too complex for any computers existing at that time.

The mathematics of growth in biological organisms was also an area of interest to Turing, and he developed mathematical models that could explain the growth of feathers and the branching pattern in the lungs.

In January of 1952, Turing's life fell apart when he was charged with homosexual acts with a 19-year old man. Turing was 39 at the time, and although the younger man received a conditional discharge, Turing was persuaded by his solicitor and his brother John, to plead guilty. To avoid a prison term, Turing accepted probation with the condition he would receive injections of synthetic female hormones to reduce his libido and thereby not re-offend. The conviction lost him the security clearance he needed to continue working for the Government, and he was barred from entry into the U.S. There was considerable anxiety at that time, following the discovery of the Soviet spy Guy Burgess, that homosexuals could be blackmailed into revealing state secrets.

On 8 June 1954, his body was discovered by his housekeeper. He had died the previous day of cyanide poisoning. It has been speculated that he took the cyanide through an apple that was found half-eaten beside him, but the apple was never tested. Alternative theories are that he accidentally poisoned himself using cyanide to dissolve gold for electroplating spoons. His body was cremated.

His Legacy

Turing is regarded as a father of modern computing, and he received an OBE for his wartime work. Numerous other awards have been made posthumously, and his prosecution and death have made him an iconic figure in the gay-rights movement.

He has been named by Time magazine as one of the 100 most important figures of the 20th century, and in a BBC poll, he was 21st of the 100 Greatest Britons. Numerous university buildings and awards have been named after him on both sides of the Atlantic.

Following a four-year campaign of petitions and parliamentary bills, Turing was granted a full-pardon on 24 December 2013, by Queen Elizabeth II under the royal prerogative of mercy.

Sites to Visit

- There is a blue plaque at Baston Lodge, 1 Upper Maze Hill, St Leonards-on-Sea, Hastings, where Turing grew up and another at 2 Warrington Cresent, Maida Vale where he was born.
- There are an additional nine blue plaques to Turing, including his family home at 22 Ennismore Avenue, Guildford, his home at 78 High Street, Hampton, his home and place of death at 43 Adlington Road, Wilmslow, as well as at King's College, Cambridge and Bletchley Park.
- A working replica of Turing's Bombe can be seen at the Bletchley Park Museum.

Further Research

Biographies of Turing include:

- Alan Turing: The Enigma, by Andrew Hodges and Douglas Hofstadter
- Alan Turing: Unlocking the Enigma, by David Boyle
- The Man Who Knew Too Much: Alan Turing and the Invention of the Computer, by David Leavitt
- The Essential Turing: Seminal Writings in Computing, Logic, Philosophy, Artificial Intelligence, and Artificial Life, by Alan M. Turing and B. Jack Copeland

A number of plays, fictional accounts and films have been made around Turing's life and work, including:

- A play, Breaking the Code (1986), also a BBC and PBS television show.
- A drama-documentary, Codebreaker (2011)
- An opera, The Life and Death(s) of Alan Turing (2014)
- A film, The Imitation Game, starring Benedict Cumberbatch (2014)

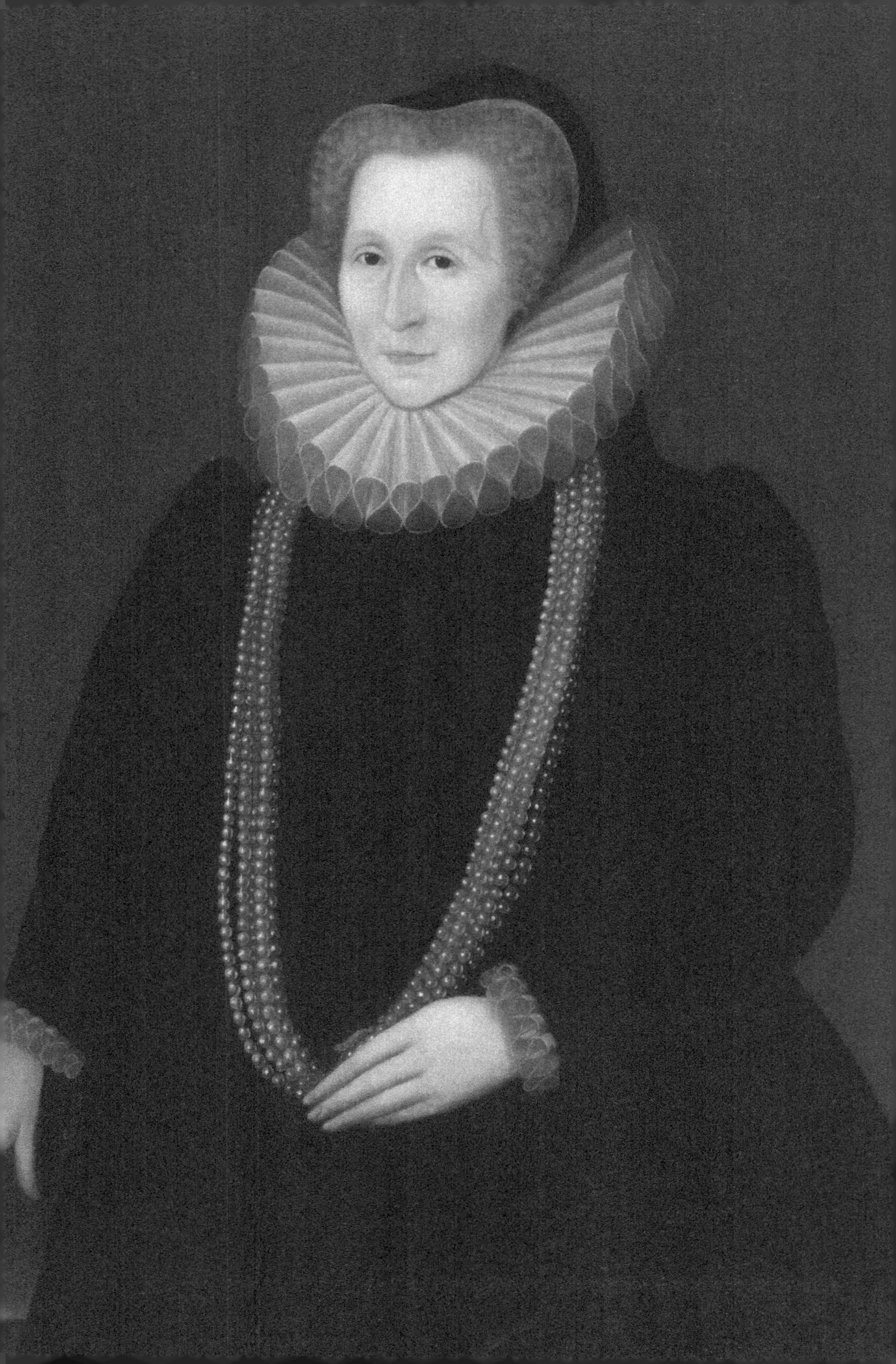

BESS OF HARDWICK
An Uncrowned Queen

Key Facts

- Born 1521, died 1608
- Became one of the richest women in England
- Left a legacy of grand homes and artifacts
- Ancestor of Queen Elizabeth II

The 16th century in England was a turbulent and dangerous time. A time of religious conflict, intrigue and plotting, where fortunes and lives could be won or lost on a whim and when anger, jealousy and naked ambition directed state affairs as much as reason and strategy. It was also a time when women had opportunities previously denied them.

With the first two female monarchs in the country's history, it was a century where it was acceptable for women to wield power and amass fortunes. Elizabeth Talbot, usually know as Bess of Hardwick was pre-eminent in this age of new-found female power.

Bess was born around 1521 – the exact year is unknown – to John Hardwick of Derbyshire. At the time this area between Lancashire and Yorkshire was heavily wooded, and remote from the southern centers of power and influence. The family-owned just a few hundred acres of farmland and were at the lower end of the social scale, being minor members of the gentry, just one step above yeoman farmers.

Bess's younger brother James was the last male heir in the family. Around 1543 Bess, perhaps 20, was married to the 13-year-old

Robert Barley, who was the heir to a nearby estate. However, he died at the end of 1544, and it seems the marriage was only on paper and that they never lived together or likely even consummated their marriage. Certainly, Bess was refused the dowry due to her when Robert died, and it was only after several years of court battles that she was awarded a share in the estate and compensation.

A few years later, in 1547, she married again, this time to a man twice her age who had himself been married twice before, his earlier wives having died. However this was a more financially favorable marriage as her husband, Sir William Cavendish, was the King's Treasurer (to Henry VIII) and had amassed a significant fortune from Henry's seizure of Church property known as the Dissolution of the Monasteries. Bess persuaded her new husband to sell his properties in the south and buy up the estates of her mother's second marriage, in the Derbyshire district of Chatsworth.

When Sir William died just ten years later, Bess inherited his money, since the land had been left to their six surviving children.

By this time Henry VIII, Edward VI and Mary I had come and gone and Elizabeth I had taken the Throne. Catholicism has been briefly and violently re-established by Mary, who imprisoned her half-sister, the future Queen Elizabeth in the Tower of London. Spain has gone from catholic enemy to husband of the Queen and back to enemy again, and Britain has lost its last foothold in France, the port of Calais.

The Captain of the new Queen's Guard and Chief Butler of England (basically the caterer to Royal Coronations) was Sir William St Loe and when he married Bess in 1559 Lady Cavendish became Lady St Loe.

Unlike her earlier marriages, this seems to have been a loving one, and they were both around the same age. Sir William owned extensive estates in the south-west, chiefly in Somerset and although his death in 1565 without a male heir was likely the result of being poisoned by his brother, he left everything to Bess, turning her into one of the richest women in the country. Her annual income of £60,000 would be equivalent to around $10 million today. Not just wealthy, Bess also had power and influence with the new Queen, since she was one of Elizabeth's personal Ladies and had daily access to her. Because of her influence, wealth and enduring good looks, she soon began to attract new suitors.

Bess took her time finding a suitable match but eventually, in 1568, now approaching fifty, she and two of her children married into the powerful Talbot family in a triple ceremony. Bess married George Talbot, the 6th Earl of Shrewsbury, one of the most powerful men in the country. Her daughter, who was 12 at the time, married Talbot's oldest son and thus his heir, while her own son, 18, married one of Talbot's daughters, who was just eight years old. This would certainly have ensured that the Earl's fortune would pass into Bess's family.

Bess now became caught up in the intrigues of the British royals. Mary I of Scotland (not to be confused with Mary I of England) was considered by many British Catholics to be the legitimate heir to the Throne. So when she was deposed by rebellious Scottish lords and fled to England seeking Elizabeth's protection the Queen had a problem.

She solved it by placing Mary in the hands of the Shrewsbury's in what was effectively a house arrest. Mary spent the next 15 years living in several of the Shrewsbury estates, out of Elizabeth's way. She was ultimately executed for treason, but the years with Bess and her husband created marital strain and resulted in their separation.

However, Bess and Mary also spent a considerable amount of time together working on embroidery and tapestry, as was appropriate to their gender and positions. Bess and the Earl had separated permanently by the time Elizabeth took Mary off their hands. The Earl died in 1590, leaving Bess the richest woman in England after Elizabeth herself and with the title Dowager Countess of Shrewsbury. She built herself a grand palace at Hardwick Hall to rival Elizabeth. The house is notable for its use of very large windows for the period.

While married to the Earl of Shrewsbury Bess made complex marriage arrangements for one of her daughters which resulted in a grandchild, Arbella Stuart, who was a potential heir to the Throne. Bess's plan did not succeed, and in the end, she was forced to ask Elizabeth to take this willful child into her care after Arbella attempted to elope. Although this plan failed, Bess did eventually have a descendant take the Throne – Queen Elizabeth II.

Bess died in 1608, outliving Elizabeth I and seeing James I take the Throne and imprison Arbella Stuart in the Tower, where she eventually died, after a plot by Sir Walter Raleigh to make her Queen – something Arbella had never personally wanted. Bess also probably heard of the settlement of Jamestown, Virginia in 1607.

Her Legacy

In an account of history dominated by male characters, Bess of Hardwick stands out as a woman who used marriage to accumulate a fortune which she then turned to her own benefit. Her romantic life in turbulent times is a story of survival and success in a constantly shifting landscape of alliances and betrayals.

Sites to Visit

- While married to William Cavendish Bess had a manor house built on the Chatsworth Estates. Although the house was significantly re-built, a room known as the Queen of Scots Room still exists in the house, which is now owned by Bess's descendant the Duke of Devonshire and is open to the public.
- The considerable collection of needlework made by Bess and Queen Mary during her imprisonment is still kept at Hardwick Hall, Derbyshire, the house she built when Countess of Shrewsbury. The property is now owned by the National Trust.

Further Research

- A number of Bess's letters can be read on-line.
- Recent biographies include: Bess of Hardwick, by Mary S. Lovell (2006) and Bess of Hardwick and Her Circle, by Maud Stepney Rawson (2012).
- Bess is the main character in the fictional account of her life Venus in Winter: A Novel of Bess of Hardwick, by Gillian Bagwell (2013).

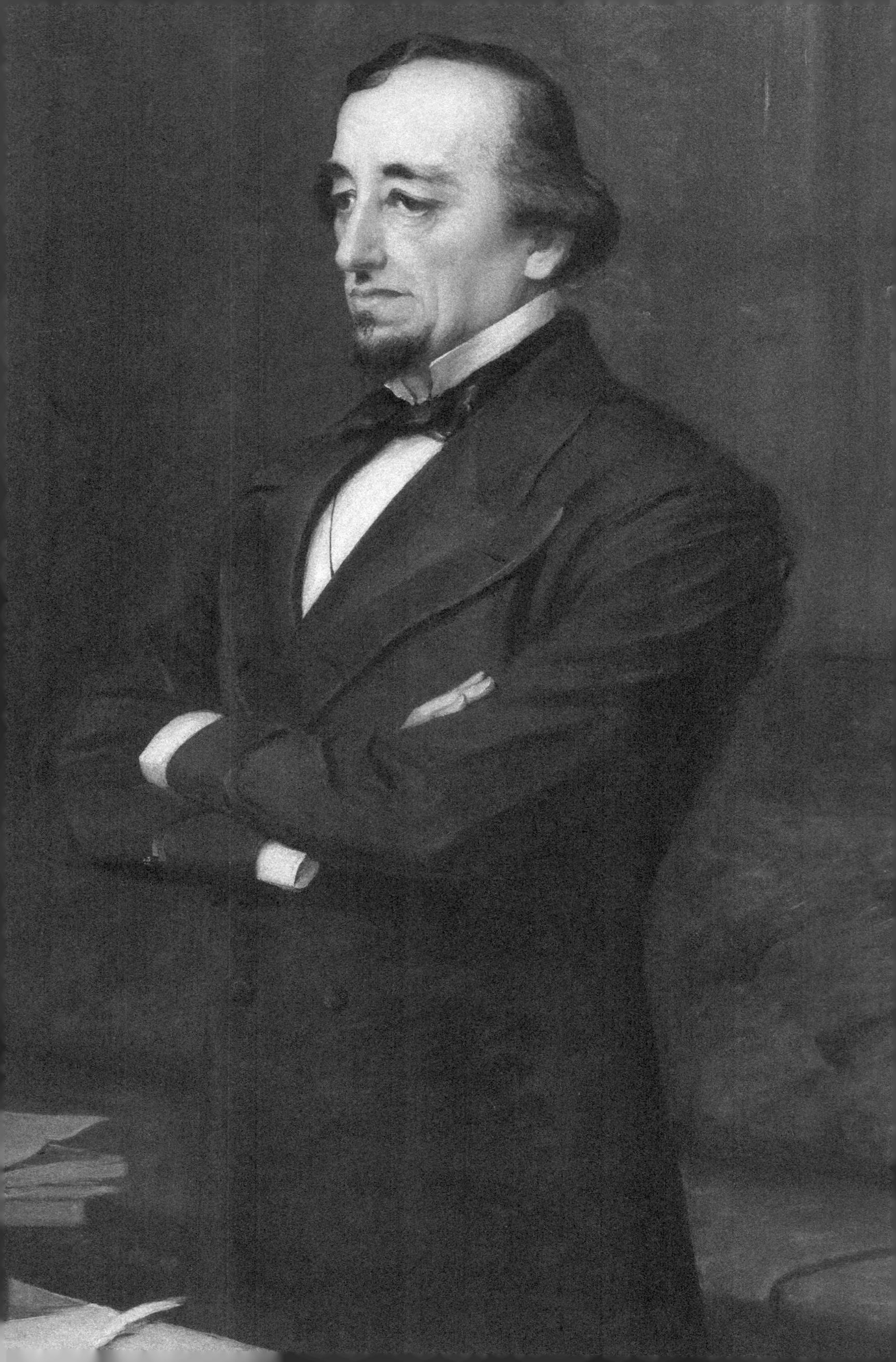

BENJAMIN DISRAELI
Prime Minister and Reformer

Key Facts

- Born 1804, died 1881
- Combined a literary career with a political one
- Became Prime Minister and was knighted by Queen Victoria
- Advanced the British Empire and Britain's international role

Benjamin Disraeli was the first British Prime Minister of Jewish descent and a controversial political figure in Victorian England. He formed the Conservative party from the Tories and established its power base. He expanded the British Empire and developed Britain's role as an international power.

Despite his later attempts to paint it as more eminent, Benjamin Disraeli was born in to a boring middle-class family at the beginning of the 19th century in the Bloomsbury district of London. His father was a Sephardic Jew of Italian descent, but in 1817, when Benjamin was 12, he had his five children baptized into the Church of England, following disputes with his local synagogue. Although England was not an openly anti-Semitic society at the time, this did open-up opportunities for Benjamin that would not have been there had he remained Jewish.

Following an education in small private schools and with private tutors that was normal for better-off children at the time, he was articled as a clerk to a firm of London solicitors. However after two years and a trip to the Continent, he briefly entered training as a barrister at an uncle's chambers, but he did not prove suitable and was advised to begin a career as a writer. However, his early writing turned out to be chiefly promotional sales pamphlets for investments in South America; he borrowed heavily to invest in the stocks he promoted and lost heavily when the bubble burst. It took him 25 years to repay the loans. Feeling tricked by the man who had encouraged him to invest, he wrote a thinly-veiled attack in the form of a four-volume novel, which sold well but made him an outcast from the upper levels of the literary society he aspired to.

Plunged into a deep depression and still living at home, in 1830 he and his sister's fiancé William Meridith, set out for Southern Europe and ended up in Egypt, where Meridith died of smallpox and Disraeli contracted an STD. Disraeli returned to England late in 1831 and wrote two novels based on his experiences, but the opinions he had formed on the broad issues of the time led him to move into politics, and he began to write political pamphlets.

At that time, there were three main political parties in Britain. The Whigs were supported by wealthy merchants and industrialists and were for a strong parliament over the monarch, free-trade and religious freedom.

The Tories, with aristocratic and gentry support, were for a powerful King, the Church of England and they were protectionist. While the Tories opposed political change, the Radicals, who were the third force, drew support from the middle-class and working-class and wanted wider suffrage and parliamentary reform.

Disraeli found himself divided in his allegiances. He was with the Radicals on reform, and he stood as a Radical candidate in the 1832 elections but did not win the seat. However he was a protectionist and through a shared mistress became a friend of the powerful Tory Lord Lyndhurst, with whom he found a common interest in political intrigue. In 1835 he began to build a public profile when he stood as a Tory in the election of that year. Although he failed to win, his performance was admired and some strong exchanges with an Iris MP, including a challenge to a duel, garnered him significant media coverage in The Times.

Now circulating in the very aristocratic circles he had satirized in his early novels, Disraeli moved firmly into the Tory camp, with his support of a benevolent aristocracy and an anti-Irish, anti-

Catholic, anti-business stance. He was rewarded with membership in the Tory's exclusive Carleton Club and a safe seat in Parliament, which he entered as a back-bencher in 1837. He continued to support himself by writing novels which usually took his own life as inspiration, but he made a lack-lustre showing in Parliament.

In 1839 he married the widow of a close political associate. Although significantly older than him, and wealthy, this marriage for money did become an affectionate and loving one. They had no children and remained together until his wife died in 1872.

In 1846 a major political crisis erupted over the repeal of the Corn Laws, which kept the price of wheat high through tariffs and impacted on the poor. The outcome was a repeal of the laws, but more importantly, the forming of a new political alliance, with free-traders from the Tory party joining the Whigs and Radicals to form the Liberal Party, and the protectionist Tories, including Disraeli, forming the Conservative Party, forming a two-party system that was to persist until the rise of Labour in the 20th century.

Early in 1852, Disraeli had his first change of office when he was appointed Chancellor in the minority government of Lord Derby, but his first budget was defeated along with Derby's government, and Disraeli found himself on the opposition benches. Following years of political turmoil and dispute, Disraeli managed to have the Reform Act of 1867 passed by Parliament, extending the franchise to male householders and removing corrupted electoral boundaries. He handled this complex reform so well that the following year he was appointed Prime Minister. His rise from relatively humble origins was particularly admired. In and out of office during the following years, he was made Earl of Beaconsfield by Queen Victoria in 1876, but at that time a Lord could be Prime Minister, so he continued in that office as well, whenever the Conservatives could win an election.

His governments passed significant reforms in working conditions, forging an alliance with the working-class that became an important power-base for the party, while simultaneously employing patronage to place Tories in powerful positions in the Public Service. In foreign policy perhaps his most famous act was to buy the Suez Canal for England, securing a stable trade-route to India. Disraeli used flattery to maintain good relations with the Queen, and jingoistic nationalism to keep political support from the electorate. He strengthened the Empire, adding South Africa and gained some control of Afghanistan. At the pivotal Congress of Berlin in 1878, in alliance with Chancellor Bismarck of Germany, Russian territorial gains in Eastern Europe as the Ottoman Empire collapsed were minimized, and Disraeli secured Cyprus for Britain as a key naval base.

Despite these successes, in the 1880 election the Conservatives were beaten by the Liberals and Disraeli, already in poor health, began to decline further. He died on the 19th of April, 1881. Fearing uncontrollable crowds, he did not receive a state funeral and was buried in the church on his estate.

His Legacy

Disraeli's literary works, although providing insight into his character, are generally considered unreadable today.

Politically, he is credited with inventing 'Tory democracy', the use of social reforms and nationalism to gain working-class support. The Reform Act of 1867 probably prevented revolution in Britain and preserved the position of the monarchy. His complex character, part dandy, sexual adventurer and master of political intrigue, part nationalist and patriot, continues to fascinate many to this day.

Sites to Visit

- Disraeli's tomb is in the Church of St Michael and All Angels, in the grounds of his country home, Hughenden Manor, High Wycombe, Buckinghamshire. The property is owned by the National Trust and can be visited.
- There is a memorial in Westminster Abbey, London, built at the urging of his life-long Liberal rival, William Gladstone.

Further Research

Biographies of Disraeli include:

- Disraeli: A Biography, by Stanley Weintraub (1993)
- Benjamin Disraeli: Scenes from an Extraordinary Life, by Helen Langley (2005)
- The Lion and the Unicorn: Gladstone vs Disraeli, by Richard Aldous (2012)
- His literary works are readily available as free e-books.

BOADICEA HARANGUING THE BRITONS.

BOADICEA
Queen of the Britons

Key Facts

- Born ? – died 60 or 61 AD
- Leader of an uprising against the Roman occupation of England
- Destroyed three cities, including London, before meeting defeat
- Remembered as a symbol of British independence from outside rule

Boadicea, or Boudica, or Boudig in Welsh, was the leader of a rebellion by English tribes against the occupation of Britain by the Roman Empire, in the first century of the modern era. Following atrocities committed against her, her daughters and her tribe, to collect debts owed, she rallied surrounding tribes to form an army. They destroyed the towns known today as Colchester, London and St Albans, slaughtering 80,000 people, mostly civilians. After defeating one legion at Colchester, she was herself defeated by two Roman legions on Watling Road, a Roman road across England. The discipline and tactics of the Romans meant that 10,000 legionnaires lost only 400 men killing 80,000 rebel troops. She died shortly afterwards, either from drinking poison or from illness. In the Victorian era, she was revived as a heroine of British independence.

In 55 BC the Roman Emperor Julius Caesar had famously attempted to conquer Britain, but he had been forced to withdraw after making an initial beachhead. The Romans however, did not forget the Island of Albion. Almost a hundred year later, in AD 43, 20,000 Roman legionnaires left from the port of Boulogne in France and crossed the English Channel, landing along the coast of Kent.

Led by a senior senator, Aulus Plautius, the ostensible purpose of the force was to re-instate Verica, king of the Atrebates tribe, who was aligned with the Romans. After days of fierce fighting against the English tribes, the Romans pushed them back across the Thames and seized a settlement that has been dated back to 1,500 BC. There they built a fort and trading post and called it Londinium.

From Londinium and other bases in the south-east, Roman troops spread out across the country, subduing the tribes they encountered along the way, even bringing in war elephants to over-awe the native populations. When Nero became Emperor in 54 AD, he decided to continue the conquest of this land, and he sent Quintus Veranius to be governor. Veranius had experience in suppressing difficult tribes in hostile terrain, having conquered the tribal areas of Anatolia – modern-day Turkey.

Veranius sent troops into Wales, where they destroyed Druid temples and settlements, massacring several tribes and seizing the Island of Anglesey. The Romans viewed the English and Welsh as barbaric and accused them of human sacrifice on their stone altars. They pushed north until they reached Caledonia, the area of modern-day Scotland. The Emperor Hadrian would build a wall there about 80 years later, to keep back the unconquerable Scots.

Some tribes had surrendered, rather than be massacred, in return for some degree of independence. One such tribe was the Iceni, who lived where Norfolk is today. Their king was Prasutagus, and his wife was called Bodica, or Boadicea, a tall woman with a piercing gaze and long hair below her waist. They had two daughters. In an attempt to preserve the little independence the tribe still had, Prasutagus named the Emperor, and his two daughters as joint heirs to his kingdom. He hoped this would cause the Romans to leave his tribe in peace, but that was not to be.

As a way of controlling the tribes, the Emperor Claudius had encouraged and even forced them to borrow money from the Empire, collecting interest on it and so creating economic dependence – a method familiar to modern consumer-capitalism. Nero's advisor Seneca seems to have been responsible for issuing the loans, and when Prasutagus died, Seneca called in his loans to the Iceni. When they could not repay it all at once, he sent in the troops.

They looted and pillaged the tribal lands; took the royal household into slavery; confiscated the estates of the leading tribesmen; had Boadicea whipped, and raped her daughters. The governor of Britain, Gaius Suetonius Paulinus, was fighting in Wales at the time, and it is possible that this was all a private action of Seneca, without sanction from the governor.

Un-bowed, Boadicea met with a neighboring tribe, the Trinovantes, and others, to plan a revolt against the Romans. Perhaps drawing inspiration from the folk-memories of the successful defeat of Julius Caesar, the army marched on Camulodunum (modern Colchester), which had been the capital of the Trinovantes before their conquest. Veteran Roman soldiers had moved in, extracting money from the locals to build a temple to Emperor Claudius, and mistreating the tribe. By offering to take their capital first, Boadicea showed a shrewd political sense of how to ensure their loyalty for her future actions.

There were only 200 mercenary troops protecting the town, auxiliaries to the legions, and after two days of fighting with the troops who had barricaded themselves in the temple, Boadicea took the town. The tribes systematically razed it to the ground. Quintus Petillius Cerialis, a future governor, who was at that time commander of one of the four legions holding Britain, the Legio IX Hispana, came to relieve the garrison. We don't know the size of Boadicea's army, but a legion at that time was 5,000 men. The tribes destroyed them, and only Quintus and some of his cavalry escaped.

Governor Suetonius heard of the destruction of Camulodunum and hastily returned from Wales to protect Londinium. When he arrived at this unassuming but busy trading centre, he had second thoughts, and looking at his weary troops, and remembering the defeat of Quintus, he decided to withdraw, leaving the 20-year-old settlement to the mercy of Boadicea. Those who could keep up with the legion went with it, but everyone else was left behind. When Boadicea and her rebels arrived, they burned the town to the ground and massacred everyone left behind. The rebels then marched to Verulamium (St Albans) and destroyed it as well.

Estimates are that 70,000 to 80,000 people were killed, with no prisoners taken. According to Roman accounts – we have no other – people were variously hung, burned or crucified. Women of high rank were impaled, their breasts removed and stitched to their mouths. The tribes celebrated their victories with banquets and orgies. The Romans estimate that by this time the rebels numbered almost a quarter million, but that may not be an accurate account, and probably includes family members and not just troops.

Suetonius meanwhile had called in a second legion to join his own and took a stand in an unknown location. There is some evidence this was on the Roman Road known as Watling Street, at a spot in the West Midlands. Lined up with their backs to a wood, the legions were completely outnumbered by the vast horde of rebels. Boadicea, in her chariot with her daughters, addressed her army:

It is not as a woman descended from noble ancestry, but as one of the people, that I am avenging lost freedom, my scourged body, [and] the outraged chastity of my daughters ... this is a woman's resolve; as for men, they may live and be slaves.

Suetonius has chosen his spot wisely. The woods created only a narrow front, so Boadicea could only send in limited numbers of her men at any one time. The skilled and disciplined legionnaires were far superior to the mob of tribesmen. As happened so often much later, when the British confronted tribes in Africa and elsewhere, a small group of trained soldiers can overcome a large number of rampaging warriors. First, the Romans decimated the tribesmen with their throwing javelins, called pila. When these were used up the legionnaires advanced in a wedge formation, trapping the tribesmen against their own wagons. They had circled the battlefield with them and left their families there, but they proved to be a self-made trap. Perhaps 80,000 of the British were killed, at the cost of just 400 Roman soldiers.

What happened next is unclear. It may be that Boadicea poisoned herself, or she may have fallen sick. In either case, she died at or shortly after the battle. Suetonius embarked on a campaign of retribution so severe that Nero, who had considered abandoning Britain when he heard of the uprising, sent a more moderate governor to replace Suetonius and restore calm.

It took another hundred years of campaigning to subdue the tribes, and Scotland was never conquered. A unique Romano-British culture and society emerged, ruled over by the goddess Britannia. Agriculture, planned cities, and industry developed, but the country was a backwater, hardly mentioned in Rome, and our knowledge of it comes chiefly from archaeology. Roman rule continued until 410 AD when the island achieved de-facto self-government. In that year the Emperor Honorius refused to send help to the ruling magistrates, telling the Roman cities to 'see to their own defence'. The legions never returned.

Sites to Visit

- The Boadicea Monument is at the north-west corner of Westminster Bridge, facing Big Ben and the Houses of Parliament, and close to the London Eye. It was created by the sculptor, artist and engineer Thomas Thornycroft in the 19th century, but not cast into bronze and erected until 1902. It depicts Boadicea and her daughters in a chariot with scythes on the wheels.
- There is a statue of Boudig by J. Havard Thomas (1916) on

the first-floor landing of Cardiff City Hall, in Wales. There are ten other statues of Welsh cultural heroes on the landing.
- Sections of Watling Street can be walked, particularly around St Albans. The remains of Verulanium can be seen.

Further Research

Film depictions:

- Boadicea (1927)
- The Viking Queen (1967)
- In Search of Boadicea (1980), by Michael Wood. BBC documentary film
- Boudica (2003) released as 'Warrior Queen' in the US) TV film

Novels:

- Dreaming the Hound (Boudica Trilogy), by Manda Scott.
- A Year of Ravens: a novel of Boudica's Rebellion, by E Knight, 2015
- Boudica, by Tristan Bernays, 2018 – a play Shakespeare's Globe, London, in September 2017

Biographies:

- Boudica: The British Revolt Against Rome AD 60, by Graham Webster, 1999
- Boudica: A Groundbreaking Biography of the True Warrior Queen, by Vanessa Collingridge, 2006
- Boudica: Iron Age Warrior Queen, by Richard Hingley and Christina Unwin, 2006
- Boudica: Warrior Woman of Roman Britain (Women in Antiquity series), by Caitlin C. Gillespie, 2018

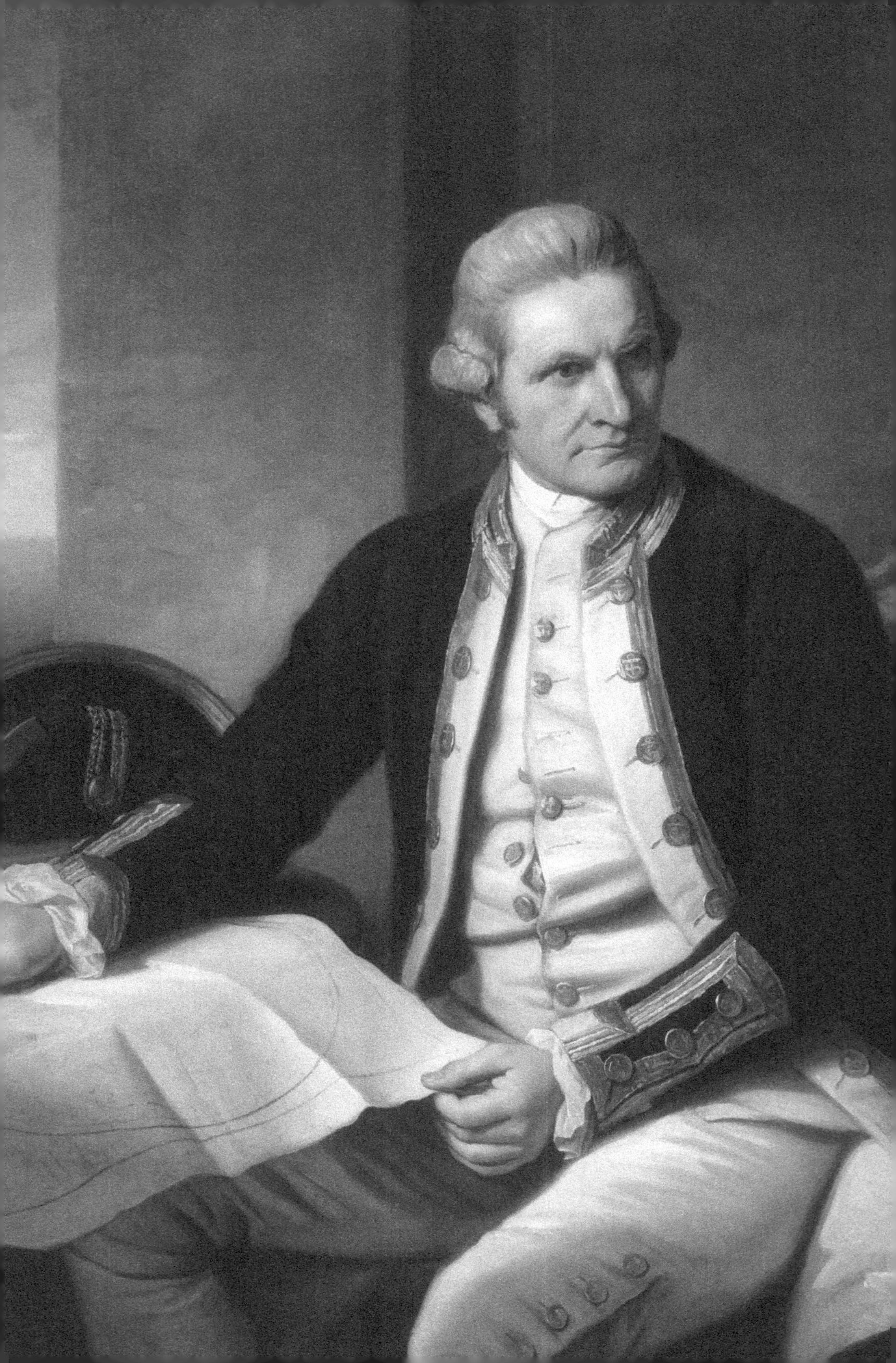

CAPTAIN JAMES COOK
Explorer

Key Facts

- Born November 7, 1728, died February 14, 1779
- Discovered Australia and many islands in the Pacific, including Hawaii
- Contributed to the accurate mapping of coastlines and improved navigation

When sailing a ship, you need to know where you are. The first equipment to help sailors do this was the compass, which indicated north. One's latitude, or distance from the pole, can be determined fairly easily by measuring the angle of the Sun at noon and knowing the date. However determining longitude – how far east or west you are – is a much more difficult problem. Many shipwrecks were caused by errors, and accurate charts were impossible to make. So in 1714, a prize was offered by the British navy for a method of accurately determining longitude at sea. The answer was a clock which would keep precisely accurate time while on a moving ship, which at that time was very difficult to do. It took John Harrison, a Yorkshire carpenter, from 1730 to 1761 and four versions to develop a sufficiently accurate clock – a marine chronometer - to win the prize of £20,000. When one realizes that this would be 40 million pounds today, the importance of this discovery to British naval strength is clear.

It was no coincidence that James Cook began his map-making career during and immediately after the development of the marine chronometer. Without it, his charts would not have had the needed accuracy.

James Cook was born in 1728 in the village of Marton, Yorkshire. He was the second of eight children his Scottish father and Yorkshire mother were to have. When he was eight, his father moved to a farm nearby, and the farmer paid for the young James to go to the local school. At the age of sixteen, he was sent to the coastal village of Staithes as an apprentice to a shopkeeper.

He did not suit shop work, but he must have made a good impression on his employer because after eighteen months he arranged for Cook to be apprenticed to a friend in the port of Whitby, who owned several ships trading in coal. He spent two years working on the merchant boats, learning mathematics and navigation. In 1752 he passed his seaman's examinations and rose to ship's mate.

In 1755 he was offered a merchant-ship to captain, but instead joined the Royal Navy which was just recruiting for what became the Seven Year's War. This was a major war between Britain, France, Spain and Prussia to determine who controlled which colonies in the Americas and elsewhere for trade.

Cook joined the HMS Eagle and within a month was back in mate's position. Within two years he was master on HMS Pembroke. A ship's master was second to the captain and was the navigator. Aboard her, Cook took part in the siege of Louisburg and surveyed the St Lawrence River, which was vital in the taking of Quebec. He was then transferred to the HMS Northumberland, in which he surveyed the coasts of Nova Scotia and Newfoundland.

On his return to England in 1762 Cook married Elizabeth Batts, from Wapping and moved to the East End of London. They ultimately had six children but no grandchildren were produced, so Cook had no direct descendants.

In 1766 Cook was asked by the Royal Society of London for Improving Natural Knowledge (called simply The Royal Society) to sail to the Pacific to observe a transit of Venus across the Sun. His expedition set sail in 1768, sailing westward around Cape Horn and continuing across the Pacific to arrive in Tahiti in April 1769. After observing the Transit, he opened sealed orders to discover that he had been commanded by the Admiralty to sail south to look for the hypothetical southern continent of Terra Australis.

He sailed south and mapped the islands of New Zealand, before turning west and discovering the east coast of Australia. His first sighting was Brush Island, where he saw indigenous people on the shore. A few days later he landed on the mainland at Botany Bay, near Sydney Harbour. It was so named because the famous botanist Sir Joseph Banks, who was traveling with Cook, collected specimens there. Turning north his ship was almost sunk when it hit coral on the Great Barrier Reef, but after repairs, they sailed on and landed in England in 1771, three years after leaving.

His second voyage of discovery began in 1772, with Cook sailing to Antarctica and Easter Island. He came within 1,250 miles of the South Pole. As was the habit at that time, he was again accompanied by a group of scientists who collected specimens and made observations. He arrived back in England in 1775.

The following year he set out on his third and final expedition, this time in search of the fabled Northwest Passage above North America to Asia. Since attempts from the Atlantic side had failed, Cook approached from the Pacific. After being the first European to see Hawaii (in 1778) he mapped the west-coast of Canada, trading for sea-otter pelts with the ethnic peoples. He attempted to sail around Alaska through the Bering Straits but failed.

He then returned to Hawaii. There disputes broke out between Cook and the Hawaiian people. Cook attempted to take the King hostage by inviting him to visit his boat, but others saw through Cook's trick, and he was attacked with a club, then stabbed and his body taken away by the people. However, out of respect, they treated his body as they would one of their kings – cleaning and preparing the skeleton. Some of the bones were returned to his ship's crew, who buried them at sea.

His ship, under temporary command, returned to England in October 1780.

His Legacy

Cook is remembered for his voyages of discovery in the Pacific, particularly his discovery of Australia. He was a consummate navigator and cartographer, using the new chronometer to produce some of the first accurate charts of the coastlines around the Pacific Ocean. By doing so, he greatly assisted Britain in becoming a major world trading nation and outstripping its rivals Spain, France and the Netherlands.

Cook and the scientists who traveled with him, particularly Joseph Banks, made important botanical, zoological and ethnographic collections of many new species from the Pacific islands and Australia.

Sites to Visit

- There is a plaque in Shadwell, East London marking his home.
- The Captain Cook Birthplace Museum in Marton was opened in 1978 on the 250th anniversary of his birth.
- There is an obelisk dedicated to Cook overlooking the village of Great Ayton, and a monument near Chalfont St. Giles in Buckinghamshire.
- There is also a monument in the Church of St. Andrew the Great, Cambridge.
- Because of his strong association with Australia, many Cook artifacts and memorials are to be found there, including his parent's house, known as Cook's Cottage, which was dismantled, shipped to Australia in crates and re-erected in Melbourne in 1934.

Further Research

- Two biographies of Cook are: Farther Than Any Man: The Rise and Fall of Captain James Cook, by Martin Dugard (2001), and Captain James Cook: A Biography by Richard Alexander Hough (2013 – reprint)
- Cook's own Journals are available in several editions.
- There is a TV miniseries – Captain James Cook (1987)
- There is a biographical DVD - Captain Cook: Obsession & Discovery (2007)

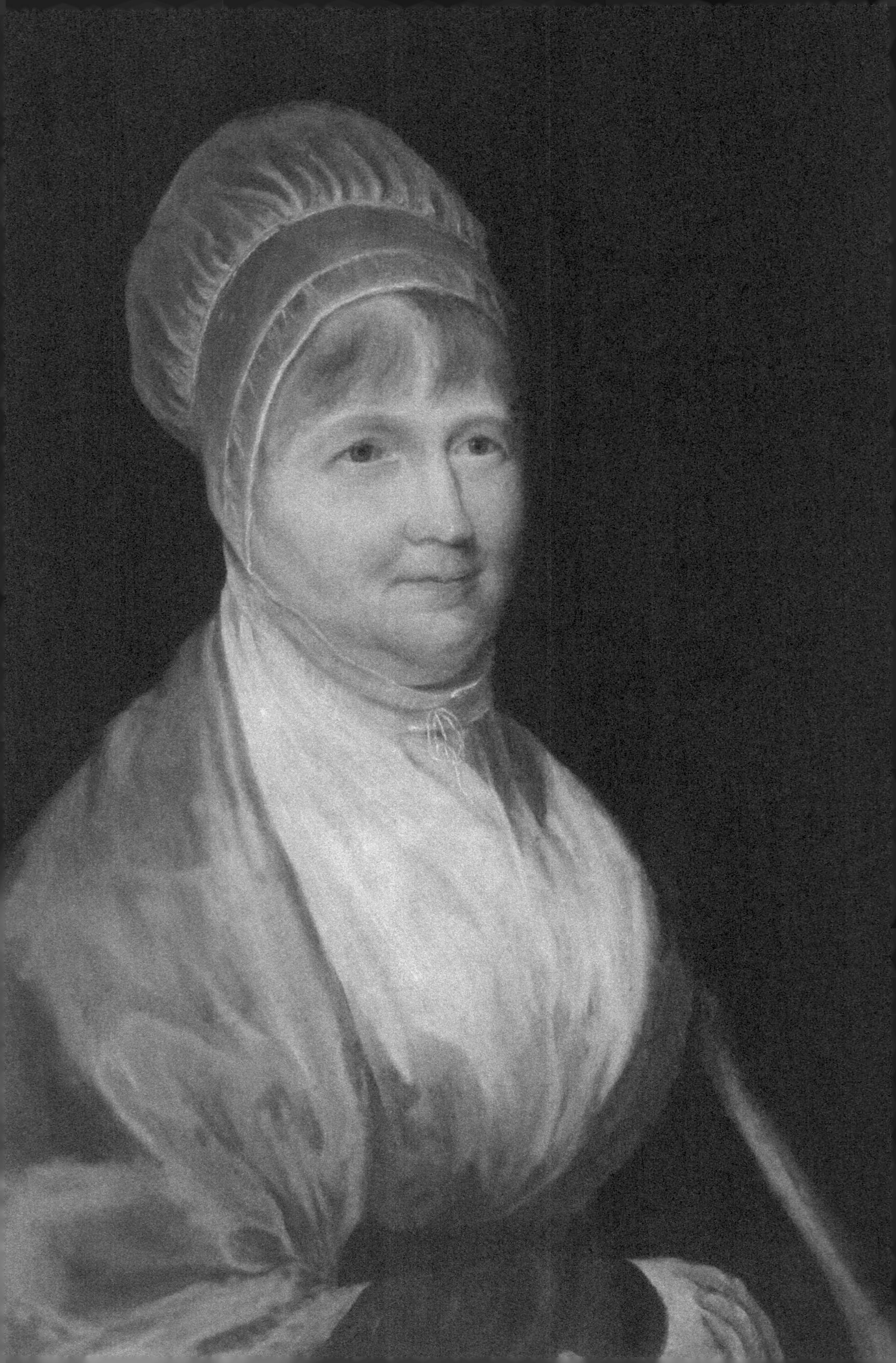

ELIZABETH FRY
Social Reformer

Key Facts

- Born 1780, died 1845
- A Quaker who worked for prison reform
- An early female activist for social justice

Elizabeth Fry was a Quaker who campaigned in the first half of the 19th century for the improvement of prison conditions, especially for women. She became famous for her philanthropic work and encouraged a social conscience among the wealthy classes for the plight of the poor and underprivileged.

Prison is never a great place to end up, but there was a time when it was a living hell. It was appallingly overcrowded, unspeakably squalid and so disease-ridden that a prison-sentence could soon become a death sentence. Few people seemed to care until one day in 1812 the wife of a London banker went to the notorious Newgate prison. Her name was Elizabeth Fry.

Elizabeth Gurney was born in Norwich into a Quaker family on the 21st of May, 1780. Her father John Gurney had founded Gurney's bank in Norwich ten years earlier with his brother. Her mother, Catherine, came from the Barclay family and by the end of the century, Gurney's had merged with Barclays Bank. Elizabeth was one of the older children, so after her mother died when she was just 12, some of the responsibility for raising the other children in the family fell to her. Her sister Louisa was to go on to write on education and promote the positive virtues of childhood.

In 1800 Elizabeth married Joseph Fry, also a banker and a Quaker and the new couple moved to London where they lived for a time in the City, before eventually moving out to what was then the rural area of Forest Gate. They had 11 children. Elizabeth was active in the Quaker church as a preacher.

Around 1810 she met Étienne de Grellet du Mabillier, who she knew as Stephen Grellet. He had been in the personal guard of King Louis XVI and had narrowly escaped execution during the French Revolution. He had become a Quaker and traveled to North America where he made his home in Burlington, New Jersey. He was an active social reformer and had met with Kings, Popes and Czars to further his reforms in education, hospitals and prisons. Knowing that Elizabeth already worked collecting clothes for the poor and visiting the sick, Grellet persuaded her to visit Newgate prison.

This prison was founded in 1188 but had recently been re-built in a style deliberately chosen to make the very appearance of the prison a deterrent to crime. The style was known as architecture terrible and had been promoted by the French architect Jacques-François Blondel. Besides a deliberately heavy, foreboding façade the building had such features as carved chains over the doorways. Inside the prison conditions exceeded the promise of the exterior. Elizabeth was especially concerned by the conditions of the female prisoners, who lived and cooked within their cells, sleeping on straw. Children lived inside the prison with their mothers. She returned the next day with food and clothing, but family issues kept her from further visits for the next four years.

When she returned in 1816 she started a school for the children, encouraged the women to sew, preached and encouraged Bible reading and by becoming a friend with the prisoners helped them improve their own conditions. She founded the British Ladies' Society for Promoting the Reformation of Female Prisoners, which is generally considered to be the first nation-wide female organization in Britain. With the influence of a brother-in-law who was an MP, she was able to give evidence in 1818 to a House of Commons committee on prison conditions, which was the first time a woman had given evidence in Parliament. She invited her wealthy friends and even members of the aristocracy to visit the prisons and stay overnight, so as to publicize the issues and gain support for her cause.

After finding the body of a young boy frozen to death during a severe winter, she established a night shelter for the homeless. She also established a system of Visiting Societies, with the first one in Brighton, where volunteers went to the homes of the poor and helped them as they could.

In 1818 she toured England, visiting other prisons and establishing more Ladies' Societies for their reform. She wrote a book called Observations of the Siting, Superintendence and Government of Female Prisoners, which suggested specific practical changes, rather than simply arguing against the existing conditions. Anyway, as Fry herself said, the conditions she saw were so appalling that she could only paint a faint picture of reality; the filth, the closeness of the rooms, … and the abandoned wickedness, … are really indescribable.

Elizabeth's husband went bankrupt in 1828 – it is not recorded if he went to Debtor's Prison – and her brother Joseph John Gurney became both an active participant in her work and her source of finance. Prime Minister Robert Peel took an interest and passed the Goals Act of 1823 and other legislation intended to reform the prisons. However, the absence of an inspection system made these early reforms ineffective.

She visited Queen Victoria several times, and the Queen took an interest in her work and made financial donations. In 1842 she established a school to train nurses, and it was from this school that Florence Nightingale took nurses to her hospital in Turkey, during the Crimean War. In 1842 the King of Prussia came to meet her at Newgate Prison while he was in England on a state visit.

Elizabeth died suddenly on the 12th of October, 1845. After her death, the Lord Mayor of London started a campaign and helped raise private funding to establish the Elizabeth Fry Refuge for Women, which opened in 1849 in Hackney. It was a place for recently-released female prisoners to live while they re-established their lives.

Her Legacy

Although John Howard had worked for prison reform earlier than Elizabeth Fry, she was the first woman to do so and one of the first women to work for the improvement of society. Although at the time she was sometimes criticized for neglecting her family, she showed that women could raise a family and also be involved in the wider world.

Her legacy can be seen in the relatively humane conditions found in most prisons today in Britain, Europe and North America. There are Elizabeth Fry societies still active in Canada. The Elizabeth Fry Refuge evolved and changed premises, and is now the Elizabeth Fry Probation Hostel in Reading.

Sites to Visit

- Her grave is in the former Society of Friends Burial Ground, Whiting Avenue, Barking, Essex.
- Her name is on the Reformers Monument in Kensal Green Cemetery, London.
- There is a bust in the gatehouse of HM Prison, Wormwood Scrubs.
- There is a statue of Elizabeth at the Old Bailey, a courthouse in central London, near Covent Garden.
- She is shown reading to prisoners in Newgate on the British £5 note.

There are English Heritage blue plaques with her name at:

- Her birthplace of Gurney Court, 31 Magdalen Street, Norwich
- Her childhood home of Earlham Hall, now part of the University of East Anglia
- St. Mildred's Court, London, where she first lived after her marriage
- Arklow House, Ramsgate, her final home and where she died

Further Research

- There is archival material related to Elizabeth Fry held at the National Archives in England.
- There are several biographies of her life, including:
- The Value of Kindness: The Story of Elizabeth Fry, by Spencer Johnson, (1976)
- Elizabeth Fry - a Biography, by June Rose (1980)
- Memoir of the Life of Elizabeth Fry, by Katherine Fry (her eldest daughter) (1848, reprinted 1974)

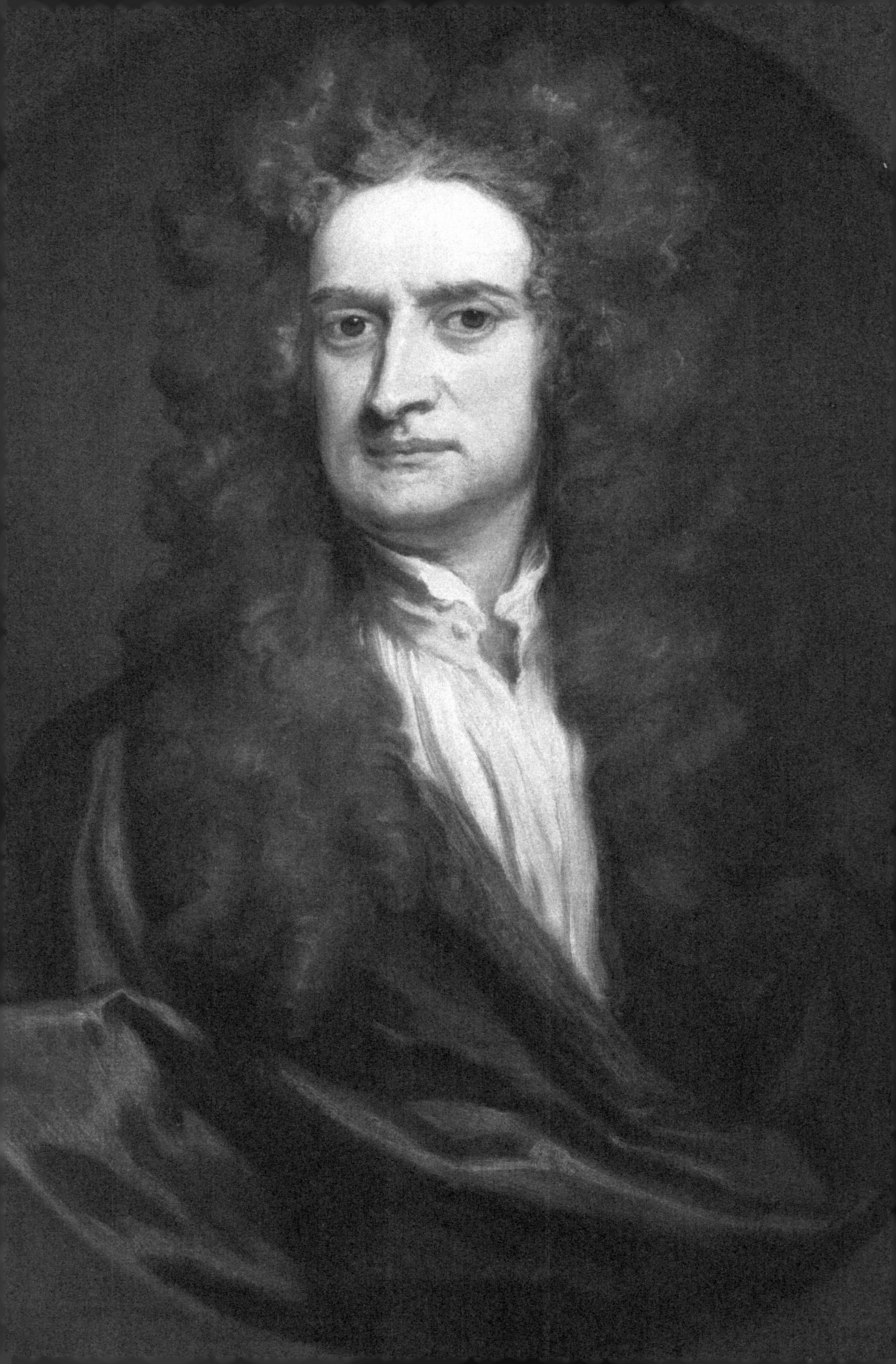

ISAAC NEWTON
Scientist and Naturalist

Key Facts

- Born 25th December 1642, died 20th March 1727
- Explained the nature of gravity and the motion of the planets
- Discovered the spectrum of colors in white light and the particle nature of light
- Developed the intellectual methodology of modern science

Motion is the fundamental activity of the universe. From planets, stars and galaxies to atoms, rocks and apples, the movement of things around us is a basic observation.

Reaching a true understanding of that motion has been a long road lined with obvious, but false, ideas, political and social battles and the genius of a few names. With Galileo at one end and Einstein at the other, one figure stands at a major junction of the road, and that is Isaac Newton.

Newton was born to a farming family at the end of 1642, into a divided Britain just starting a Civil War to decide if authority should be from a hereditary king or an elected parliament. The split was also between a conservative Church of England and the Puritans – radical Protestants – who supported parliament. When Newton was a child, the King was deposed.

Throughout Newton's life, these religious and political wars continued to rage in Britain with power shifting from one group to another and back again. Towards the end of his life, the Monarch was restored, but this background of strife and intolerance created issues for Newton's work. Science has never been socially neutral.

Newton's father was already dead when he was born, and his mother re-married when Isaac was three.

He was raised chiefly by his maternal grandmother and animosity towards his step-father and mother continued throughout his youth. He himself never married.

In 1661 he entered Trinity College, Cambridge, first working as a valet to support himself and later winning a scholarship to complete his M.A. While still a student he discovered the binomial theorem and set the groundwork for modern calculus.

He became Professor of Mathematics at Trinity in 1669 and remained at Cambridge until 1696. These were his most creative years. It was in this period that he carried out his famous experiments with glass prisms and studied the color spectrum in white light.

He proposed the particle theory of light – today called photons – and the reflection and refraction of light by different materials. This was highly controversial as light at that time was believed to be homogeneous, not particulate.

Newton often did work which was not published until several years later. For example, his mathematical work at Cambridge was not published until 1707, after he had left his Professorship.

It was around 1665 when the famous event of his observing the falling of an apple and realizing the universal nature of gravity occurred. This insight led him to apply the concept to explain the motion of the Moon and the orbits of the planets. This work continued and refined the earlier work by Galileo which had established that the Earth revolved around the Sun and not the other way around. Such false ideas, along with many others, came from the teaching of Ancient Greece, particularly Aristotle. Newton had been taught Aristotle at Cambridge, but he soon completely overturned those ideas and developed the fundamental concepts of motion which form the basis of modern physics.

Aristotle's views on motion did not distinguish the effects of friction, so he taught the common-sense observation that objects in motion slow down unless a force is applied to keep them moving. Newton realized this was only because friction (another force) from the ground, from air-resistance or from gravity caused this slowing down and that in the absence of any forces to change them, the object would continue forever in motion, once they were started to move. This understanding opened the door to the development of mathematical equations and methods to explain the motion of all objects, from atoms to galaxies.

He also developed a fundamental approach to experimentation and the explanation of natural phenomena which became the scientific method still used today.

In 1696 Newton became head of the Royal Mint, which was a position he kept until his death. Although intended as a sinecure – payment for a job that required no work – Newton took it seriously and undertook a major re-coinage of the currency and battled counterfeiters.

Although his work set the stage for modern physics and mathematics, Newton stood at the bridge between superstition, religion and science. He spent a large part of his life and energies involved with the minutia of religious dispute and working to find the mythical 'philosopher's stone' of Alchemy, which would turn lead into gold.

In 1703 he was made President of the Royal Society, and in 1705 he was knighted – ironically not for his work in science but for political reasons. He moved into his niece's house near Winchester as he became older and died in his sleep in 1727. He is buried in Westminster Abbey, London.

His Legacy

Newton consolidated the discoveries and work of earlier scientists like Galileo. He developed theories to explain and predict the movement of objects that would persist until the development of relativity by Einstein in the early 20th century.

His theories on the nature of light are still considered at least partly valid.

As a scientist, he developed sound methods for solving problems and developing sound explanations for natural phenomena – methods that are the foundation of modern science.

Sites to Visit

- There is a statue of Newton at his tomb in Westminster Abbey. There are more modern statues at the British Library in London and at the Museum of Natural History, Oxford University in Oxford, England.
- His image was used for the last issue of one pound notes (1978-1988) by the Royal Mint.

Further Research

- An excellent biography is The Life of Isaac Newton, by Richard Westfall (1993)
- A collection of articles, illustrated, on Newton's life, work and impact on culture is Let Newton Be!, Ed. John Fauvel (1988).
- A film biography Isaac Newton exists, from 1998.

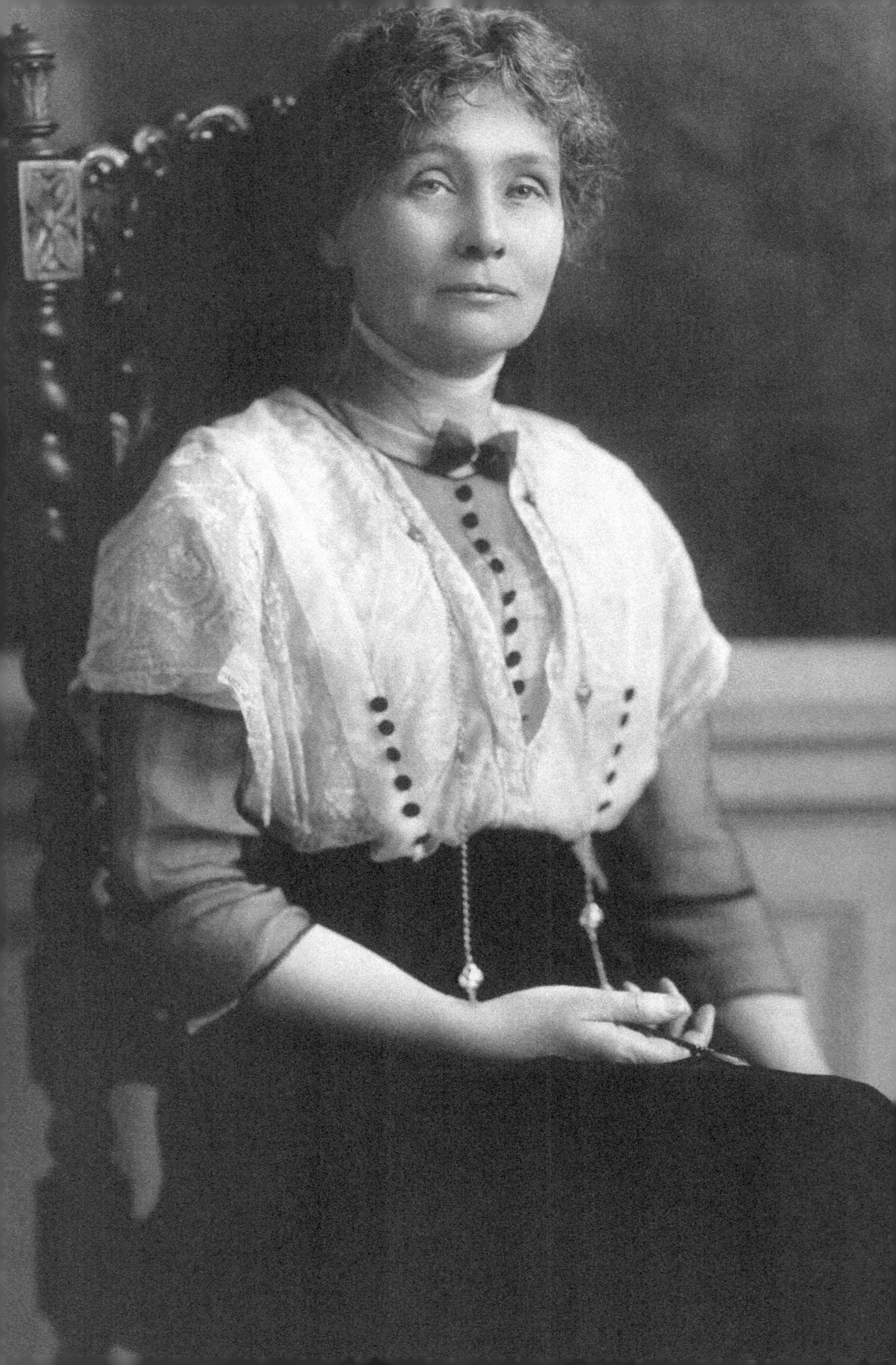

EMMELINE PANKHURST
Suffragette

Key Facts

- Born 1858, died 1928
- The most well-known name in the movement for the vote for women
- Used radical tactics to publicize her campaigns

Although later destined to become a densely-populated working-class neighborhood of Manchester, Moss Side in the 1850s was still a rural village when Emmeline Pankhurst was born there on July 14 in 1858 (her birth certificate states the 15th, but this was apparently some kind of error). Being the child of politically active parents in a time of great social turmoil, Emmeline had already been exposed to the campaign for women's right to vote by the time she was eight. She attended her first women's suffrage meeting at fourteen and came away inspired with the goal of getting women the vote and greater social equality.

Emmeline was highly intelligent, she was reading by the time she was three and went on to attend the école normale supérieure de jeunes filles in Paris. This was the women's section of the famous grande école which has produced many famous French military, political and intellectual leaders since its founding shortly after the French Revolution. July 14 – her birthday - is Bastille Day, the event usually considered to be the start of the French revolution. Emmeline felt that this was a significant fact and grew up reading Thomas Carlyle's three-volume 'The French Revolution', so studying in Paris must have felt like a further sign of her revolutionary future.

On her return, she had adopted Parisian fashions and was a striking, beautiful woman. She attracted the attention of Richard Pankhurst, who had already made a reputation as a reformer and fighter for women's suffrage. The attraction was mutual and in 1879 the 21-year-old Emmeline and the 45-year-old Richard married. Emmeline had actually wanted them to live together unmarried, a very radical act for the time. Richard persuaded her to marry because being unmarried would hinder her political career.

By 1885 their fourth child was born. In 1886 they moved to London and following the death of their only son moved again to a house in Russell Square, London, which quickly became a centre for gatherings of their socialist and suffragette friends.

Emmeline's father had known the socialist philosopher and activist John Stuart Mills and she too mixed with many famous people – William Morris, Kier Hardy, and Eleanor Marx were just a few of their socialist and radical friends.

Emmeline became involved in several causes of the time. In 1886 she became involved in the Matchgirls Strike. Annie Besant had unionized the women workers – who were mostly in fact children – and led them to strike over pay and safety. This was a seminal event in the history of unions, being the first strike to gain national attention. Its success - the Bryant & May Match Company capitulated in three weeks – led to the formation of many more unions across the country.

In 1889 the couple formed the Women's Franchise League.

This was a group actively working for women's right to vote in local elections.

In 1893 the family returned to Manchester and became even more involved in activist politics. Emmeline held regular outdoor meetings attended by tens of thousands of people, despite them being declared illegal and marked by the arrests of often famous speakers.

Following the death of Richard in 1898 Emmeline formed, with her young daughters, a group called the Women's Social and Political Union (WSPU).

Her campaigning for universal suffrage for women at a time

when only around one-third of men had the vote led to a split with many of her old allies.

By 1905 the campaign for women's suffrage had foundered on public indifference. The media no longer reported their activities or published their letters to the editor. Pankhurst decided more radical tactics were needed and began to develop a new, more confrontational approach. At a speech by a government minister, the Pankhurst's jeered and disrupted the meeting and fought with the police who came to arrest them. When found guilty of assault, they refused to pay the fines and were jailed.

The resulting publicity – the first time women had used violence to promote their goals – shocked the public and re-activated the issue.

A number of prominent women joined the WSPU, and they began marches and civil disobedience activities to further their goals. Despite a split in the group over leadership, the WSPU went on to more radical activities.

In 1908 she and other suffragettes were jailed for throwing stones through the windows of the Prime Minister's house in Downing Street.

The suffragettes began to be arrested and jailed frequently. They began hunger and thirst strikes in the prisons and continued activities such as stone-throwing outside of prison, ensuring their quick return.

Several suffragettes, including Emmeline's sister Mary Clarke, died as a result of being force-fed during their hunger strikes.

The violent tactics caused further splits and disagreements within the WSPU, but their activities continued. They adopted arson as a tactic, setting fire to homes of members of parliament, cricket pavilions, golf clubs and other premises. Everything reached a climax in 1913 when a suffragette called Emily Davidson threw herself under a horse at the Grand Derby race and was killed. The public saw her as mentally ill and were more concerned for the horse and jockey.

The outbreak of World War II triggered patriotic fervor in Emmeline. She and her group postponed the demand for the vote and began to campaign for both the war itself and the right for women to work in the factories left short-handed by the workers joining the army. Her radical approach shifted to a radical hatred of Germany and of attempts by socialist pacifists to broker a peace. This caused a permanent split in the family between Emmeline and some of her daughters. Her new party, the Women's Party, called for equality in all areas of life but opposed socialist institutions such as trade unions.

In 1918 a new law allowed women to run for parliament and gave the vote to women over 30 with some property.

Emmeline resisted pressure to run, but her daughter Christabel ran instead but lost by a narrow margin to the Labour Party candidate. Emmeline was heart-broken and the Women's Party collapsed shortly afterwards,

Following the end of the war and several years of living in Canada, Emmeline returned to Britain, and in 1926, after a brief period in the South of France, she joined the Conservative Party as a candidate in working-class areas of London. Her break with socialism was final, to the horror of her daughters.

With her family relationships in ruins, Emmeline entered a nursing home in Hampstead, where she died on June 14, 1928, just short of her seventieth birthday. Just a few days later, on July 2, a bill passed parliament unopposed giving the vote to all women over 21. Her funeral was a huge event with many suffragettes attending.

Her Legacy

Historians continue to disagree over the contribution to women's suffrage of Pankhurst's campaigning and the radical tactics of the WSPU. There is, however general agreement that her tactics brought massive publicity even if they may have hindered public acceptance of her goals.

Her model of the defiant woman resisting the roles of wife and mother was important in defining the later feminist movement and also in fostering radical methods of political protest still in use today by campaigners for a variety of causes.

Sites to Visit

- There is a statue of Emmeline Pankhurst in Victoria Tower Gardens, a park on the Thames in London.
- Her portrait hangs in the National Portrait Gallery in Trafalgar Square, London.
- The Pankhurst Centre in Manchester has been developed in one of her homes. There is a small museum and a centre for women.

Further Research

- There is a BBC mini-series of her life called Shoulder to Shoulder (1974).
- A film called Suffragette with Meryl Streep as Pankhurst in a cameo role (2014).
- A documentary called The Suffragettes (2008) combining original footage and recreated scenes is also available in North America.
- There are many biographies and writings by Emmeline, her daughters and sister suffragettes available. There are also many books on the broader subject of women's suffrage.
- A recent biography Emmeline Pankhurst: A Biography, by June Purvis was published in 2002.

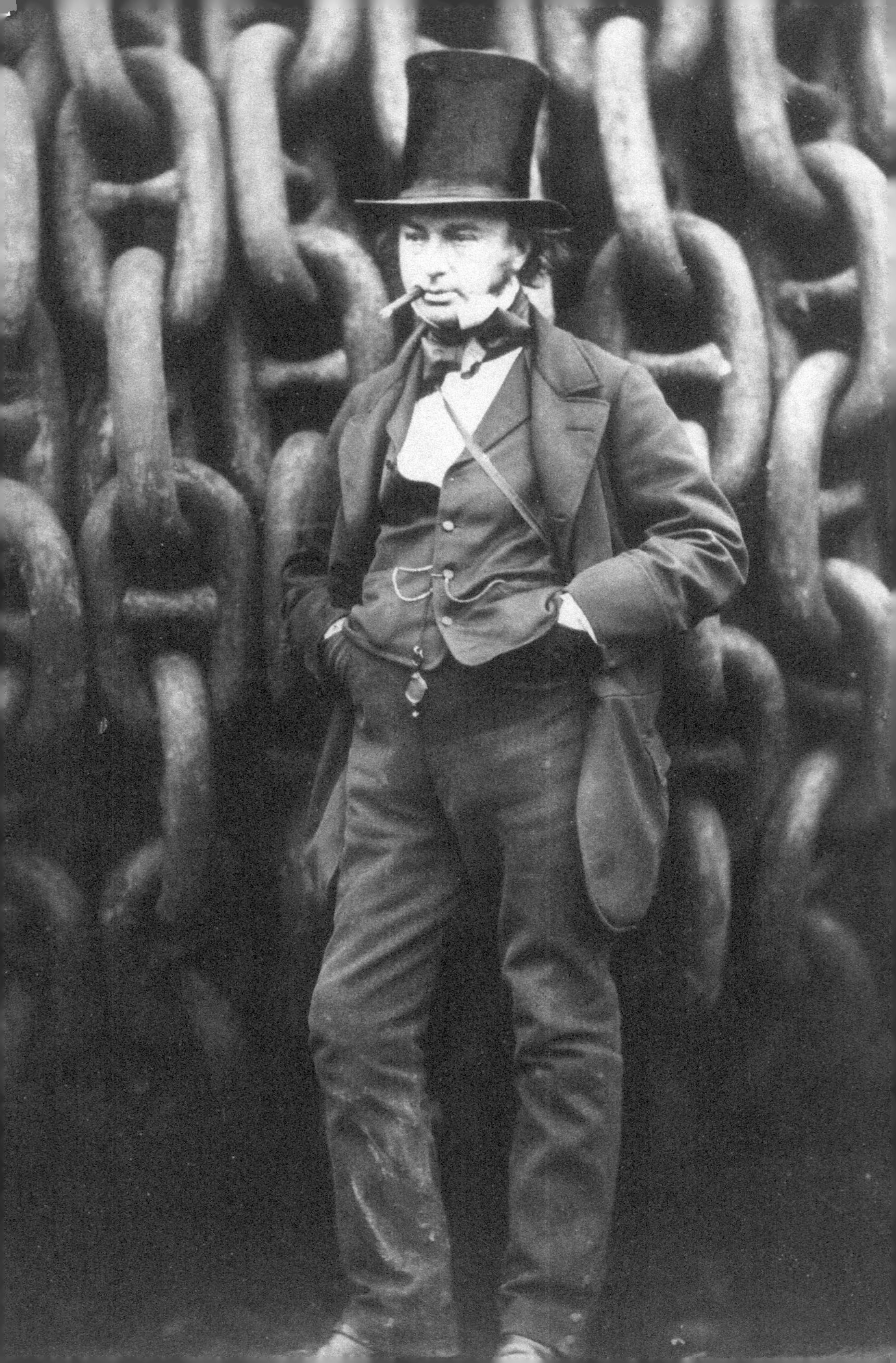

ISAMBARD KINGDOM BRUNEL
Engineer and Greatest Name Ever

Key Facts

- Born April 9, 1806, died September 15, 1859
- Developed modern rail and shipping transport
- Showed the power and ability of engineering to change the world

The Industrial Revolution used new technologies to turn raw materials into manufactured goods. However, transportation of these materials to and from factories and the transportation of people was a limitation on the development of industry. So in the 19th century, there was a great need to move on from the canals, dirt roads, and horses and carts then in use. Isambard Kingdom Brunel was a key figure in the Transportation Revolution that took place in the middle of the 19th century and largely shaped the modern world.

Sophia Kingdom was a young English woman of eighteen when she met the Frenchman Marc Isambard Brunel. He was a naval cadet when the French Revolution broke out, and while living in Rouen hiding his Royalist sympathies, he met Sophia. Forced to leave her behind to escape the Revolutionary government, he sailed to America. There he became a citizen and the Chief Engineer for the City of New York. In 1796 he traveled to England with a design that he wanted to present to the Royal Navy. Sophia had been able to leave France the previous year and was waiting for him. His invention was adopted by the Royal Navy, and he went on to design other equipment for sawmill engineering and dock construction. He and Sophia were married in 1799.

Their only son, Isambard, was born in 1806 and was schooled from an early age by his father in drawing, French, and engineering. At eight, he was sent to boarding school to learn classics, and at fourteen, he went to a top rank school in France, the Lycée Henri-IV. There were plans for him to move on to the renowned Ecole Polytechnique, a famous engineering school in Paris, but he was refused entry because he was not French.

When he returned to England, he joined his father working on a project to build a tunnel under the River Thames in the East End of London. To protect the workers while they built the tunnel, Marc Brunel devised a tunneling shield, which was later to be used to build the early tunnels of the London Underground – his Thames Tunnel itself later became part of the Underground tunnel network. Despite many problems during the construction of the tunnel, including the serious injury of the younger Brunel, it was eventually officially opened in 1843, after 18 years of intermittent work. Marc Brunel was knighted, and the project brought his son Isambard into public prominence.

Isambard became involved in the growth of the railway system, which was revolutionizing transportation at that time, and in 1833 he was appointed chief engineer of the Great Western Railway, which was going to build a line from London to the important city of Bristol. Brunel dreamed of connecting the train to a steamship, which would make it possible to buy a single ticket from London to New York. He chose to use a broad-gauge track (the distance between the rails), which did not match the existing track in Britain at the time. Despite his claims that this made for a smoother ride, after his death, the track was converted to standard gauge to link with other track systems in the country.

The track featured viaducts, bridges, and what was then the longest train tunnel in the world, the Box Tunnel. He designed most of the stations, including London Paddington Station, where the line began. The first trains began to run in 1838.

Brunel's work caught the imagination of the British, who were showing a great enthusiasm for mechanical development and railways in particular.

While working on the GWR, he met and married Mary Elizabeth Horsley, whose father was a famous composer of the time. Even before the GWR was opened, Brunel had begun working on the steamship section of his London to New York vision. At that time, Atlantic crossings were by sailing ships as steamboats could not carry enough fuel for the long trip. Brunel reasoned that larger ships would be more efficient in their fuel use and that if a ship was big enough, it would be able to carry all the fuel it needed to cross the Atlantic.

He and a group of investors formed the Great Western Steamship Company to build the world's largest ship, the Great Western. The ship was 72 meters long, constructed mostly of wood but with steel-beam reinforcements.

It ran on paddle-wheels, and it also had four masts for sails. The maiden voyage took place in 1838, and the ship had one-third of its fuel still left on arrival, proving Brunel's theory and the viability of trans-Atlantic steamships. In all, the Great Western made 64 crossings.

In 1843 Brunel launched the first 'modern' ship – the Great Britain – 98 meters long with a steel hull and the more efficient screws or propellers replacing paddle-wheels. In 1852 he began the Great Eastern, a 210-meter luxury vessel designed to sail from London to Sydney, Australia, and back on a single load of fuel.

Its maiden voyage was in 1859, and it remained the world's largest ship until the beginning of the twentieth century.

Brunel pioneered pre-fabricated construction techniques when he built the Renkioi Hospital for the British Army during the Crimean War. In five months, his team designed, constructed, and shipped 16 modules consisting of a building with two 50-man wards. The hospital met the highest standards of the time for hygiene, ventilation, drainage, and temperature control. They cut the death toll to one-tenth of what it had been in the other hospitals of the war-zone.

Brunel also designed a house and gardens for his retirement in Torquay, Devon. However, before its completion, he suffered a stroke and died shortly thereafter at the young age of 53.

His Legacy

Although several of Brunel's projects were failures – including his visionary vacuum-powered train system – his problems were more economical than technical and largely due to his vision being so far ahead of the times he lived in. He is remembered for his vision and his role in the development of Britain as a major industrial and shipping nation.

Sites to Visit

- The Brunel Museum is inside the Brunel Engine House at Rotherhithe, London.
- London Paddington Station is still largely in the form it was originally designed by Brunel. Other stations of his design can be seen at Mortimer, Charlbury, Bridgend, and Culham.
- The Swindon Steam Railway Museum features the Great Western Railway.

- Swindon was the construction center for locomotives of the GWR.
- In the Welsh coastal town of Neyland, which was the original terminus of the Great Western railway there are, at the dock, a number of information boards showing various aspects of Brunel's life. Sections of the original broad gauge tracks can be seen as safety barriers. There is also a bronze statue of Brunel with a steamship in one hand and a locomotive in the other.
- There are several other statues of Brunel to be seen, including at Brunel University, Uxbridge, at the Temple Underground station, and in Bristol, Milford Haven, Plymouth, Saltash, and Swindon.
- The Great Britain can be visited in Bristol Harbour.
- The main mast of the Great Eastern can be seen being used as a flagpole at Liverpool Football Club.
- Brunel's family grave can be seen in Kensal Green Cemetery, London.

Further Research

- Brunel has been the subject of several films, including the animated Great (1975) and part of Seven Wonders of the Industrial World (2003), a BBC TV series and book.
- Many of his papers and books can be seen at the Brunel Institute beside the Great Britain in Bristol.
- Two recent biographies are Brunel: The Great Engineer (1999), by Tim Bryan, and Brunel: The Man Who Built the World (2005), by Steven Brindle.

JANE AUSTEN.

JANE AUSTEN
Novelist

Key Facts

- Born December 16, 1775, died July 18, 1817
- Considered transitional in the development of the modern novel
- Only became famous long after her death
- Has developed near-cult status among her many fans

Author Jane Austin was born and lived her whole life among the lower ranks of the gentry. The English gentry was and to some extent still are part of the upper-middle-class, distinguished by the possession of country homes and often surrounding land leased to farmers. They differ from the nobility, who have titles, large estates, and considerable wealth. The gentry usually enjoy comfortable lives and private educations but often lack significant wealth or power. Uncorrupted by the struggle for power, they represent a gentler, kinder English class of refined manners, charity, and modest learning.

It was of these people that Jane Austin wrote. Her novels generally involve kind, polite people who fall in love and, while tugging at the strings of convention, rarely break with it. Her main theme was the need for women to marry for the sake of social and economic security and the personal issues this raised. So her work strikes a chord with modern middle-class women who balance independence and family while still cherishing romantic love.

Jane's father, George, spent most of her life as a pastor at the Anglican church of Steventon, Hampshire. He also farmed and took three or four boys at a time into his house, where he tutored them. This was a time when schooling was not a state responsibility. Jane had six brothers and one sister. The two sisters never married, and they must have seen the advantages and opportunities their brothers had compared to themselves.

Just as her father took in children to educate, so Jane, when aged seven, and her sister Cassandra, who was two years older, were sent away to the home of a Mrs. Ann Cawley who lived in Oxford and later in Southampton. Both became ill with typhus, and Jane almost died, so she returned home but was sent - again with her sister – to boarding school in 1785. They only spent one year at school before returning home because her family could not afford to any longer pay for their education. The rest of Jane's education was acquired through reading from her father's library and that of a wealthy uncle, Warren Hastings. Her father encouraged her writing and drawing and bought expensive paper and equipment for both her and Cassandra. She spent the rest of her life living in her parent's homes.

One attribute of the gentry was tolerance and good manners, so ideas seem to have been freely debated in the house. As was common before radio and television, the family entertained itself by the children putting on plays and performances, so by 1787, while still in her early teens, Jane began writing poems, stories, and plays for family amusement.

In these early writings, she shows a satirical side, writing parodies of the history books she had read and of the novels of sensibility popular at the time. Novels of sensibility emphasized the emotions of the characters rather than the plot and were meant to be models for the proper way to show feelings, at that time an important social skill.

In 1800 her father, by then seventy, decided to move the family to a house in Bath and being near the coast, summers were spent at the sea-side. In 1805 her father died, and her mother, Jane, and Cassandra were left as the household since all her brothers were now married and had their own homes.

While her father was alive, Jane lived the typical life of a single young woman of her class. She passed her time playing piano, sewing, directing servants, caring for sick and pregnant female relatives, and writing letters. She loved to attend dances, which were a common social activity of the time and a place for young women to meet prospective husbands. However, Jane seems to have had few romantic involvements. There was a brief interest in a Thomas Lefroy who was, however, too poor to be a suitable husband. Later there was a mysterious possible romance with an unknown man who died suddenly. She did at one time accept a proposal from a Harris Bigg-Wither but changed her mind the following day.

With the death of her father, the three women had a much-reduced income and became dependent on support from her brothers. In 1806 they moved from Bath to Southampton to be near her brothers Frank and Charles, who were in the navy and based at nearby Portsmouth.

Jane had already sold one of her novels – Northanger Abbey – in 1803, for £10. In 1811 she sold Sense and Sensibility, with the author named as 'A Lady.' She made £140 from the first edition. She received favorable reviews, and the novel became fashionable to read. This was followed by Pride and Prejudice and in 1814 by Mansfield Park. Her brother Henry lived in London and acted as an informal literary agent for her. He was well-connected, and through him, Jane mixed in social circles that would otherwise have been outside her social milieu.

In 1815 she published Emma, but this was not as well received as her earlier novels had been.

During 1816 she became ill and had to abandon work on her latest novel – Sanditon. By the middle of 1817, she was moved to Winchester, where on July 18, she died, aged 41.

The cause of her death has been variously described as Addison's disease, Hodgkin's lymphoma, bovine tuberculosis, and Brill-Zinsser disease.

Her brother Henry arranged for her to be buried in Winchester Cathedral. He also arranged for her novels to be re-published and revealed who she was in a prologue.

Her Legacy

Jane's novels were continuously in print from the 1830s on. However, they did not conform to Victorian tastes, which favored Dickens and George Elliot. It was not until the 1880s, with the publication of a memoir of her life, that her popularity grew. This popularity developed into the first 'subculture' – perhaps best defined as people who were obsessed with every detail of the life and work of someone.

The term Janeites was and still is used to describe these people, who read her works repeatedly, have teas and costume balls, take pilgrimages and attend readings. The term is usually meant in a derogatory way.

However, unlike most other subcultures, Jane Austen is read and studied in universities and discussed at a serious academic level as an important precursor of the modern novel, which broke with both the 17th-century style of writing novels as an exchange of letters (epistolary novels) and the novels of sensibility.

Sites to Visit

- Her house in Chawton, Hampshire, where she spent the last eight years of her life, is a museum.
- There is an annual Jane Austen festival in the city of Bath. A house where she lived in Bath can be seen. The whole city is Regency style and very evocative of the period.
- Chatsworth House, Derbyshire, can be visited. It is mentioned in Pride and Prejudice.
- Steventon and the village Jane was born in can be visited, but the rectory where she lived has been demolished.
- There is a plaque in Winchester Cathedral where she is buried.

Further Research

- Films of Austen novels include Pride and Prejudice starring Greer Garson and Laurence Olivier (1940); Sense and Sensibility starring Emma Thompson (1995); numerous BBC productions that closely follow the text, including the mini-series Pride and Prejudice with Colin Firth and Jennifer Ehle.
- All her books, including incomplete works completed by other family members, are in print.
- There are many biographies of her too numerous to mention and books covering life during the Regency period.

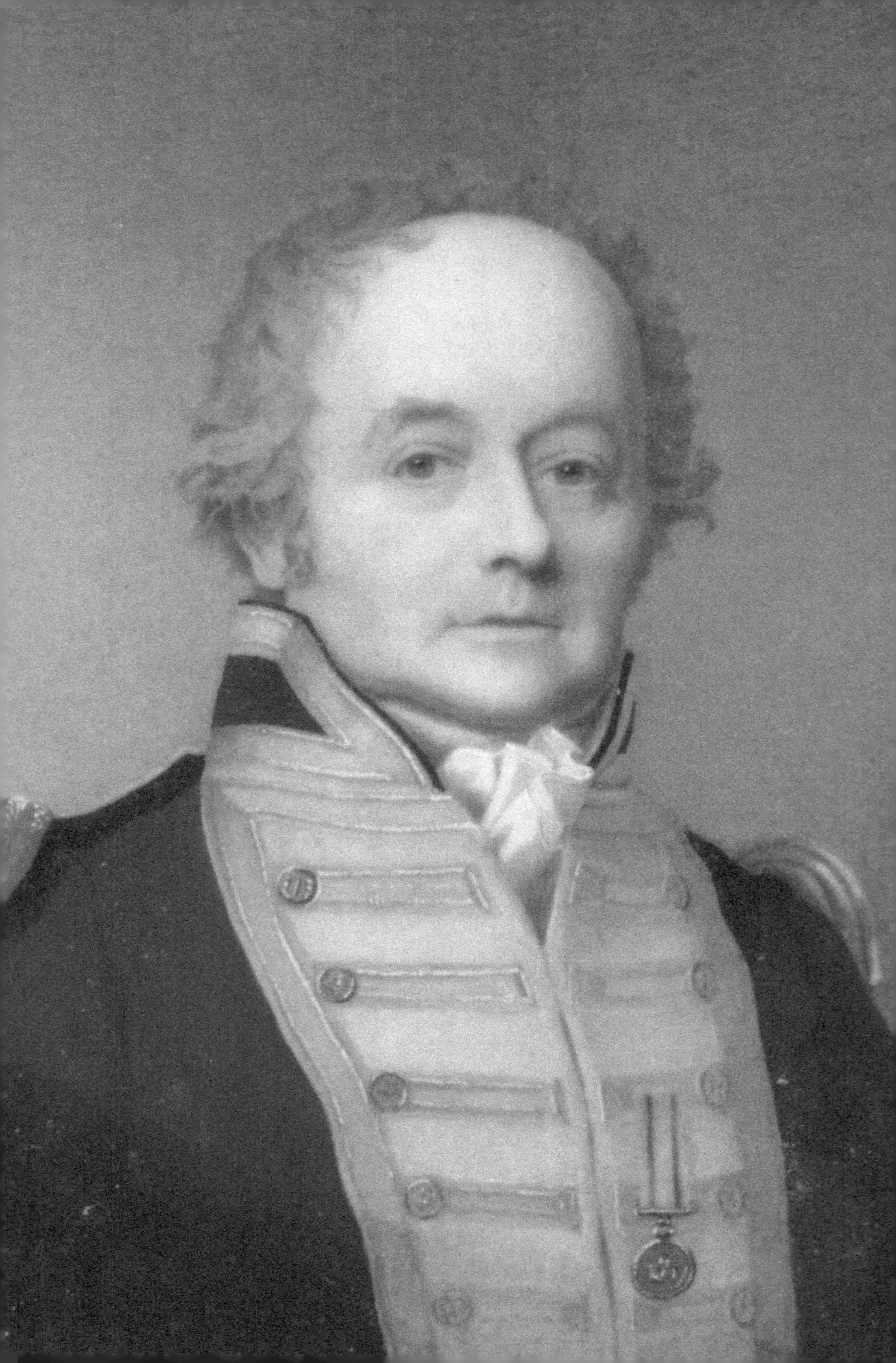

WILLIAM BLIGH
The Maligned But Skilled Seaman

Key Facts

- Born 1754, died 1817
- Sailor, Captain, and Vice-Admiral in the British Navy
- Governor of the colony of New South Wales, Australia
- Remembered for his role in the infamous 'Mutiny on the Bounty'

William Bligh was a sailor and ship's Captain best remembered for his role in the famous mutiny, which took place on his ship HMS Bounty while attempting to transport breadfruit trees from Tahiti to the Caribbean. He was also the Governor of New South Wales when Australia was a British colony and was deposed by a rebellion. He rose to Vice-Admiral, sailed with Captain James Cook, and served under Horatio Nelson.

William Bligh was born on the 9th of September, 1754, probably in Plymouth, Devon, where his father was a customs officer, although his family home was the modest, but grandly-named, Tinten Manor, near Bodmin, Cornwall. By the age of seven, he was already in the Navy, a not-uncommon practice at that time and the first step on a naval career. At 16, he became a midshipman, the most junior rank in the Navy, and spent three years serving on the HMS Crescent.

In 1776, now aged 22, he was appointed by Captain James Cook to be the sailing master on the HM Sloop Resolution for Cook's final voyage. A sailing master was what we would today call a navigator, responsible for the complex task of keeping the ship on course, using a compass, sextant, and the recently invented marine chronometer. This last instrument – a very accurate clock – made precise chart-making possible for the first time, and the British Navy was engaged in charting the world.

This was Cook's third voyage of discovery in the Pacific Ocean, and he was searching for the fabled Northwest Passage above North America that would link Europe and Asia. He did not discover the Northwest Passage, but he did make formal contact with Hawaii. It was in Hawaii that he was killed while trying to take the Hawaiian king hostage. Bligh and the rest of the ships arrived back in England in 1780, and Bligh was able to give important information about Cook's voyage.

In 1781, he married Elizabeth Betham and almost immediately set sail again with the Royal Navy as a senior master, being involved in the Battle of Dogger Bank and the Siege of Gibraltar, both battles in Europe between Britain, Spain, France, and Holland connected with the American War of Independence.

After America won its independence, much of the Royal Navy was demobilized, and berths were hard to come by for younger officers, so Bligh joined the Merchant Navy as a commanding lieutenant, a position that was effectively Captain, on smaller ships without other officers. Such was his situation in 1787 when he was given command of the HM Armed Vessel Bounty, a 90-foot, 215-ton, three-mast ship. Bligh was the only officer, with 43 sailors and two botanists on board.

The ship was tasked with sailing to Tahiti to collect breadfruit trees and transport them to the Caribbean. This was a scheme devised by his patron, the wealthy botanist Sir Joseph Banks, whose fame had been made with his plant collections from his travels with Cook on his first voyage, discovering the east coast of Australia. His breadfruit scheme was intended to provide a cheap source of food for slaves in the Caribbean working on the sugar plantations.

Failing, due to bad weather, to round Cape Horn at the southern tip of South America to reach the Pacific, the Bounty turned east and sailed around the Cape of Good Hope to enter the Pacific from the West. The delay meant that when they finally arrived in Tahiti in October 1788, the trees were not ready, and Bligh had to remain in Tahiti for five months.

Life in the British Navy at that time was harsh, with flogging and hanging routine punishments for sailors. The work was hard, living conditions barbaric, and the diet appalling. So when Bligh allowed the sailors to live on land to take care of the 1,015 potted breadfruit trees, the easy and free life of the island was an irresistible draw. Many of the sailors' went native', entering into relationships with island girls and, in the case of Master's Mate and Acting Lieutenant Fletcher Christian, marrying one. Christian had been appointed by Bligh during the voyage to replace his original Lieutenant, John Fryer.

So it's not surprising that when the ship finally did set sail, the crew were not happy to be leaving Paradise. They were so unhappy, in fact, that less than a month out, on the 28th of April, 1789, Christian and 18 of the crew mutinied and took control of the ship, without loss of any life. Their plan was to return to Tahiti, so Bligh and several of the crew that had remained loyal were set adrift in the ship's 23-foot row-boat, with some supplies. Bligh used his impressive skills in navigation to guide the boat 3,618 nautical miles to Timor, the nearest European settlement in present-day Indonesia – at that time, a trading colony divided between the Dutch and the Portuguese.

The mutineers did eventually return to Tahiti, where most of them stayed, to be captured by the Royal Navy two years later. Fletcher Christian, some sailors, and some Tahitian men and women sailed on to the uninhabited Pitcairn Island, where the last survivor and the remains of the Bounty were discovered 35 years later.

On his return to England, Bligh was court-martialed, acquitted, published an account of his amazing voyage, and returned to Tahiti as the Captain of HMS Providence to complete his transportation of those breadfruits. They did not prove popular with the slaves, but while in Jamaica, Bligh collected the Ackee Fruit, which was named after him as Blighia sapida.

Mutinies over conditions were relatively common during these times, and Bligh was also involved in the 'Spithead' and 'Nore' Mutinies, which affected a number of vessels. He also went on to command HMS Glatton under Horatio Nelson at the Battle of Copenhagen in 1801.

His old friend, Sir Joseph Banks, then arranged for him to be appointed Governor of the colony of New South Wales in Australia. His arrogant manner and failure to make friends with those he controlled led him into trouble, and in 1808, Australia's only uprising, the Rum Rebellion, occurred with wealthy settlers raising a petition and marching soldiers on Government House, deposing Bligh. He was again set adrift, this time in a full-sized boat, the HMS Porpoise, in which he sailed for Hobart, on the island of Tasmania. He could not get permission to re-take the rebellious colony and remained on board the vessel for two years before finally sailing for England. A new system of governance of the Australian colony was introduced.

Back in England, Bligh continued to rise through the Navy, reaching the rank of vice-admiral, but never really engaged in any further significant voyages or duties. He died at his home on Bond Street, London, on the 7th of December, 1817.

His Legacy

Much maligned in the past, today, Bligh's reputation has been largely restored with a more balanced view of his abilities and shortcomings. The Bounty Mutiny has become a by-word for rebellion against oppression, even though the conditions on the ship were certainly no worse than on other vessels of the time. Breadfruit did not take hold as a food in most of the Caribbean Islands, except for Puerto Rico.

Sites to Visit

- His grave is in St. Mary's churchyard, Lambeth. His tombstone is topped with a carving of a breadfruit.
- There is a blue plaque on Bligh's house, at 100 Lambeth Road, London. The house is now a B&B.
- Tinten Manor is a listed building and still stands in St Tudy, Cornwall.
- There is a statue of Bligh on George Street, Sydney, Australia. It was erected in 1987 to "restore the proper image of a much-maligned and gallant man."

Further Research

There are several biographies and accounts of the mutiny available, including:

- BLIGH: William Bligh in the South Seas, by Anne Salmond
- The Bounty Mutiny, by William Bligh and Edward Christian
- The Fortunate Adversities of William Bligh, by Roy Schreiber
- Captain Bligh's Portable Nightmare: From the Bounty to Safety - 4,162 Miles Across the Pacific in a Rowing Boat, by John Toohey
- Captain Bligh: The Man and His Mutinies, by Gavin Kennedy
- Vice Admiral William Bligh RN FRS: A Biography by J.H.Bligh, by John Heath Bligh

There are numerous film versions of the mutiny, including:

- George Cross in The Mutiny of the Bounty (1916)
- Mayne Lynton in In the Wake of the Bounty (1933)
- Charles Laughton in Mutiny on the Bounty (1935)
- Trevor Howard in Mutiny on the Bounty (1962)
- Anthony Hopkins in The Bounty (1984)

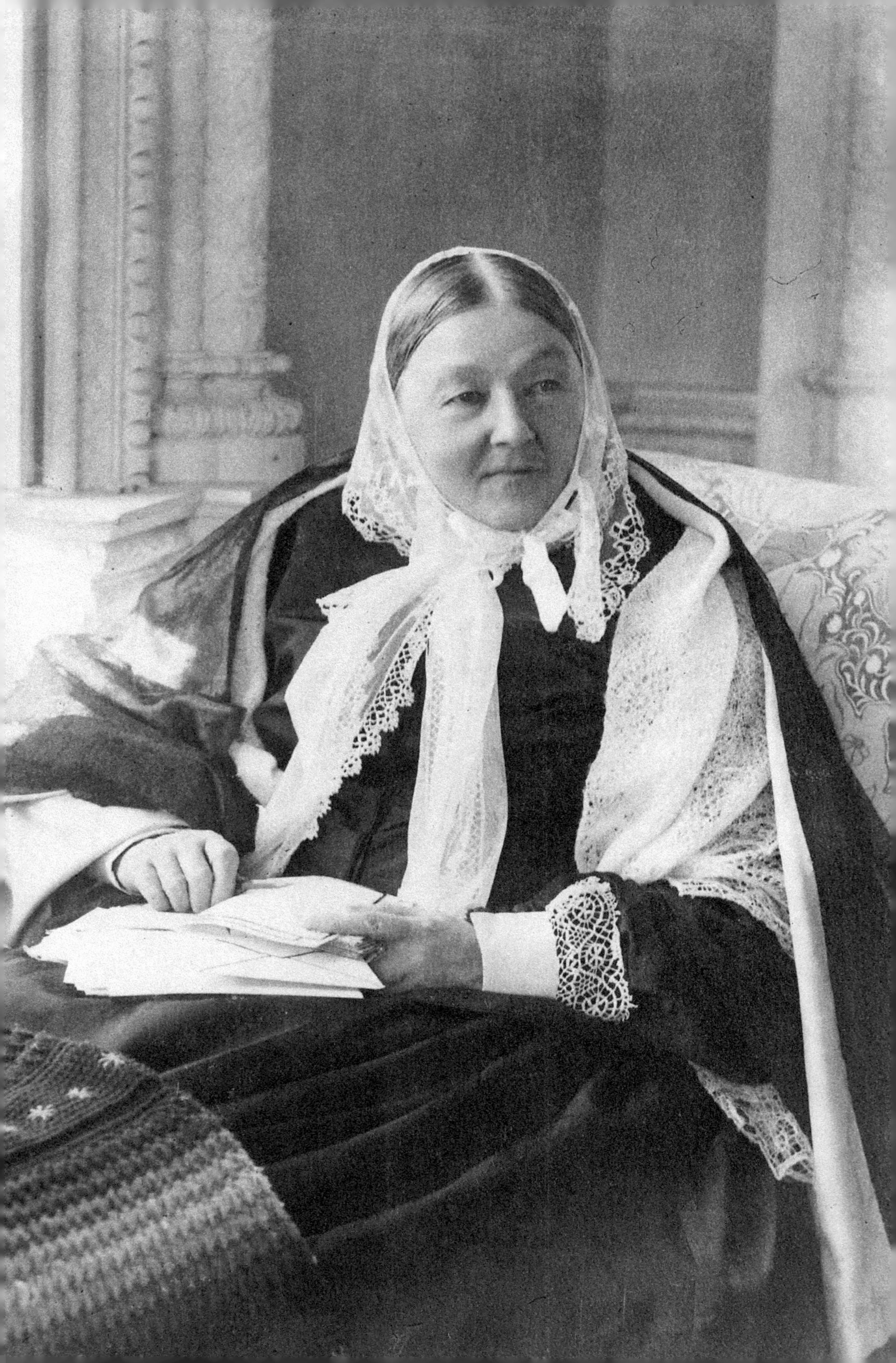

FLORENCE NIGHTINGALE
The Founder of Modern Nursing

Key Facts

- Born 1820, died 1910
- Known as "The Lady with the Lamp" for her night-time visits to wounded soldiers
- Famous for her work on the battlefields of the Crimean War
- Established the profession of nursing as a career and the first secular nursing school

The Grand Tour of Europe was a nineteenth-century tradition for wealthy British people. Florence Nightingale was born in and named after the city of Florence in Italy, which her parents were visiting as part of their own Grand Tour. She was born on May 12, 1820.

Her father – William Shore Nightingale – was a wealthy landowner and Florence grew up at Lea Hurst in Derbyshire, one of her father's two large estates. There she received the typical education of an upper-class girl and learned French, German, and Italian as well as studying classical literature.

Her mother wanted Florence to marry well and be an upper-class lady. This was not at all Florence's wish, so the two were often in conflict, despite her desire to also be a good daughter. She may have inherited her strong temperament from her mother's father, who had been active in the movement to abolish slavery.

Florence showed an early interest in philanthropic work with those less privileged and was often found in the villages of her father's estates helping the poor and sick. Being also very religious, she became convinced by the time she was sixteen that God had chosen her to nurse the sick. Nursing at that time was not a profession at all, and nurses were untrained menial servants. So this idea did not meet with the approval of her mother, who had very different plans. She tried to marry Florence to a 'suitable' wealthy young man, Richard Monckton Milnes, who had been pursuing Florence for some years, but Florence quickly rejected him.

She then went on her own extensive and extended travels in Europe, Greece, and Egypt. She eventually visited a Lutheran Hospital in Kaiserswerth-am-Rhein, Germany, run by Pastor Theodore Fleidner, and was impressed both his work with the sick and poor and by his training of the nurses. She studied there for four months, and this formed the basis of her skills. On her eventual return to England, she took a position at the Institute for the Care of Sick Gentlewomen. Within a year, she was promoted to Superintendent.

The Crimean war began in 1853. When reports came back to England of the terrible conditions for the wounded, she assembled a team of 38 volunteer nurses she had trained and, using the influence of her personal friend and then Secretary for War, Sydney Herbert, had herself and her team sent to the British Army Headquarters in modern-day Turkey. She arrived in November 1854.

It was during her time in the Crimea that the title The Lady With the Lamp was given her, from an article in The Times describing her moving among the sleeping wounded at night with a lamp to help her give them any aid she could.

Although highly regarded at the time and with her activities publicized in the media of the day, her work was, in fact, not always impressive. The death-toll in her hospitals actually rose during her time there, and more men died from disease epidemics than from their wounds. This was because she believed at the time that nutrition was more important than hygiene in caring for the soldiers. A 'Sanitary Commission' was sent from England to clear sewers and clean the hospitals - the death-toll fell.

On her return to England, however, she reconsidered her position in the face of the statistics she had gathered and became an advocate for sanitary conditions in hospitals. Indeed her work in statistics is recognized as ground-breaking, particularly in methods of presentation and her early use of pie-charts to show her results.

She became the first female member of the Royal Statistical Society.

In 1859 she published Notes on Nursing, which became the basic text for her early courses. It emphasized knowledge of hygiene is vital for patient care, distinct from medical knowledge.

In 1860 she opened the Nightingale School for Nurses, the first secular nursing school, now part of King's College, London. The initial funding came from contributions raised from the public on the strength of the publicity surrounding her work in the Crimean War.

From 1857 to her death, she became increasingly bed-ridden, it is believed with severe brucellosis — a disease usually contracted from unpasteurized milk, which leads to severe joint pain. Despite this, she continued to work on hospital planning, and only in her later years did her work output diminish. She may also have suffered depression suggested to have been triggered by guilt over her slowness in recognizing the importance of hygiene in inpatient care.

She received the Royal Red Cross from Queen Victoria in 1883, and she was the first woman to receive the Order of Merit in 1907. She died at her home in central London on August 13, 1910.

Her Legacy

Florence Nightingale is still a role-model for nurses around the world. She was the first person to give nurses professional status and serious training. After her, nurses changed from being servants to being skilled essential aids to physicians. International Nurses Day is held each year on her birthday.

She is also a symbol of the determined woman who makes her mark on the world in spite of her gender and who resists the pressures to lead a genteel life as a wife and mother. She was critical of women for not showing leadership and seems indeed to have largely dismissed them, preferring to work with men to reach her goals. This could have, of course, been a pragmatic recognition of the times she lived in, rather than a firm position on gender issues.

In more general terms, she stands for self-sacrifice and determination to serve others.

Sites to Visit

- The Florence Nightingale Museum is at St Thomas' Hospital in London. There is also a museum at her sister's family home, Claydon House in Buckinghamshire. There is also a museum in the Selimiye Barracks building in Istanbul.
- Statues of Florence Nightingale can be seen in Waterloo Place, London, and at several locations in the town of Derby, England.
- There is a stained-glass window dedicated to her, which has been in several locations since its construction in the 1950s. It is currently in St Peters Church, Derby.
- There is a blue plaque at her house in South Street, Mayfair, London. A plaque can also be found in the Haydarpasa Cemetery, Istanbul.

Further Research

- Florence Nightingale's voice can be heard in a preserved recording from 1890, which is kept in the British Library Sound Archive and can be accessed online.
- A play called The Lady with the Lamp was produced in 1929, and a film version of the same name made in 1951. There have also been several television documentaries made of her life.
- There are numerous biographies of her life. Her official biography by Edward Cook was published in two volumes in 1913. Lytton Strachey, husband of Virginia Woolf, wrote a chapter on Nightingale in his book Eminent Victorians. Her most recent biography by Mark Bostridge was published in 2008.
- Her collected writings have been published starting in 2001 by Lynn McDonald. The series is expected to reach sixteen volumes.

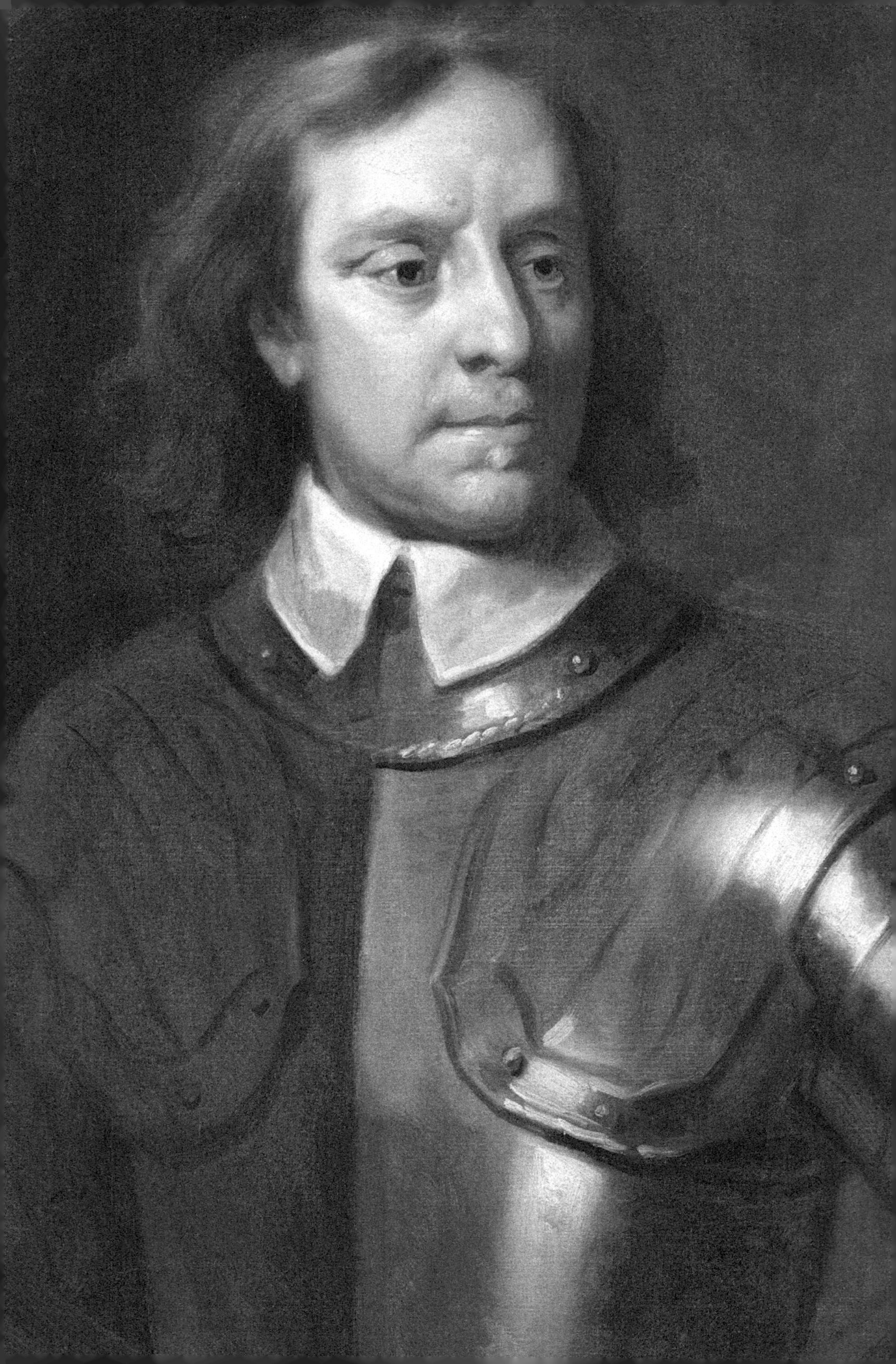

OLIVER CROMWELL
England's Dictator

Key Facts

- Born April 25, 1599, died September 3, 1658
- Led the Parliamentary army to victory over the Royal army
- Briefly dictator of England
- Remains highly controversial in British history

The British are usually considered to be moderate in their views, very tolerant, and open-minded. But that was not always so. In the 17th century, intolerance was widespread on a scale that today we would consider to be religious fanaticism. It led to a Civil War, the execution of the King, and the establishment of a dictatorship. Oliver Cromwell was a key figure of that period, whose actions remain highly controversial while he is at the same time considered a major figure in British history.

Cromwell was born in 1599, on the cusp of the new century. He was a member of the gentry – a landowner and therefore of some social rank, but not a member of the nobility.

His early life was relatively uneventful. He married in 1620 and fathered nine children. His wife, Elizabeth Bourchier, came from a family of somewhat higher social position, and the network of associations Cromwell made through his wife's family served him well in his later political career.

During the 1620's Cromwell, seems to have had a personal crisis. He was treated for depression (called at that time valde melancolicus) and discovered God. This turned him from a moderate figure into someone who believed that God had chosen him to carry out God's will on earth – which he proceeded to do.

In 1628 he became a Member of Parliament but seemed to have made only one speech before the Parliament was dissolved by the King, Charles I. The King ruled without Parliament for the next decade, but in 1640 he called a new one to pass financial bills since he had bankrupted himself waging war with Scotland. This Parliament became known as the Long Parliament because it continued in various forms until after Cromwell's death in 1658.

There were several divisive issues in British society at the time. On the religious front, there was a battle between two views of church governance. On one side were the episcopal churches – Catholics and Anglicans – who believed in centralized church control through the system of bishops appointed by a leader such as the Pope or an Archbishop. On the other were the presbyterian churches – particularly the Church of Scotland – that had a more democratic system of elected elders running the church.

A growing third side was the puritans, who believed in a congregationalist approach with direct control of each church by its members and no centralized power-structure. Cromwell belonged to this last group, although he was not as extreme in his views as some other puritan churches.

There were also a number of serious issues between the King and the Parliament, involving taxation, religious freedom, the introduction of Presbyterianism in Scotland, and an apparent plot by supporters of the King to raise an army in Ireland to suppress freedoms in Britain. Finally, in 1642 Parliament declared itself able to pass laws without Royal Assent and began to raise an army to defend its rights.

Cromwell had very little military experience, but he quickly joined the army of Parliament, which won some early victories over the Royalist forces. Cromwell quickly showed himself to be a brave leader, riding at the head of his cavalry and using novel tactics to ensure victory. He led with the authority of his own commitment and developed more disciplined tactics for what were basically amateur soldiers. By 1644 he had risen to the rank of Lieutenant-General of the cavalry.

Following a period of indecisive military campaigns, the Parliament created a brand new centralized form of the military, called the New Model Army. This was the beginning of a national army and developed into the present British Army. This new force quickly defeated the royalist troops at the decisive Battle of Naseby in 1645.

Parliament attempted to reach a political settlement with the King, but they were hampered by factions within their own side, most notable the Levellers, a radical group that had developed within the New Model Army and who demanded universal suffrage for men. The King escaped from imprisonment, and pro-Royalist uprisings broke out in Wales and Scotland, where a Royalist army invaded Britain. Cromwell quickly put down the Welsh uprising and, finally in sole control of the army, defeated a Scottish force twice his size just below the Scottish border.

Following a military coup by Thomas Pride, only those MPs who supported a trial of the King were allowed to sit in Parliament. Cromwell returned to London to lend his support, and along with the other remaining MPs, he signed the death warrant for Charles I, who was beheaded on January 30th, 1649.

A republic was declared, called the Commonwealth of England. As the royalists had re-grouped in Ireland, Cromwell was ordered to invade and crush this opposition. While organizing for the invasion, he destroyed the Levellers, whose demands for universal suffrage were denounced as anarchy. The vote was restricted to male landowners only, and Leveller leaders were executed.

Cromwell had both religious and political reasons to attack Ireland. He was vehemently anti-Catholic, and his nine-month campaign in Ireland is still remembered by the Irish for the slaughter of captured soldiers and civilians. Many historians consider Cromwell's actions in Ireland to be genocidal. Perhaps 600,000 Irish died from battle, disease, and famine.

Having dealt with Ireland, Cromwell turned his attention to Scotland, wherein a relatively gentler campaign, he seized control of the country for the Commonwealth. Presbyterianism was allowed, but the powers of the Scottish Church were reduced.

After a period of transition, a new constitution was adopted for the Commonwealth, which made Cromwell Lord Protector. In all but name, he was a King – he was even addressed as "Your Highness" – or as we would say today, a dictator. As dictators do, he took power with the declared aim of "restoring order" to the country. In 1657 there was a coronation of Cromwell as Lord Protector, complete with a throne, ermine robes, and a sword of justice.

However, the following year Cromwell fell ill with malaria and kidney infections, and he died on September 3rd, 1658. He was buried in Westminster Abbey.

Cromwell was succeeded as Lord Protector by his son Richard, but he lacked a strong power-base, and the Commonwealth was short-lived. The attempts to impose puritanism on the public were hated, and in 1660 Parliament invited Charles II back from exile in France to restore the Monarchy. Cromwell's corpse was dug up, hung in chains, and beheaded. The body was thrown into a churchyard crypt and his head put on a pole outside Parliament, where it remained until 1685.

His Legacy

Cromwell is perhaps the most controversial figure in British history. To some, he is an admirable early republican; to others, a genocidal fascist dictator. In Ireland in particular, he is universally hated.

He was perhaps best described by one Royalist writer as a "Brave Bad Man." At a time when brutal executions and slaughter were more "normal," it is perhaps difficult to judge him by modern standards, but his fanatical religious intolerance seems strangely familiar in the present period.

At such an early time, theories of equality and democracy were so poorly developed that it is no surprise that the Commonwealth failed. A hundred years later, the same ideas succeeded with the French and American Revolution and a little after that in Britain with universal suffrage and women's suffrage in the 19th and early 20th centuries.

Sites to Visit

- Some of the Civil War Battlefields have monuments, but most are now simply agricultural land, often with limited access.
- Banqueting House, in Whitehall, London is all that remains of the Palace of Westminster where Cromwell's Parliaments met. Charles I was executed on the balcony of this building.
- The Museum of London has a large collection of Cromwell artifacts, including his bible and death mask. This collection was made by Richard Trevithick Tangye, a Victorian businessman.
- There are statues of Cromwell which were erected in the 19th century outside Parliament, in London, and also in Manchester, St-Ives, and Warrington.
- There is a small stone in Westminster Abbey recording his brief burial there. In what is now the RAF chapel at St Margaret's, Westminster, there is a stone in the floor marking the pit where his body and those of his family were buried.

Further Research

- A film called Cromwell, starring Richard Harris was made in 1970.
- He is a main character in a TV miniseries called "The Devil's Whore" (2008).
- Some recent biographies are "Oliver Cromwell: King in all But Name" by Roy Sherwood (1997), "Cromwell" by Antonia Fraser (2011), and "Oliver Cromwell: God's Warrior and the English Revolution" by Ian Gentles (2011).

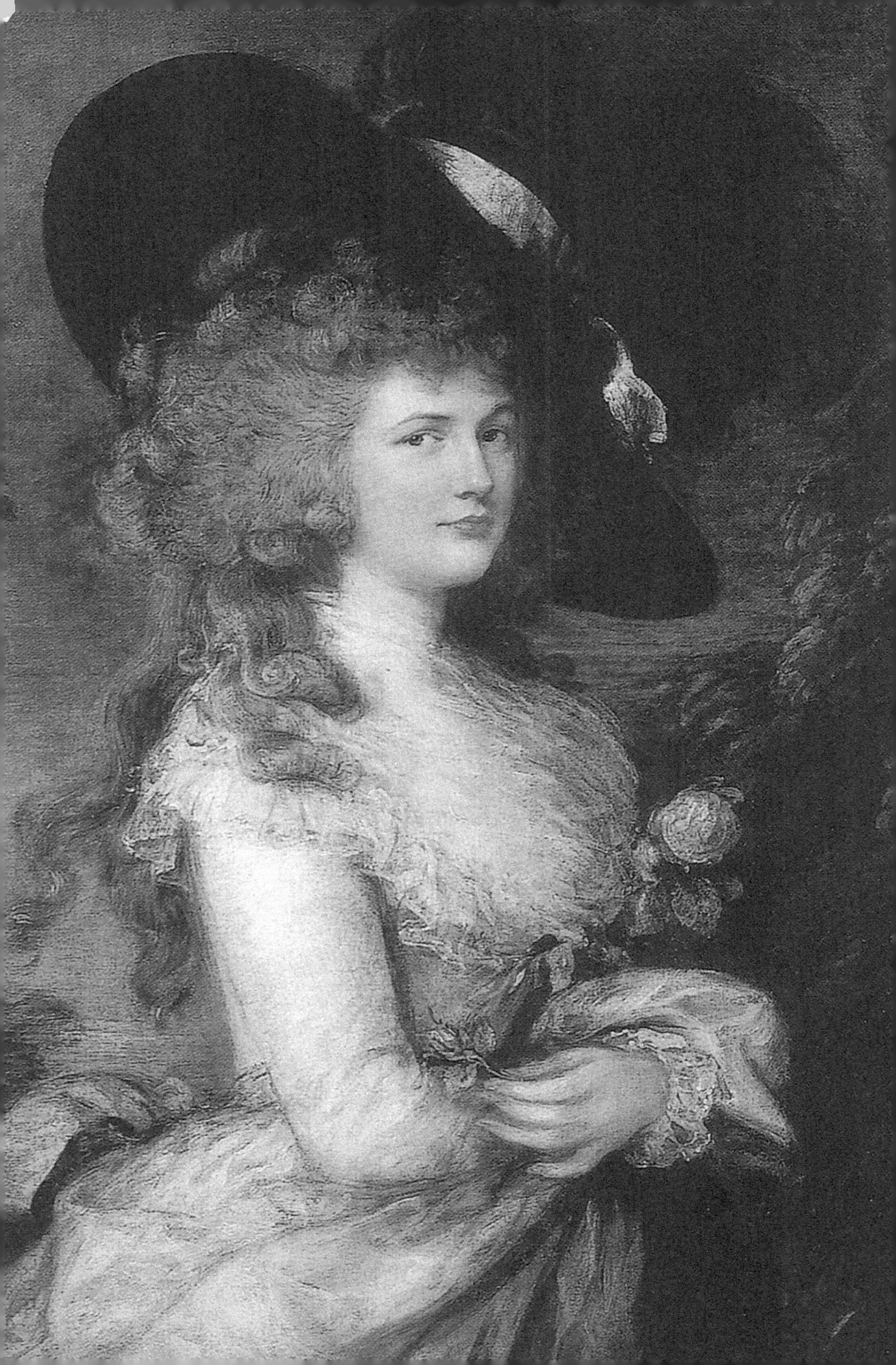

GEORGIANA CAVENDISH
The Duchess of Devonshire

Key Facts

- Born 1757 – died 1806
- Born into the wealthy Spencer family
- Married at 17 to the young Duke of Devonshire
- Lived for 25 years in an infamous ménage à trois

Idle and frivolous rich woman, or oppressed early feminist? Political activist or vote-buyer? Tricked by her best friend, or fully in control of her actions? Best-bred woman in England or dissolute gambler? One's view of Georgiana Spencer, who married William Cavendish, the 5th Duke of Devonshire, will inevitably be colored by one's view on class and privilege in general, but either way, the life of the Duchess of Devonshire makes an exceptional story. She lived the fairy-tale life until her husband, after a string of mistresses, brought her best friend into his bed. She was undoubtedly a loving mother to the children she bore him and finally produced the requisite male heir. Following the custom of the time, she was then able to take a lover of her own, which she promptly did. The great-great-great-grand-aunt of Diana, Princess of Wales, she shared with her descendant high periods and low ones, love, and disappointment. There was also scandal and intrigue, although the Duchess had the good fortune to die surrounded by a loving family.

If anyone could be said to have been born, as the saying goes, with a silver spoon in her mouth, it was Georgiana Spencer. Her birth on the 7th of June 1757, as the first child of John and Georgian Spencer, took place at the Spencer family home, Althorp. The mansion, which dates from 1688, was filled with art treasures and valuable objects, deriving from the family's lucrative sheep-raising business. John Spencer was just 23 years old when his daughter was born, and at the age of twelve, he had received the largest inheritance ever seen in Britain. That family wealth would only increase in her teenage years by the imposition of the brutal Inclosure Act (1773), which took common land away from the rural people and transferred it, often for sheep-raising, into the hands of the wealthy. Althorp today sits on 13,000 acres of prime, rolling agricultural land.

Georgiana was adored by her mother, who, unusually for the time, had married for mutual love. She was a noted philanthropist, well known for the concerts and plays frequently staged at their London residence, Spencer House. She seems to have favored Georgiana over her other children and called her 'My little Gee.' She must have passed on to her daughter her proficiency in language, her love of the arts, and perhaps even her 'accomplishments in botany.' After an uneventful childhood, she was placed in an arranged marriage at 17 to another wealthy family. At a small private ceremony in Wimbledon Parish Church, she was married to William Cavendish, the 5th Duke of Devonshire, who was 25 at the time. The Cavendish family were wealthy aristocrats and politically powerful. They supported the Whig faction and the government of Sir Robert Walpole.

From the start, Georgiana's marriage was not a happy one. Like most men of the time – although not like her father – William had little interest in a close relationship. He was emotionally distant and spent most of his evenings playing cards at the newly-founded Whig club, Brook's in St James, London. Any illusions Georgiana may have had about her husband were shattered when he tasked her with the upbringing of his illegitimate daughter, Charlotte Williams, born from a brief encounter with a hat-maker before their marriage. When her mother died, Charlotte was given to Georgiana to raise. Although she seemed to take well to the child, Georgiana's mother warned her not to mention her origins to anyone. William continued to have numerous affairs.

While 'taking the waters' in the spa town of Bath in 1782, Georgiana met a woman of her own age, Lady Elizabeth Foster, daughter of the Earl of Bristol. Lady Elizabeth had separated from her husband, John Thomas Foster, an Irish politician, the year before. Largely destitute after the separation and with two sons in her care, Georgiana took pity and invited them to move into Althorp. This may have been a fatal mistake since quite soon, the Duke and Lady Elizabeth became lovers. She continued to live in this a ménage à trois for the next 25 years, bearing him a son and a daughter. Along with his legitimate children by Georgiana, all these children would be raised together at Devonshire House, the London residence of the Duke.

The three-way relationship was complex. The Duke and Elizabeth were clearly lovers, but the relationship between Georgiana and Elizabeth is unclear. They seem to have had genuine affection for each other – certainly from Georgiana, who wrote to Elizabeth of her 'heart crying to you', but if any sexual relationship occurred, which on balance seems quite likely, it cannot be verified. They exchanged many letters expressing affection, and it is not inconceivable that Elizabeth's relationship with the Duke was a cover for a deeper, more emotional relationship with Georgiana. Neither was Lady Elizabeth true to the Duke, having numerous liaisons with other men, but where Georgiana stood in all this was and continues to be a topic for speculation. Many feel that the popular portrayal of Georgiana as betrayed by her best friend is far from being the whole story.

Georgiana had her first child in 1783 when her daughter Georgiana Dorothy was born. She was followed in 1785 by Harriett Elizabeth – whose middle-name is perhaps telling. The male heir, de rigueur among the aristocracy, would not arrive until May 1790, when William George Spencer Cavendish was born. Ironically, he never married and left no heirs, becoming known as the 'bachelor duke.'

During the 1780s, Georgiana became involved in the political activities of her husband. The Whigs were the party of the 18th-century version of liberalism, against the monarchy and for the then-novel idea of Liberty. Many supported both the American and French Revolutions. Dinner parties at the Devonshire houses often became political meetings, and Georgiana was known for encouraging women (who did not, of course, have the vote) to support Whig policies. She gained notoriety during the elections of 1784, where she supported a distant cousin, Charles James Fox. Fox was an important politician who had been gaining power against the opposition of King George III and signed the Treaty of Paris, ending the American Revolutionary War. Dismissed by the King, Fox was fighting for re-election in his Westminster constituency. Georgiana campaigned vigorously in his support, walking the streets, talking to commoners as equals, and even bribing a shoemaker with a kiss to vote for Fox. Her efforts attracted considerable satirical attention, and she retreated to working for the Whigs behind the scenes.

As well as attracting literary figures, including the great Dr. Samuel Johnson, to her home, Georgiana is credited with writing two novels anonymously. Both were epistolary, that is, written as an exchange of letters, the normal style for novels in the 18th century. The first, Emma; Or, The Unfortunate Attachment: A Sentimental Novel, is attributed to her with some reliability, but the second, The Sylph, is more doubtful and may have been ghost-written by Sophia Briscoe, an obscure novelist of the time. She also had two poems published.

What is more certain than her literary talent was her talent for losing at cards. Early in her marriage, she began to gamble, a habit that would keep her heavily indebted for life. At first, she turned to her parents to pay, but they ordered her to tell her husband, who repaid her parents and from then on was obliged to pay more and more. Her mother admonished her regularly, but she too had the same problem and lost most of the Spencer fortune gambling. The Duke at one point threatened to end the marriage but relented. It must have been a powerful tool for him to stay in control of his complex household.

Under the social rules of the time, Georgiana could only take a lover once her duty to produce an heir was discharged. Following the birth of William George, she was free and chose Charles Grey, a Whig politician and a future prime minister who would abolish slavery. It was perfectly acceptable for a married woman to take a lover, but much less so to bear his child, so when she became pregnant in 1791, she was sent to France to have the child – a daughter – in secret. Lonely and fearing she would die in childbirth, her time there was miserable. In the event, there were no complications at the birth, and she returned home, but her daughter was brought up by the Grey family. Grey was almost certainly not the only man Georgiana had affairs with, and she lived the rather dissipated life of parties, elaborate clothes and hair-styles, gambling, drinking, and secret liaisons that were especially common among the wealthiest classes.

Older now and worn down by the tribulations of her life, the Duchess became more domestic, spending time with the Duke and writing. Her health declined, her gambling continued, until in 1806, only 48 years old, she died of an infected liver. There was great mourning in her family and across society for someone who had always been a shining star of the social world. The Duke was left with a mountain of gambling debts to repay, estimated at the equivalent of about $4 million today. 'Is that all?' was his response when told this. Three years later, the Duke married Elizabeth, to the consternation of Georgiana's children.

Sites to Visit

- Althorp, the Spencer family home in Northamptonshire, 75 miles northwest of London, is open to visitors during July and August.
- Spencer House, the Spencer's London home, 7 St James's Pl, St. James's, London SW1, is open on Sundays, except for August.
- Chatsworth House, Bakewell, Derbyshire, is the seat of the Dukes of Devonshire. The house and grounds are open from 11 a.m. to 5 p.m. every day from late March to late May and in September and October.
- Devonshire House was demolished in 1924, but many of the items in it were moved to Chatsworth House.
- A portrait by the artist Thomas Gainsborough of Georgiana hangs in the dining room of Chatsworth House.

Further Research

- The Duchess, 2008, is a film biopic portraying Georgiana as both a victim and a social activist.

Biographies

- Georgiana, Duchess of Devonshire, by Brian Masters, (1981)
- Georgiana: Duchess of Devonshire, by Amanda Foreman, (2001)
- Elizabeth & Georgiana: The Duke of Devonshire and His Two Duchesses, by Caroline Chapman, (2003)

Earl of

ROBERT WALPOLE
The First Prime Minister

Key Facts

- Born 1676 – died 1745
- Britain's first Prime Minister
- Established the foundations of the British parliamentary system
- Kept his party – the Whigs – in power for 50 years

Robert Walpole came to prominence just as power in Britain was shifting from the Crown to the Parliament. He was the first, and the longest-serving, Prime Minister under the newly-developed balance of power. Although he ruled more by influencing the King than by using Parliament, he laid the foundations for the present constitutional monarchy. By avoiding wars for an extended period, he allowed the country to grow in wealth and establish itself as a powerful nation, ready to build an Empire. He also personally enriched himself and retained power by using the corrupt political system which existed at that time.

The Glorious Revolution in 1688 was a turning point in British history, shifting the balance of power away from the Monarch and toward the Parliament. After the English Civil War abolished the Monarchy, Charles II returned to the throne when the Commonwealth collapsed in 1660, but when Charles II died in 1685, his already-unpopular Catholic brother, James II, took the throne. English Protestants were outraged, and a group of nobles arranged for his nephew and son-in-law William, Prince of Orange, to invade England and ensure that a Protestant dynasty ruled. James II fled, and William and Mary took the throne, establishing a Protestant succession that has continued in various forms into the present. But William got the throne at a price – The Bill of Rights of 1689.

The Bill of Rights listed 12 things that James had done to subvert the laws and liberties of this kingdom and asserted a list of ancient rights and liberties which were to be protected. These lists repeatedly used the term without the consent of Parliament, effectively limiting the power of the King in matters such as raising an Army, the election of MPs, levying taxes; establishing fines and punishments; and limiting free speech within Parliament. Britain does not have a written constitution, so the transfer of these powers to Parliament represented a major shift of power towards a constitutional monarchy, such as exists in Britain today.

What the King could still do was select the person who was his Prime Minister, who must, however, be the person most likely to command the confidence of the House of Commons. The first person to effectively hold that position was Robert Walpole, 1st Earl of Orford.

Walpole was born in the small Norfolk village of Houghton on the 26th of August, 1676. He was the fifth of what were to become 19 brothers and sisters. His father was a member of the local gentry and an MP for the Whig party. Robert was educated privately and then went on to Eton School and King's College, Cambridge. Although he had intended to enter the clergy, plans changed after his two elder brothers died, leaving him the heir. He returned home to help his father, and two years later, in 1700, his father died, leaving the family estate of ten manor houses and land to the 24-year-old Robert.

It was relatively easy to take advantage of the corrupt nature of the electoral system of the time – there was no secret ballot, and since those eligible to vote were limited, a rich man could buy all the properties with voting rights, install obedient tenants, and ensure a seat for perpetuity – a so-called pocket borough. This Walpole did in 1702 with the borough of Kings Lynn, in the same year that William died, and the popular protestant Queen Anne took the throne. Like his father, he was a Whig, whose rivals in Parliament were the Tories. The Whigs were largely responsible for curtailing the freedom of the Monarch, preferring to exercise power themselves. Their political descendants became the current Liberal Party. They supported Protestantism and were largely responsible for the Glorious Revolution.

Walpole caught the eye of the new Queen and became a member of the advisory council to her husband, Prince George of Denmark. He entered the Cabinet of Lord Godolphin as Secretary of War and Treasurer of the Navy. When power shifted to the Tories at the election of 1710, the new Lord High Treasurer was a defector from the Whigs, Robert Harley, who attempted to entice Walpole to join him, but failed, leaving Walpole as a major critic of the new government and defender of the Whig cause. To eliminate him from the opposition, he was found guilty of accepting bribes and expelled from Parliament. He spent six months as a prisoner in the Tower of London, where he continued to attack the government, but in 1713 he was re-elected to his seat of Kings Lynn.

The death of Queen Anne the following year brought her distant German cousin, George I, to the throne, a triumph for the Whigs, who retained power for the next 50 years. Walpole became a powerful member of the Cabinet as a Privy Councillor and Paymaster of the Forces. He also condemned without trial prominent members of the previous Tory government. He quickly rose to Lord of the Treasury and Chancellor of the Exchequer. In a dispute over foreign policy with other cabinet members, Walpole chose to resign and join the opposition, but after being influential in ending a rift in the royal family, he returned to the Cabinet.

As a younger man, Walpole had purchased shares in the South Sea Company, a joint-stock company with a monopoly on trade with South America. Walpole enjoyed a 1,000% profit, but others were not so fortunate, and when the highly inflated value of the stock began to fall in the event known as the South Sea Bubble, prominent cabinet members were implicated. Although Walpole protected them from punishment, he benefited from their resignations and was able to eliminate several long-standing rivals, leaving him the most prominent and powerful figure in the Cabinet. He simultaneously became First Lord of the Treasury, Chancellor of the Exchequer, and Leader of the House of Commons; with his brother-in-law

Lord Townsend by his side, they effectively controlled the entire government. He became, in fact, if not in the title, the King's 'Prime Minister,' the first since the Glorious Revolution established the importance of such a position. He devised a scheme to partially repay those most injured by the South Sea debacle and reduced the damage to the reputation of the King and the Whig party.

Throughout the reign of George I, the power of the Cabinet and the Prime Minister rose, as that of the King declined. When George II took the throne, he retained Walpole and even Townsend, despite a personal dislike of him. When Townsend died in 1730, Walpole was left in sole charge and clearly the most powerful person in the country. Despite opposition and ridicule from many social liberals, like Jonathan Swift and Dr. Samuel Johnson, Walpole was able to remain popular with the people by keeping Britain out of wars and thus keeping taxes low. Despite a succession of crises, he retained power, even managing to silence critics like Alexander Pope and Henry Fielding by regulating the theatres, so reducing their power to parody and satirize him.

As time passed, however, his popularity waned, and an unsuccessful war with Spain further damaged his reputation. Finally, corruption and his immense personal enrichment led to a parliamentary inquiry, and rather than face the outcome, he resigned from office, ending his political career. Always one to land on his feet, however, George II, grieving at the loss of his favorite minister, made him Earl of Orford, thus giving him a seat in the House of Lords. He continued to wield considerable influence with the King and became known as the 'Minister behind the Curtain.' As he grew older, he retreated more and more to his country estate to hunt and admire his extensive collection of art acquired during his years of power. However, his health continued to deteriorate, and he died on the 18th of March, 1745.

His Legacy

Although usually regarded as Britain's first Prime Minister in the modern sense, in fact, Walpole governed more by personal influence with the King than by using the House of Commons. He did, however, reduce the Tories to insignificance and ensure Whig dominance for half a century. By keeping Britain away from the older pattern of perpetual wars, he greatly enriched the country, doing that also by protectionist trade policies that allowed the wool industry to thrive and produce revenue for necessary imports.

The use of 10 Downing Street as the official residence of the Prime Minister also dates back to Walpole's time. The house was a personal gift to him from George II, although he only used it as his residence when he was First Lord of the Treasury.

As for corruption and personal gain, he was probably no more corrupt than most of his peers, although he was known to advise new MPs to rid themselves of their principles and become 'wiser.'

Sites to Visit

- Walpole is buried in his family vault in St Martin Churchyard, Houghton, Norfolk.
- There is a statue of Walpole in St. Stephen's Hall, Palace of Westminster (the Parliament Building).
- There is a blue plaque on a house where Walpole lived, at 5 Arlington Street, Westminster, SW1.

Further Research

- The Great Man: Sir Robert Walpole: Scoundrel, Genius and Britain's First Prime Minister, by Edward Pearce
- Sir Robert Walpole, by B.W. Hill
- Walpole, by John Morley
- Sir Robert Walpole: A Political Biography, 1676-1745, by Alexander Charles Ewald
- Walpole and the Whig Supremacy, by H.T. Dickinson

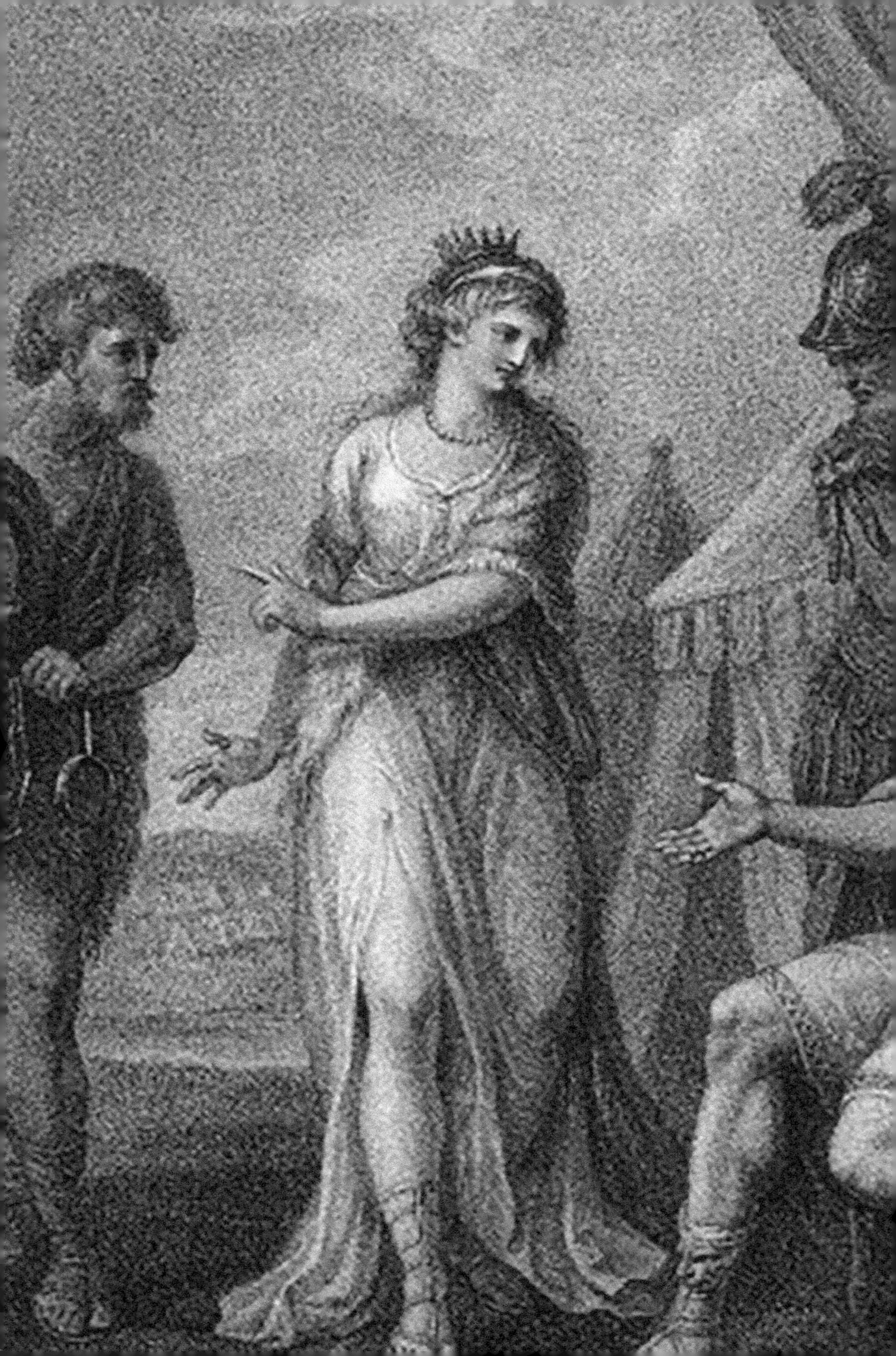

CARTIMANDUA
Queen of Brigantia

Key Facts

- Died around 70 AD
- Allied with the Romans following their invasion
- Replaced her husband with another, leading to a civil war
- Rescued by the Romans before disappearing from history

The times of the Roman invasion of Britain are shrouded in mystery and only accessible from Roman accounts or archaeology. From the little we know, Cartimandua was Queen of Brigantia, the area that is today Yorkshire, and allied with the Romans, growing rich as a client state. She re-payed them by betraying the Welsh rebel Caratacus, handing him over to Emperor Claudius. When she replaced her husband Venutius with his armor-bearer, Venutius waged a civil war against her. She was aided by the Romans in putting down the rebellion, but she had lost the trust of her people. When Venutius returned at a time when the Romans were facing rebellions everywhere, they were able to rescue Cartimandua, but Venutius won his kingdom back. Cartimandua is heard of no more, and after years of warfare, the Romans seized Brigantia, finally bringing it permanently under their control.

History belongs to the victor, the saying goes. When looking at the history of ancient Britain, this is most certainly true, since the only written sources are Roman, and once the Roman Empire set its sights on that island in the North Sea, its fate was sealed. It took about 200 years to complete that conquest, from Julius Caesar's famous failed attempt in 55 BC, but their control continued until 410 AD, creating a unique Anglo-Roman culture whose form is still today being newly discovered and excavated. We only know details of the conquest from Roman authors, notable Tacitus, a Roman senator, and historian. He wrote two major works, the Annals and the Histories, which cover the history of the Roman Empire from the death of Augustus (14 AD) to the First Jewish–Roman War (70 AD). Tacitus was close to the events, as he lived from 56 to 120 AD.

The Roman invasion met with varying levels of resistance. In the south, the tribes fought back fiercely, best remembered in the uprising of Boadicea. In the north, the tribes took a more realistic view and quickly conceded without a fight. The Emperor Claudius, who launched the successful invasion of 43 AD, proudly inscribed on his triumphal arches, the words, Father of the Fatherland, because he received the surrender of eleven kings of the Britons defeated without any loss. Presumably, there were arches saying this in England once, but today they can only be found in Rome, France, and Turkey. The eleven kings referred to were the leaders of a federation called Brigantia, occupying the territory that would become the Roman province of Britannia Secunda. This area is thought to have been today's Yorkshire and northern England, below the Scottish border. The federation was ruled by a Queen called Cartimandua. Her base may have been a heavily-fortified site at Stanwick, a hill-fort near Richmond, North Yorkshire.

Cartimandua was the living incarnation of the goddess Brigantia, ruling over the Brigantes tribes. Horses were an important part of the culture, and 'mandu' means a pony. Her husband, Venutius, was the warlord of the tribes, but it was Cartimandua who wielded ultimate power, choosing Venutius, rather than the other way around. This must-have confused the Romans since, in Rome, women could not hold any official political positions. Having battled so many tribes already, the Romans were surely relieved that Cartimandua wanted to form an alliance rather than confront an overwhelming force. By 40 AD, Brigantia was a client state of Rome, paying taxes and doing the bidding of the conqueror. The federation grew rich, and then Cartimandua had a chance to prove her loyalty – by betrayal.

Further south, in Wales, the tribes were less accommodating.

Caratacus (or Caractacus) was the chief of the Catuvellauni tribe, and he had waged a successful campaign of guerrilla war against the Romans for a decade or more. He was less successful on a formal battle-field (a venue also fatal to Boadicea) and fled north to escape capture. Seeking refuge, he was instead taken prisoner by Cartimandua, who handed him over in chains to the Romans. Taken back to Rome for execution, his eloquent death-row speech persuaded Claudius to spare his life.

It may have been guilt, or perhaps he was unhappy that Cartimandua had put him aside for another, but Venutius decided to overthrow the queen after she married his armor-bearer, Vellocatus, and made him king. The tribes were not happy, but Cartimandua was a goddess with a fiery temper too, so there was little they could do at first. Venutius switched sides, and he turned to anti-Roman factions in the tribes for support. A civil war broke out, and as she began to lose power, Cartimandua called on the Romans for support. Wanting to show loyalty to an ally and concerned with the possibility of losing the territory, they sent a Roman officer called Caesius Nasica with a full legion, the IX Hispana. They were successful in crushing the rebellion around 55 AD.

Venutius must have escaped because, in 69 AD, he was back, with the help of several surrounding nations. This was a time of instability, and Rome had a tenuous grip on the country. They could only spare some mercenaries, and Cartimandua was forced out of the kingdom, surrendering power to Venutius and the rebels. It took the Romans several decades to regain full control, and for some time, Britain was effectively independent. In the end, though, Venutius did lose his kingdom to the Romans. As for Cartimandua, we hear nothing more about her after she flees under Roman protection.

Some people have seen fascinating parallels between Cartimandua's story and that of King Arthur's Queen Gwenhwyfar (Guinevere). Legend has it that Gwenhwyfar replaced her husband Arthur with his trusted commander Mordred, as Cartimandua did Venutius with Vellocatus. In the resulting civil war, both sides in the Arthurian legend recruited outside forces, Saxons and Angles. Here too, the displaced husband – Arthur – finally defeats the upstart Mordred. The ultimate outcome was the same, too – the kingdom was lost to a foreign power. Could it be that the oral history of Cartimandua's story was passed down, eventually reaching the ears of Geoffrey of Monmouth, to be woven into the legend of King Arthur? Or are adultery, betrayal, and civil war such common tropes that it is merely a coincidence?

Sites to Visit

- Stanwick Iron Age Fort is 10 miles north of the town of Richmond, in Yorkshire, on the edge of the Yorkshire Dales National Park. Almost 6 miles of ditches and ramparts enclose a 700-acre site. Excavations have found an Iron Age sword in a wooden scabbard, iron horse-fittings, and the burial of a man with a horse's head placed under the body.
- Maiden Castle is another Iron Age fort from the Anglo-Roman period, near Grinton, North Yorkshire.

Further Research

- Cartimandua: Queen of the Brigantes, by Nicki Howarth Pollard, 2008. The only researched biography available.
- The Sword of Cartimandua, by Griff Hosker – a 12-book series of fictional stories built around the Roman conquest of England.

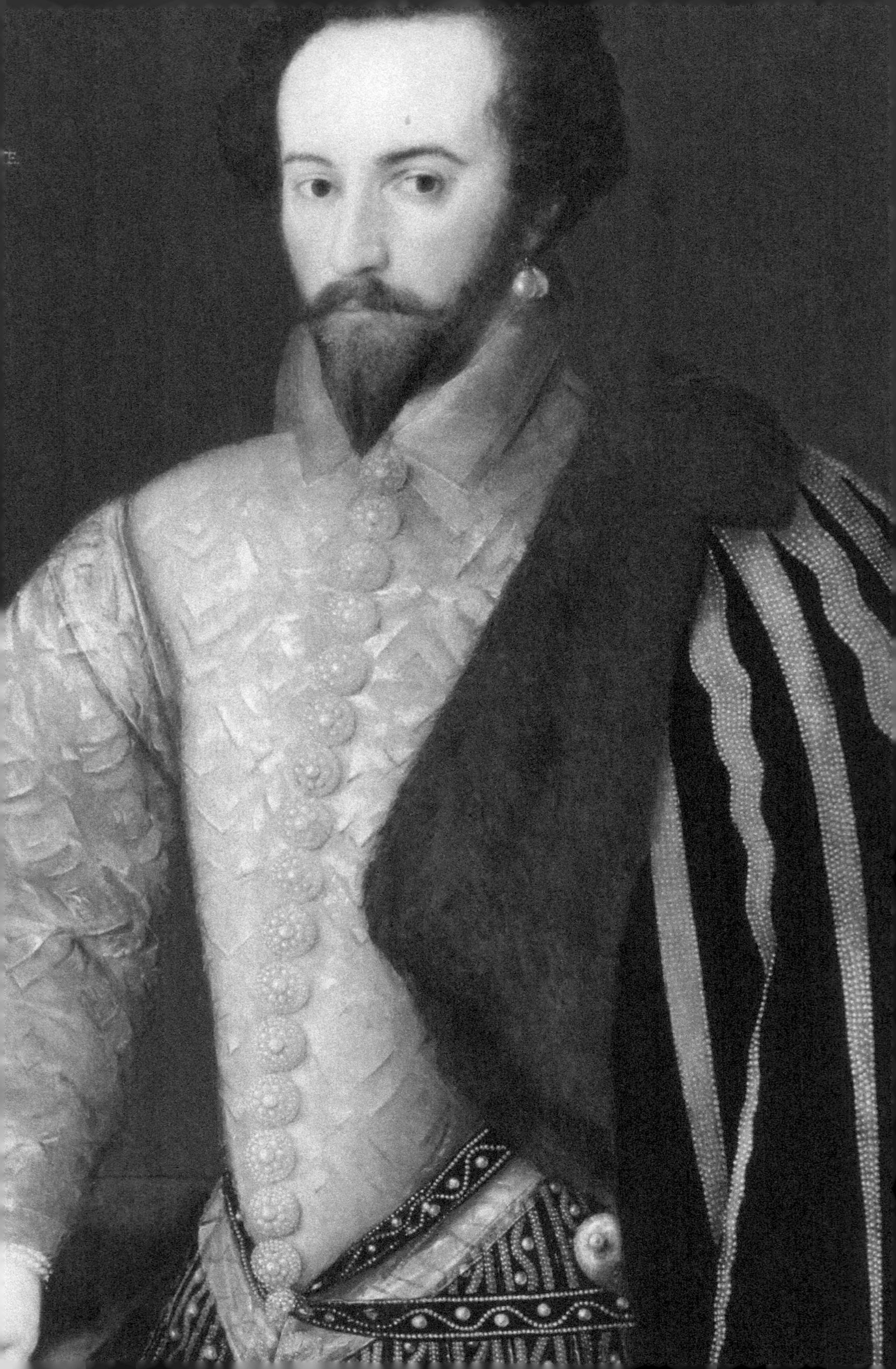

SIR WALTER RALEIGH
Explorer and Adventurer

Key Facts

- Born 1554, died 1618
- Founded the settlement in North America that became the state of Virginia
- Tried to find 'El Dorado' in South America
- Popularized the smoking of tobacco

Not much is known of Raleigh's early life. He was born into an England divided by religious differences between Catholics and Protestants. During his childhood in Devon, the Catholic Queen Mary I was on the throne, and this led to problems for Raleigh's protestant family, with his father having to go into hiding on more than one occasion to avoid execution. His mother, Catherine Champernowne, was married twice and had a total of 5 sons. Because of his staunch Protestant upbringing and the persecutions suffered by his father, Raleigh developed a life-long hatred of Catholics.

All of her sons became prominent in various ways as Catherine was a niece to the governess of Queen Elizabeth I and was, therefore, able to obtain court introductions for her sons. At that time, connections to the court were an essential means of social progress, and Raleigh exploited this to the full, writing poems to the Queen and becoming famous for his loyalty and affection for the monarch.

While still a teenager, Raleigh went to France to fight for the Huguenots – who were Protestant – in the French civil wars. In

1572 he spent a brief time at Oxford University and then seems to have returned to France, coming back to England finally around 1575 to become a member of the Middle Temple, one of the Inns of Court, which would have made him a lawyer of the time.

In 1579 he was back fighting Catholics, this time in Ireland, where he advised Elizabeth and also took an active part in the suppression of the Desmond Rebellions, which were an attempt by the FitzGerald dynasty to re-establish their authority over their historic lands in the province of Munster. Raleigh was so prominent in the resulting British victory that he was awarded 40,000 acres of seized land and the towns of Youghal and Lismore. Raleigh was able to persuade tenant farmers to come from England to rent these lands from him and kept them for 17 years, but in 1602, when in financial difficulties, he sold the land to the 1st Earl of Cork, Richard Boyle. Boyle was a major landholder – the Donald Trump of his time – who, although a Protestant, was able to stay in favor with both sides of the religious conflicts.

During his time in Ireland, where he lived in Killua Castle, County Westmeath, Raleigh seems to have taken up smoking the tobacco only recently brought back from the New World. Although also attributed to other locations associated with Raleigh, this seems to be the actual setting of the famous story of a servant throwing a bucket of water over Raleigh, thinking he was on fire. As well, during his stays in Ireland, he became friendly with another receiver of seized land, the writer of the Faerie Queene, Edmund Spenser.

While holding these lands in Ireland, Raleigh was often busy elsewhere. He rose to a favored position at the court and received numerous honors and sources of income from the Queen as well as the use of Durham House, on the Thames. Raleigh successfully flattered Elizabeth with poems comparing her to the goddess Diana and they both dressed in jewels, pearls, and ruffles. The apocryphal story of his throwing his expensive velvet cloak across a puddle to keep Elizabeth's feet dry probably helped too.

The Spanish and French had been active for several decades in colonizing eastern North America, so Elizabeth was interested in gaining a foothold in these new and potentially rich areas. When Raleigh's half-brother Sir Humphrey Gilbert was lost at sea, Elizabeth granted him Gilbert's royal charter to establish a colony in the area that was to become Virginia. In 1585 he was knighted as 'Lord and Governor of Virginia.' Raleigh himself never traveled to the area, but he sent three expeditions to colonize Roanoke Island, one in 1584, which returned with information and two Croatoan Native Americans, and the second in 1585, which established a settlement but was rescued the following year by Sir Francis Drake, who brought back tobacco, potatoes, and corn as well as the settlers. In 1587 a third group was sent, but this colony eventually disappeared completely, gaining them the title of the Lost Colonists. A permanent settlement was eventually established by James I in 1607.

In 1587 Elizabeth appointed Raleigh responsible for her personal safety, and with that mandate, he raised a fleet to defend England against Spain. Commanded by Sir Francis Drake, the fleet succeeded in scattering the Spanish Armada and saving the nation, but Raleigh quickly fell out of favor at the court and was forced to retire to his Irish estate.

He did not stay out of favor long, and by 1591, he was back at the court and doing well, at least until he secretly married Elizabeth Throckmorton, who, being a royal attendant to the Queen, needed her permission to marry. Furious, Elizabeth threw both of them into the Tower of London, but they were soon out again. In 1595 Raleigh received the Queen's patent to explore Guiana and set out to find El Dorado, the fabled City of Gold. His book of his voyage was more successful than his expedition and played a part in keeping the legend alive.

Raleigh continued to enjoy Elizabeth's support for the rest of the century, but after her death in 1603, the Catholic James I took the throne, and Raleigh's successes at the royal court were over. After most of his privileges were rescinded by the new King, Raleigh found himself on trial for treason within months of Elizabeth's death. Although found guilty and sentenced to be hung, drawn, and quartered, his sentence was commuted, and he spent the next ten years in the Tower of London. He won the support of the King's eldest son (and thus heir to the throne) Henry, Prince of Wales, partly by tutoring him in navigation, but when Henry died of typhoid fever in 1612 at the age of eighteen, Raleigh lost that support too.

Nevertheless, in 1616 he was able to persuade the King to release him in return for promises to sail to Guiana again to bring back the gold for the depleted Royal Treasury. While away, he foolishly defied his orders and attacked a Spanish settlement – Spain was now briefly a friend of England – and the Spanish demanded his execution. In 1618 James obliged them by having him beheaded. Raleigh's wife received the head and had it embalmed. She kept it in a special case right up to her death twenty-nine years later.

His Legacy

Raleigh is widely regarded as a key figure in encouraging the British to develop settlements in North America. Although sometimes credited with the introduction of the useful potato to Europe, his popularization of smoking is a more dubious legacy. His poetry and chronicles of his and others' voyages made him one of the most important writers of the time. His character as a proud, bold, and sometimes head-strong man has an archetypal quality to it that continues to inspire.

Sites to Visit

- There is a statue of Raleigh in Raleigh, Virginia, and one in the Royal Naval College, Greenwich. There is a recently erected statue in his home town of East Budleigh, Devon, partly funded by the British American Tobacco Company.
- Mount Raleigh is in the Pacific Ranges in British Columbia, Canada.
- Several museums, including the British Museum, have portraits of Raleigh in their collections.

Further Research

- Recent biographies are Sir Walter Raleigh in Life and Legend by Penry Williams (2011) and Sir Walter Raleigh: Being a True and Vivid Account of the Life and Times of the Explorer,

Soldier, Scholar, Poet, by Raleigh Trevelyan (2004).
- There was a biographic film of Raleigh made in 1925, and he appears as a character in Elizabeth: The Golden Age (2007). There is a DVD of his life entitled Great Adventurers: Sir Walter Raleigh (1999).
- Most of his works can be found in print or on-line.

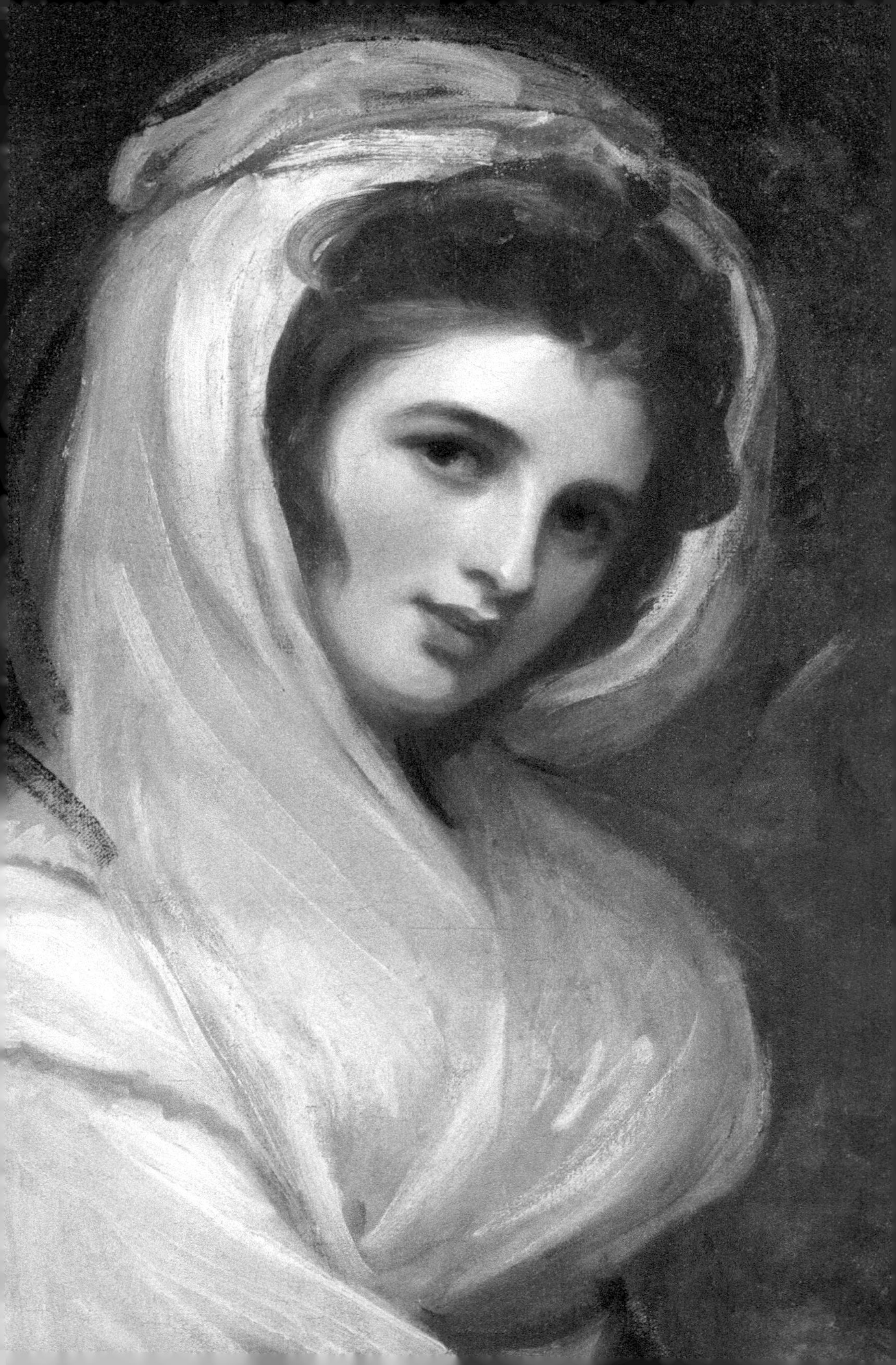

EMMA HAMILTON
Nelson's Great Love

Key Facts

- Born 1765 – died 1815
- Muse for artist George Romney
- Mistress of Horatio Nelson
- Went from poverty to riches and back again

A dancer, a muse for artists, traded for an inheritance, and mistress to the greatest admiral in British history. Emma Hamilton had it all, rising from obscure roots to become the toast of the town and the subject of endless gossip. Perhaps the first 'celebrity' in the modern sense, she began as an entertainer for stag parties and gained celebrity as the muse of George Romney, who painted numerous portraits of her as classic figures. She then became a trophy bride for the British Ambassador to the Kingdom of the Two Sicilies, taking his name, Hamilton, and living in luxury in Naples. She entertained party guests with scantily-clad 'Attitudes' based on her portrait work with George Romney. When she met Horatio Nelson, Hamilton permitted them to live and love in his home, creating a scandalous ménage à trois that was the subject of sensational items in the media of the day. After Nelson died at the Battle of Trafalgar, she becomes destitute and drunken, dying in poverty in a room in France.

For women, the combination of natural beauty and a willingness to break boundaries has often been a potent path to success. For Emma Lyon, it certainly worked. When she was born on the twenty-sixth of April 1765, the future did not look promising. Her blacksmith father died shortly after she was born, leaving her widowed mother to bring her up. She was born south of Birkenhead but brought up in the village of Hawarden, on the Wales-England border. As was common for working-class girls of the time, she was 'put into service,' that is, she went to work as a maid for Doctor Honoratus Leigh Thomas, an eminent surgeon who had a house in the village. She was twelve years old.

Emma moved to a house in London, the home of the Budd family, in Chatham Place, Blackfriars, and there she befriended another maid called Jane Powell. Like many teenagers, Jane, and quickly Emma too, wanted to become actresses, and the pair would rehearse together and dream of fame and fortune. Emma did, in a sense, join the theatre because she became the maid to actresses at the Drury Lane theatre in Covent Garden.

The traditional view of 18th-century theatre is that the boundary between acting and prostitution was porous for actresses, but more modern writers suggest that female actors were shrewd businesswomen who knew how to profit from the gender stereotypes they performed, both on and off the stage. So when we hear that Emma Lyon, aged 15, was dancing nude on the table at the raucous dinners of young, dissolute aristocrats, we might just as much admire her business acumen in using her only marketable asset, as we might see her as an exploited working-class child. The organizer of these events was Sir Harry Fetherstonhaugh, who hired Emma for an extended engagement as hostess and entertainer for a stag party at his Uppark house on the South Downs. The party apparently lasted several months and perhaps only ended when Emma became pregnant in the summer of 1781 with Fetherstonhaugh's child.

She was sent to one of his houses in London, and after the birth, her daughter, Emma Carew, was raised by a certain Mr. and Mrs. Blackburn, although Emma saw her frequently. While pregnant, Emma became the mistress of the MP Charles Francis Greville, whom she had met at the extended stag party. Greville seems to have been dull but sincere and loved Emma. After the birth, he kept her at a house on the Edgware Road and changed her name to

Emma Hart. There he encouraged her development with music and drawing lessons, such as would have been de rigueur for the daughters of the well-to-do.

Wanting a portrait of her, Greville hired the fashionable society artist George Romney to create one, and Romney was immediately smitten, making Emma his most famous muse. Besides numerous sketches in various poses, both clothed and nude, he did 60 full portraits, portraying her often as mythological figures, such as the Greek enchantress Circe, who turned men into pigs. These paintings caught the eye of the wider London society, and Emma, with her witty manners, intelligence, and beauty, found herself the center of attention.

Greville, however, was finding Emma an increasing embarrassment. He needed to marry money to escape his debts, and being known for his mistress was not endearing to respectable prospective brides. So he devised a scheme that was little short of a sale. He had a rich uncle, Sir William Hamilton, whose wife had died in 1782. Hamilton saw Emma's portraits, and as a collector of art and beautiful objects, he wanted to add Emma to his collection and acquire a female companion. He agreed to make Hamilton his heir, while Greville's marriage would relieve Hamilton of financial responsibilities while still alive. In return – and Hamilton even paid the transport costs – Greville would deliver Emma to him in Naples, where Hamilton was the ambassador of King George III to the Kingdom of the Two Sicilies.

Emma thought she was going on holiday with Greville, and she was understandably furious when she learned the true purpose of their voyage. Perhaps she had little choice in the matter, but it seems that Hamilton's passion for her won her over, and she stayed. Hamilton moved in the highest circles of Naples' society, and Emma became a close friend of Maria Carolina of Austria, Queen of Naples and Sicily, and sister of Marie Antoinette.

Emma had never given up her dream of becoming an actress, and while in Naples, she developed a unique performance art which became known as 'Attitudes.' Drawing on her experience modeling for George Romney, she combined posing with mime, flimsy costumes, and shawls, to create solo tableau that evoke

Greco-Roman mythology. She performed at parties when Hamilton had guests from all over Europe staying at his Naples home. Just how much clothing came between Emma and the guests is a matter of speculation, although judging from contemporary accounts and cartoons, the answer is 'very little.'

After five years together, the couple were married in 1791. Emma was 26, and Hamilton was 60. Trophy wives are not a 21st-century invention. Just two years after the wedding, Emma met Horatio Nelson, the captain of HMS Agamemnon at that time. Nelson was in Naples to negotiate reinforcements from the King of the Two Sicilies for the war against the Revolutionary Government of France. With Hamilton's help, he got his reinforcements – and fell hopelessly in love with Emma. Five years later, in 1798, Nelson was back, but his battles had weakened the famous captain, so Emma and Hamilton took him into their home, the Palazzo Sessa, where he was nursed, entertained, and fêted as a hero. The times were troubled, and following skirmishes with local revolutionaries, Nelson was recalled. Hamilton requested to be relieved of his post too, and all three traveled together back to England, taking the long route home via Austria.

They arrived in London in November of 1800, where the unlikely threesome openly set up house first in Piccadilly, and later in Merton, where Nelson bought a house and land in what was then a rural community south of Wimbledon. On the first of January 1801, Nelson became a vice-admiral, and on the 29th, Emma gave birth to their daughter, Horatia. Nelson was still married to Fanny Nisbet, but they had parted completely after her failed ultimatum to him the Christmas before. Hamilton, now 70, seemed not to object to their ménage à trois, and Emma was described as 'leading Nelson around like a bear.' The newspapers were fascinated by the trio, reporting daily on them, and Emma set trends in clothes, home decorating, and fashionable dishes for dinner parties. Emma had put on weight, and Nelson did not enjoy the whirl of social events, so they entered a quieter phase of life.

Hamilton died in 1803, Nelson returned to his ships, and the next year Emma gave birth again. The baby girl died a few weeks later, and Emma used gambling and lavish spending to keep her spirits up, anticipating the possibility of now marrying Nelson. It was not to be, and in 1805 an emissary from the Admiralty delivered the fatal message – Nelson had died at the Battle of Trafalgar. Emma was distraught with grief.

Now doubly-widowed, Emma had a small annuity from Hamilton, and Nelson had left her Merton Place. Unsuited to genteel poverty, the annuity was soon gone, Merton Place proved too expensive, and she was forced to sell it. She fell heavily into debt, and in 1813 she was committed to debtor's prison in Southwark. Because of Horatia, she was permitted to live in rooms nearby. Once the toast of society, now she found almost no support, and in the summer of 1814, with the help of her few remaining friends, she fled to Calais, France, to escape her creditors. There, drinking heavily and living in a dismal room with Horatia, she lingered a few months until January 1815, when she died of amoebic dysentery contracted in Naples, or perhaps of cirrhosis of the liver from her drinking. She was buried in Calais, but the site was destroyed by war.

Horatia went on to have ten children, but she never publicly acknowledged her mother.

Sites to Visit

- There are numerous paintings and other drawings of Emma Hamilton by Romney and other artists at the National Portrait Gallery, St Martin's Place, London WC2.
- Uppark, the home of Harry Fetherstonhaugh, in South Harting, Petersfield, West Sussex, is a National Trust property and open to the public.
- There is a memorial to Emma Hamilton, erected in 1994, in Parc Richelieu in Calais.
- There is a blue plaque at Merton Place, near Doel Close, Merton, 200 yards from the location of Nelson's house, which was called 'Merton Place.'
- There is a blue plaque at East Rock House, an unassuming building on St Julian Street, Tenby, Wales, where the three briefly stayed.

Further Research

Film depictions of Emma's life:

- That Hamilton Woman (1941) Vivien Leigh as Emma and Laurence Olivier as Horatio.
- Emma Hamilton (1968) Michèle Mercier as Emma.
- The Nelson Affair (or, Bequest to the Nation), (1973) Glenda Jackson as Emma and Peter Finch as Horatio.

Novels:

- The Volcano Lover: A Romance, (1992), Susan Sontag

Biographies:

- Emma Hamilton: Seduction and Celebrity, by Quintin Colville and Kate Williams
- Emma Hamilton, by Norah Lofts
- Beloved Emma: The Life of Emma, Lady Hamilton, by Flora Fraser
- That Hamilton Woman: Emma and Nelson, by Barry Gough and Andrew Roberts

Other books:

- Emma Hamilton and Late Eighteenth-Century European Art: Agency, Performance, and Representation, by Ersy Contogouris

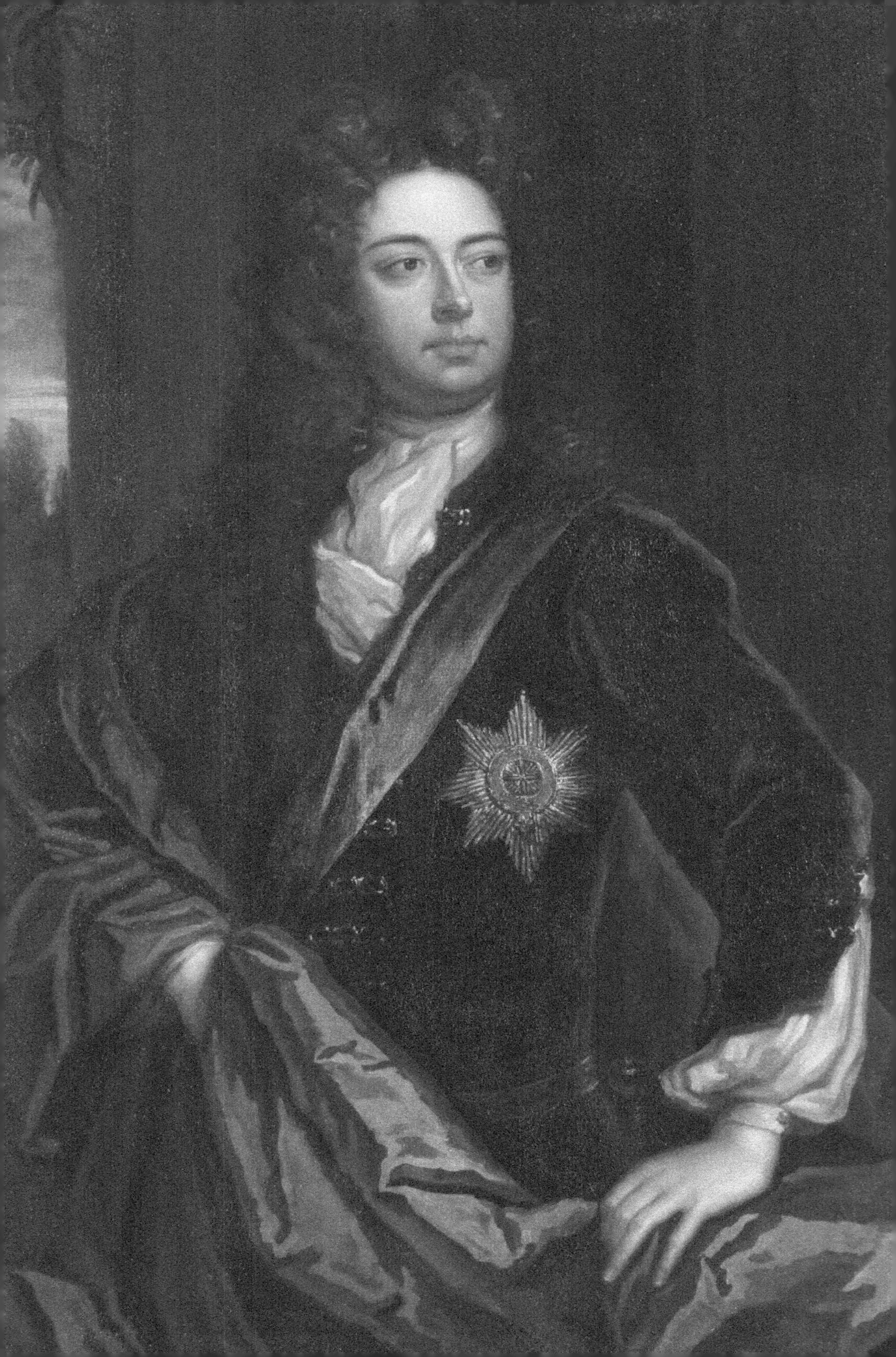

1ST DUKE OF MARLBOROUGH
Victor of the Battle of Blenheim

Key Facts

- Born 1650, died 1722
- Considered by many to be the greatest British military leader
- Went through several changes of fortune in a long career under five monarchs.
- Amassed great wealth and built Blenheim Palace
- Ancestor of Sir Winston Churchill

The 1st Duke of Marlborough was a larger-than-life creation of the complex politics of the 17th century, going from power to the Tower and back again. He was an important military leader and won decisive battles that helped draw the map of Europe for the next two centuries. He accumulated wealth and power and built one of the greatest homes in England, Blenheim Palace. Sir Winston Churchill was a direct descendant.

At the death of Oliver Cromwell, there was a good chance that the protestant revolution that had beheaded Charles I in 1649 would continue. However, Cromwell's son failed to hold the loyalty of the army, and in 1661 monarchy was restored when King Charles II was crowned the King of England.

At the time, John Churchill was approaching his 11th birthday, living in his father's house in Devon. His father, Winston Churchill, had chosen the wrong side in the revolution and had been fined for his misplaced loyalties, an event that placed him in serious financial hardship. It has been suggested that the two chief personality traits of his son, a fear of poverty and the ability to disassemble, developed during the harsh times of his father's relative poverty.

So when the monarch returned and Winston's fortunes began to improve, by 1664, the young John found himself at St Paul's School outside London, one of the first of the British public schools. The new monarch may have had relatively empty coffers, but he did have court positions to reward those loyal to him, so in 1665 John became a page to the King's brother, James, the Duke of York, while his sister Arabella was Maid of Honour to the Duchess of York.

James had a love of all things military, and John followed him and joined the Grenadier Guards, spending three years in Tangier fighting Moors for the King. When he returned to England, his good looks and charm made him popular at court, so much so that he was even able to survive the King's discovery that he was having an affair with his favorite mistress. He became a captain in the Admiralty Regiment, an early type of Marine Corps, and distinguished himself in numerous battles.

On his return to the Palace, he fell in love with Sarah Jennings, from another loyal Royalist family like his own and also a Maid of Honour to the new Duchess of York. Despite her relative poverty, John and Sarah were married during the winter of 1677–78. They went on to have seven children.

Following the death of Charles II, the Duke of York became King James II, and John Churchill became Baron Churchill, member of the House of Lords, governor of the Hudson's Bay Company, and most importantly of all, a Gentleman of the Bedchamber. Since this last gave him direct access to the King on a daily basis is was a position of great power.

The Protestants had, however, not given up, and in 1685 there was a rebellion against the Catholic James, who was not as willing to show religious tolerance as his Catholic father had been. Baron Churchill was sent to join the Earl of Feversham to put down the rebellion led by the first-born but illegitimate son of Charles II, the Duke of Monmouth. At the Battle of Sedgemoor, in Somerset, the Duke was defeated and subsequently beheaded, as were many sympathizers.

Alarmed at James' growing religious intolerance, Churchill, himself a Protestant, began to draw away from the Crown, a process helped by his feeling of having been inadequately rewarded for his service at Sedgemoor. Within three years, he had switched sides and joined what became known as the Glorious Revolution. The plan was that on the death of James II, his eldest daughter, Mary, who was married to William of Orange, de facto head of state of the Netherlands, would take the throne in a joint protestant monarchy. However, the plan was derailed when James produced an heir, assuring an unbroken Catholic succession.

At this point, a group of prominent Englishmen petitioned William of Orange to invade England, promising him the loyalty of most of the country. Churchill was not senior enough to sign the petition, but he did express his loyalty to William. When he was sent to resist the invasion, he led 400 men to join William instead, and with James' confidence gone, an almost bloodless transfer of power took place.

In 1689 Churchill was rewarded with the title Duke of Marlborough, but the coveted Order of the Garter eluded him. William wisely distrusted someone who had already switched sides once. The Duke proved his disloyalty by entering into secret negotiations with the exiled James II, which, when discovered, put him into the Tower of London awaiting trial for treason. After six weeks, he was released as there was insufficient evidence for a trial to be held, his power was gradually restored, but he struggled right up to the death of William to regain his full confidence.

His life entered a new phase when Anne, the sister of Mary and therefore an heir to Charles II, became the new Queen of England. Marlborough was close to Anne through the long friendship of Sarah, his wife, and the new Queen, and this gave him renewed power and authority. Most importantly, it gained him his coveted Order of the Garter. He also gained control of the military, and with Sarah also holding powerful positions at court, they were second only to the Queen in power and privilege.

The Duke's military high-point came during the War of the Spanish Succession, when an alliance of England, Holland, and the Holy Roman Empire fought to prevent France from gaining control of Spain through inheritance. The battles raged from 1701 to 1714, including the early Battle of Blenheim and the Battles of Ramillies, Oudenarde, Malplaquet, and Bouchain. Marlborough proved himself a great general and was decisive in beating the French in battle, but a diplomatic peace remained elusive. Eventually, Marlborough found himself on the wrong side of the Queen, who didn't want a total French defeat, as the Duke and the other Allies did – she just wanted a non-French Spain. Marlborough was replaced, although he remained popular in Europe.

It took the death of Queen Anne and the installation of the new and protestant House of Hanover, in the person of George I, to put Marlborough back in favor. However, by now, failing health restricted his powers, and he stayed mainly at Blenheim, overseeing the construction of his Palace there. Following two strokes, he died on the 16th of June, 1722.

His Legacy

Variously considered Britain's greatest military leader or an avaricious villain, the Duke certainly created a lot of history and left his mark on England. Many would perhaps chiefly thank him for eventually producing another enigmatic figure, Sir Winston

Churchill. At a time when many were lining their large pockets and building the fortunes of the future British upper-class, Marlborough stands out as especially relentless in his pursuit of wealth, power, and privilege. He was a first-rate military administrator and an excellent if conventional battle tactician who certainly won many more battles than he lost.

Sites to Visit

- Blenheim Palace, the Duke's reward for his victory at the Battle of the same name, is in Woodstock, near Oxford. It is the birthplace of Sir Winston Churchill, and the house and grounds can be visited daily.
- Marlborough's grave was briefly in Westminster Abbey but was moved to Blenheim Chapel when Sarah died. They lie beside each other.

Further Research

Biographies of the 1st Duke of Marlborough include:

- Marlborough: His Life and Times, in Four Volumes, by Winston S. Churchill (1933–1938)
- Marlborough: England's Fragile Genius, by Richard Holmes (2008)
- First Churchill: Life of John, 1st Duke of Marlborough, by George Malcolm Thomson (1979)

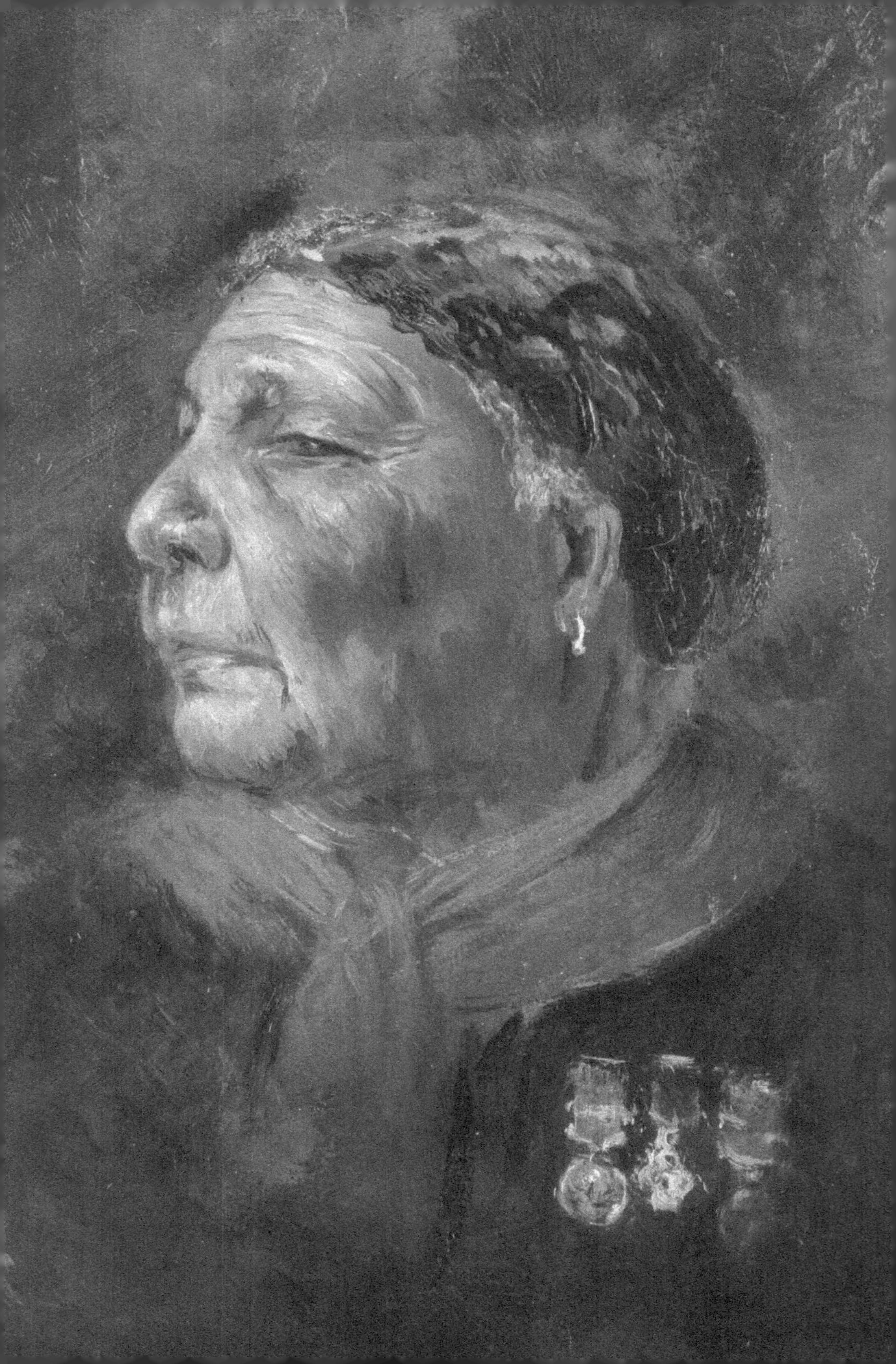

MARY SEACOLE
Britain's Other Nursing Pioneer

Key Facts

- Born 1805, died 1881
- Ran an officer's restaurant and gave basic nursing aid in the Crimean War
- Showed care and compassion for even the poorest soldier
- Enjoyed the support of many powerful and generous military men

Mary Seacole has become the center of some controversy over her place in the history of nursing. She was a Creole from Jamaica who ran a restaurant and sold supplies to officers in the first Crimean War, and gave basic nursing assistance to wounded soldiers there. She traveled widely as a single woman and enjoyed business success as well as failure, overcoming them to show resolution and determination as well as a compassionate heart.

In the 19th century, the island of Jamaica, in the Caribbean, was part of the British Empire and ruled from England. So it is no surprise to find a Scottish soldier living there and marrying a woman who was herself probably the result of a relationship between an Englishman and a black slave, one of the thousands who had been brought from Africa to work the sugar plantations that were a vital part of the trans-Atlantic trade routes. Slavery in Jamaica was abolished by Britain during the 1830s.

Mary Jane Grant, who was born in Jamaica in 1805 to a mixed-race mother and that Scottish soldier, always proudly declared herself to be Creole and Scottish, 'only a little brown' and distanced herself from other Creoles and blacks, who she frequently referred to as 'good-for-nothings' and described with the N-word.

Her mother ran a boarding house called Blundell Hall, which was one of the better hotels in Kingston at the time. She was also a 'doctress,' a traditional healer in the African tradition using herbal and folk remedies, and Mary learned those skills from her. Mary spent some time in the house of an elderly lady she described as her 'patroness' and seems to have been educated at that time so that by the time she became a woman, she was well-educated, relatively wealthy, and a part of the upper echelons of Jamaican society.

Between 1821 and 1825, she visited London several times, probably accompanying shipments of Jamaican products purchased by merchant relatives in England. She developed the habit of traveling alone as an unaccompanied woman, which was unusual at those times.

In 1836 she married Edwin Horatio Hamilton Seacole in Kingston. There was a family legend, unsupported by any facts, that Edwin was either the illegitimate son of Horatio Nelson and his mistress Lady Hamilton or Nelson's godson.

In 1843 the family hotel was destroyed by fire and rapidly replaced with an improved 'New Blundell Hall.' However, the following year both her husband and mother died, causing Mary considerable grief, which she however quickly overcame and went on to become a popular and well-known part of Kingston life, and friendly with many military officers who frequented her hotel. In 1850 there was a serious outbreak of cholera in Jamaica, and Mary drew on the skills she had learned from her mother to help.

In 1849 the California Gold Rush created many business opportunities, and a half-brother of Mary set up a Hotel on the Chagres River in what is today Panama. This was a crossroads in the circuitous route used to travel from eastern North America to California in the absence of Route 66. The following year Mary went to stay with him and helped in another cholera epidemic that broke out in 1851. As the only person in the town with any medical knowledge, she did everything she could to help, using her herbal and folk remedies. She had some success but became frustrated with her failures and later admitted that some of her 'cures' had been disastrous, a recognition of the limits of medical knowledge at that time.

She opened a small restaurant, called the British Hotel, with a barber's shop attached. As she had in Kingston, she became popular with the many men, mostly American, who passed through. She does not seem to have found Americans to her liking, with their rough speech, far from her 'King's English' and their racism, which deeply offended her.

She arrived back in Jamaica in 1853 and was asked for her assistance with an outbreak of Yellow Fever, but there was little that could be done. If cholera patients can be kept hydrated, the death rate is only around 1%, so even basic nursing makes a huge difference, whereas, with yellow fever, the death rate is around 40% and can only be prevented by vaccination, which was of course not available at that time.

In 1854 she returned to Panama to stay with a relative of her husband at a gold mine. She was in London dealing with gold mining shares when she read of the outbreak of the Crimean War, and perhaps having heard so many tales of the glories of battle from her hotel guests, she decided to experience it herself. Although the newspapers at the time carried advertisements for nurses to go to the front, there is no evidence she applied for them, but she would have seen the publicity surrounding Florence Nightingale and her contingent. She did try unsuccessfully to join a later contingent of nurses, but she was 50 and had no actual hospital experience. It is not clear if her race also played a part, but it seems reasonable to assume that it may have.

Undaunted, she set out for the Crimea herself, intending to establish a second 'British Hotel' in Balaclava. On the way, she met a doctor in Malta who gave her a letter of introduction to Florence Nightingale, who she visited at her hospital in Scutari. They had a friendly meeting, and Seacole stayed the night at the hospital before continuing her journey.

By the middle of 1855, the hotel was finished, built mostly of salvaged materials. She only served meals since the British headquarters were only a mile away and officers slept there. She did a thriving business, selling not just meals but other supplies, catering events, and doing what today would be called a 'take-out' service. She also operated as a sutler, a term used to describe someone who went among the troops with a cart selling food and supplies. She also voluntarily gave lemonade and food to wounded troops waiting on the docks to be sent to the main hospitals. Regular soldiers would not have been able to afford the prices at her hotel or have been welcomed by the officers and dignitaries who frequented it.

As the major battles were already over before she arrived, she missed them, but she did see three minor battles. It was still common at that time for officer's wives and others to view a battle from a suitable vantage point, bringing a picnic with them. Warfare, and the life in military camps, was very different indeed before the carnage of WWI forced the creation of a more professional army. After the battles, she went onto the field and to the military hospitals with drinks and to help bind-up wounds.

Following the peace in 1856, her business naturally declined, and she returned to England, destitute and in poor health. There she was a guest-of-honor at a large celebratory dinner, but her debts had mounted up, and pursued by creditors, she was eventually declared bankrupt at the end of 1856.

Her plight caught the public eye and the interest of officers who knew her from the war, and a fund was set up to free her and her business partner from bankruptcy, which happened early in 1857. Later the same year, she published her memoirs.

She divided her time for the remainder of her life between Kingston and London. She enjoyed a good reputation in London and was able to raise more funds through her connections with high society so that she could build a bungalow in Kingston and lead a comfortable life with a good social position. She died in London on the 14th of May, 1881, probably of a stroke.

Her Legacy

Largely forgotten after her death, Mary Seacole has become the center of controversy in recent years, when attempts have been made to elevate her to the level of Florence Nightingale, who has been denigrated as part of that process. An exaggerated version of her nursing activities is taught in British Primary Schools as part of educational multiculturalism. There are plans for a statue of her at St Thomas' Hospital in London, although she has no association with that hospital, which was, in fact, the base for Florence Nightingale's work for over 40 years.

The truth seems to be that Mary was an adventurous and bold woman with a generous and caring spirit who did what she could to help wounded soldiers while attending to her own business affairs. She is a role model for care and compassion during times of hardship, but her work does not rank with that of Nightingale and others who developed the modern profession of nursing.

Sites to Visit

- Her grave is in St. Mary's Roman Catholic Cemetery, Harrow Road, Kensal Green, London. It has been restored with a large headstone.
- There is an English Heritage blue plaque at 14, Soho Square, London, where she lived in 1857.

Further Research

- Mary Seacole's memoir, Wonderful Adventures of Mrs. Seacole in Many Lands, first published in 1857, is still available.

Both sides of the debate on her place in the history of nursing can be found in biographies about her:
- Black Nightingale: Mary Seacole, hero of the Crimean War, by Julia Buss (2011) (described by the publisher as a novel)
- Mary Seacole: The Making of the Myth, by Lynn McDonald (2014)

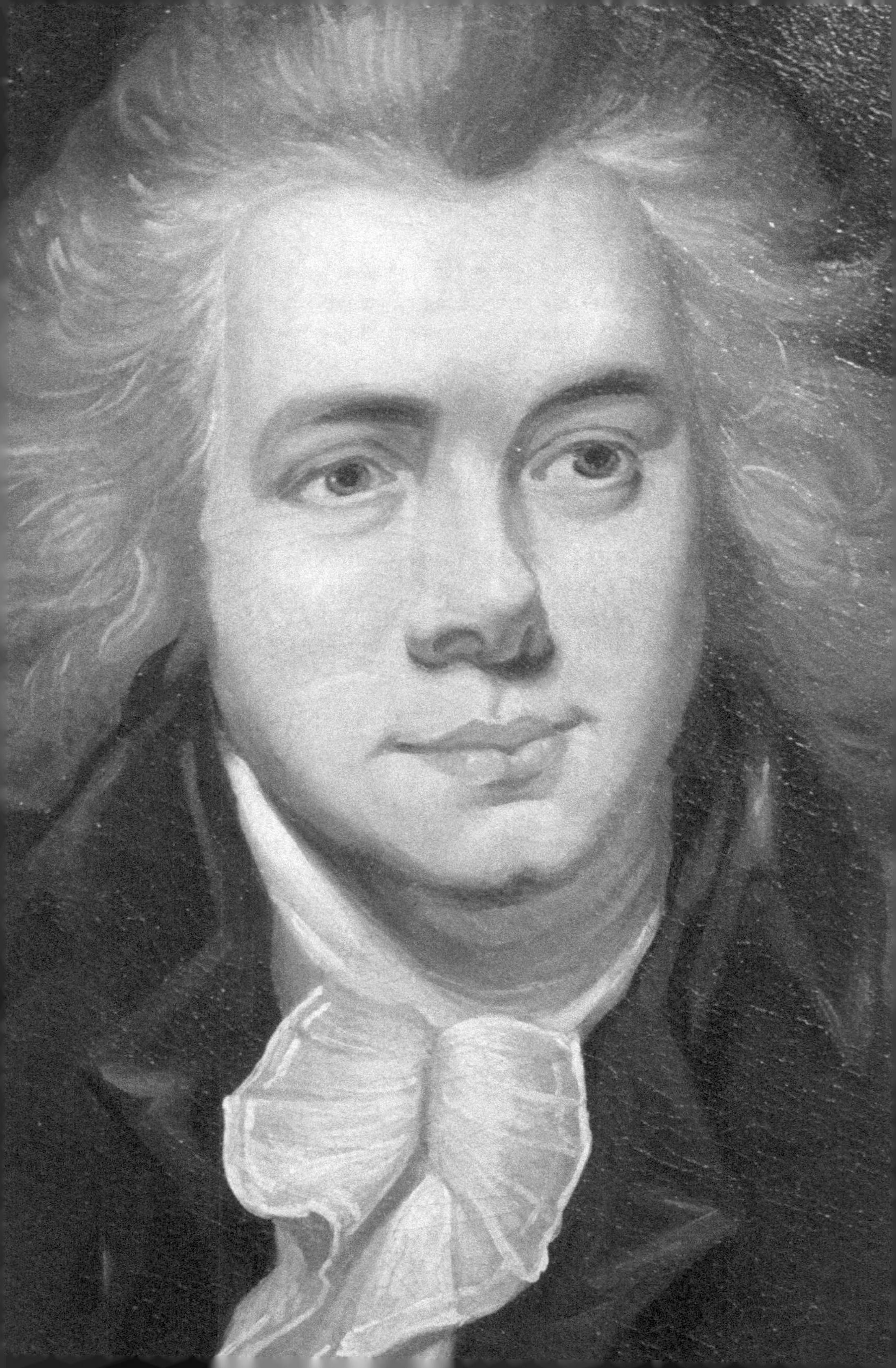

WILLIAM WILBERFORCE
Abolitionist Leader

Key Facts

- Born 1759 – died 1833
- He fought for most of his life for the end of slavery
- Died days after achieving his goal
- Evangelical conservative Christian opposed to many other social reforms

William Wilberforce was a 19th-century Member of Parliament (MP) and writer who devoted much of his life to the campaigns to first abolish the slave trade and, secondly, to abolish slavery itself in British colonies. He was converted to evangelical Christianity by friends, and his beliefs played an important role in his political life. After a campaign lasting 42 years, slavery was abolished in British territories three days before his death.

William Wilberforce was born on the 24th of August, 1759, in the town of Hull, Yorkshire. His father was a wealthy merchant, and his grandfather had been the mayor of Hull and made the family fortune trading in the Baltic. He was sent to Hull Grammar School, but upon the death of his father, his situation became more uncertain, and he was sent to live with an aunt and uncle in Wimbledon. He attended boarding school in Putney and came under the evangelical influence of his relatives, causing some concern among his Church of England mother and grandfather. They were sufficiently alarmed by his exposure to radical non-conformism to bring him back to Hull. The 12-year old was very reluctant to return, but over time his religious zeal diminished, and he began to attend balls, the theatre, and even play cards.

When he was 17, he attended St John's College in Cambridge, but the recent deaths of his grandfather and uncle had made him independently wealthy, so he had little inclination to study, preferring to continue gambling, drinking late into the night, and generally living a highly sociable student life. He became a popular figure in the College and began a life-long friendship with William Pitt, a fellow student who would go on to become Prime Minister. Despite his apparent lack of application to study, he graduated B.A. and then M.A. in 1788.

Encouraged by his friend Pitt to become involved in politics, Wilberforce was elected MP for Kingston upon Hull, a Yorkshire constituency, spending £8,000 to secure the votes, a practice considered perfectly acceptable during this time of limited franchise, where the eligible voters were a small group of landowners.

Wilberforce sat as an independent, supporting the government when he approved of their actions, and he became well-known for his eloquent speeches. Outside of Parliament, he frequented various gentlemen's clubs to gamble at cards.

Wilberforce spent the winter of 1784/5 on the French Riviera and in Switzerland in the company of his mother and a friend named Isaac Milner. Milner was a non-conformist opponent of slavery, which was a major cause at the time among many non-conformists, and he brought about an evangelical conversion in Wilberforce, who abandoned his old ways and took to rising early to study his Bible. Evangelicals were viewed with suspicion and ridicule, and his new friends among this group had some difficulty in persuading him to stay in politics. But he did, returning to Parliament a deep conservative, opposed to change in the God-given social order, a protector of the Sabbath and promoter of moral education for the masses. He was rejected by both the establishment Tories, who saw him as an enemy of Church and State and by political radicals, who distrusted his conservatism.

The campaign to abolish the British slave-trade, long-established as the major source of slaves for all the European colonies in the West Indies and elsewhere, had begun a few years earlier among the

Quakers. They had presented a petition to Parliament for abolition in 1783. Although in the same year Wilberforce had met James Ramsay, a ship's surgeon turned abolitionist after his experiences on the plantations of the Leeward Islands; it wasn't until 1786 that he was approached by reformers to support the cause. He began to read on the subject and often met with an abolitionist group called the Testonites, based in Teston, Kent.

At a dinner party in March of 1787, a diverse group, including James Boswell, the biographer of Dr. Johnson; the painter Sir Joshua Reynolds; Thomas Clarkson, a friend of Wilberforce who provided him with much anti-slavery material; and assorted MPs and abolitionists, persuaded Wilberforce to act as the spokesman for abolition in Parliament. He agreed in principle but remained reluctant, doubting his ability to bring such a controversial matter forward. A few weeks later, a pivotal conversation with William Pitt persuaded him to make a full commitment.

His planned motion in Parliament was delayed by illness, and it wasn't until 1789 that he made his first speech in Parliament in support of abolition. This was made on the back of a Privy Council report commissioned by Pitt himself, but Parliamentary tactics and delays, plus an election, meant that it was April 1791 before Wilberforce could introduce a Bill for the abolition of slavery.

A protracted campaign followed, during which Wilberforce joined an evangelical community living around Clapham Common, known as 'The Saints'. A year after his first speech, Wilberforce took the floor again to push his bill, but it was cleverly side-tracked with an amendment from the Home Secretary to make the change gradual, but with no definite timetable.

The outbreak of war with France in 1793 effectively sidelined the abolition issue. The association in the public mind between abolition and the French Revolution, which had abolished slavery in 1794, caused the campaign to falter during this period of hostilities, with the most important groups ceasing to meet, although Wilberforce continued his attempts to introduce various abolitionist bills.

A confirmed bachelor and now in his late 30s, Wilberforce was introduced to the twenty-year-old Barbara Ann Spooner, and after an eight-day romance, they were engaged. They were married in

1797 and had six children over the next decade.

With the rise of Napoleon in France, who reintroduced slavery, the cause was no longer seen as pro-French, and public interest returned. With the new Whig government, abolitionists were now in the Cabinet, and a bill was passed banning British subjects from taking part in or supporting the slave trade with the French colonies.

A general election in 1806 saw abolition become a campaign issue, and many MPs who opposed slavery were returned to Parliament. With his years of research, Wilberforce wrote a 400-page book which became the corner-stone of the arguments for abolitionists. Lord Grenville, the new Prime Minister, put forward an Abolition Bill, which passed first the House of Lords and then the Commons by large majorities, and The Slave Trade Act became law on the 25th of March, 1807. This was not emancipation, which was not on Wilberforce's immediate agenda; just the end of the trade with slave owners calculating that there were sufficient slaves in the colonies to provide the needed workforce indefinitely. Wilberforce himself did not believe that slaves were ready for freedom but may one day become so.

In 1820, he began to withdraw from public life due to ill health, but in 1823 he changed his position on emancipation and began to support the complete freedom of all slaves. During his last years as an MP, he attempted but failed to pass emancipation legislation.

In 1826, he moved from Kensington to Mill Hill, then a rural area, but in 1830 most of his personal fortune was spent salvaging his son William's failed attempts at farming the property. In April of 1833, he made his final emancipation speech, and the next month the Bill for the Abolition of Slavery was introduced with a formal tribute to Wilberforce's influence. On the 26th of July, he heard the news that the Bill would pass, and on the 29th, he died at a cousin's house in Cadogan Place, London.

His Legacy

Wilberforce was the figurehead of abolition and emancipation for over 40 years, and his dedication and commitment to that cause were instrumental in swaying public opinion to support the election of abolitionist MPs. His name will always be associated with Britain's progress in the liberation of their fellow human beings. His family tried to downplay the vital role of his friend Thomas Clarkson, but historians today view both of them as more or less equal partners in the work.

In other areas, Wilberforce remained a conservative. He supported the suspension of habeas corpus and bans on public meetings of more than 50 people. He opposed the formation of trade unions and an inquiry into the Peterloo Massacre. He was against women engaging in political activity and opposed the rights of Catholics. He supported all attempts to suppress public vice, from drinking to swearing in public. Many of these activities brought him into direct opposition with prominent reforming radicals of the time, who felt him much more concerned with the behavior of the poor than of the ruling classes. He was often ridiculed by them for what they perceived as his double standards.

He did, however, support prison reform, opposed capital punishment for some crimes, and supported education for the poor. He was also instrumental in forming what was to become the Royal Society for the Prevention of Cruelty to Animals.

Sites to Visit

- Wilberforce is buried in the north transept of Westminster Abbey, near the grave of William Pitt.
- There is also a statue of him in Westminster Abbey.
- The Wilberforce Monument, a 100-foot column topped by a statue, is in the grounds of Hull College, Hull, Yorkshire.
- There are blue plaques at 44 Cadogan Place, London, where he died; Lauriston House (originally called Laurel Grove) on Southside, Wimbledon where he grew up; and on the Holy Trinity Church, in Clapham, where he and 'The Saints' worshipped.

Further Research

Biographies of Wilberforce include:

- Amazing Grace: William Wilberforce and the Heroic Campaign to End Slavery, by Eric Metaxas
- William Wilberforce: A Biography, by Stephen Tomkins
- William Wilberforce: The Life of the Great Anti-Slave Trade Campaigner, by William Hague
- Amazing Grace in the Life of William Wilberforce, by John Piper and Jonathan Aitken

Books of or based on his writings include:

- William Wilberforce, by William Wilberforce
- A Practical View of the Prevailing Religious System of Professed Christians, in the Middle and Higher Classes, by William Wilberforce

There is a film about his life and the fight against the slave trade, based on the book by Eric Metaxas:

- Amazing Grace, starring Benedict Cumberbatch

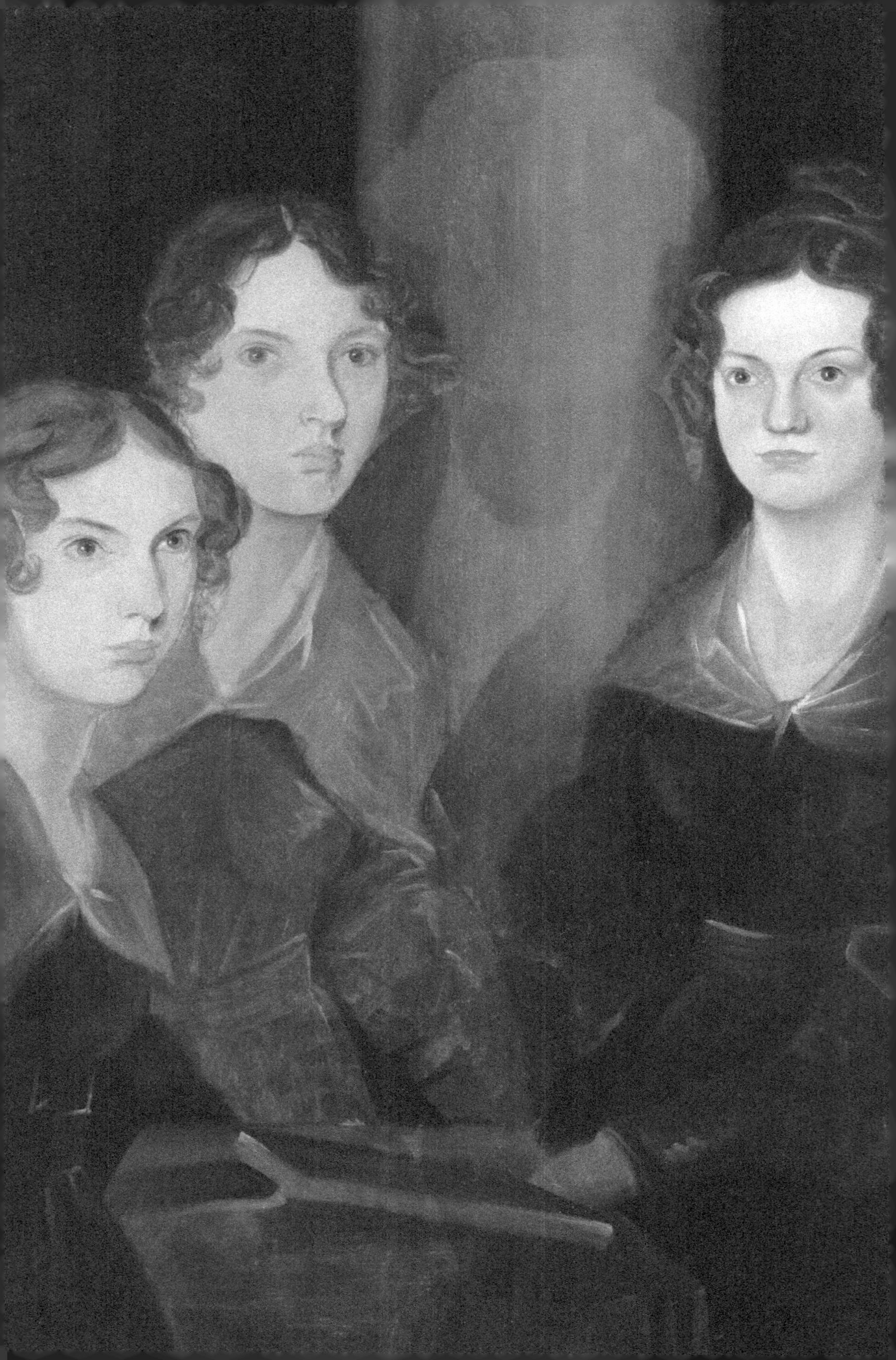

THE BRONTË SISTERS
A Literary Dynasty

Key Facts

- Three sisters, Charlotte (1816 – 1855), Emily (1818 – 1848), and Anne (1820 – 1849)
- A unique group of novelists who developed in the isolation and harsh life of the Yorkshire moors.
- Most famous for 'Wuthering Heights' and 'Jane Eyre.'
- Much admired as early feminist writers and literary icons.

The Brontës were a nineteenth-century family who spent their brief lives in the isolated moorlands of Yorkshire. The three sisters are well known as poets and novelists. They originally published under the pseudonyms Currer, Ellis, and Acton Bell, to avoid the prejudice of the time against female writers. They have attracted a cult-following only rivaled by that of Jane Austen.

Patrick Brontë was an Irishman and born a Catholic on St. Patrick's Day, 1777. Intelligent and aspirational, he won a scholarship to St. John's College, Cambridge, but on graduation, he joined the Church of England – a common practice at the time for educated men with no private means – and no particular indicator of piety. After marrying a young Cornish woman named Maria Branwell, he became curate of the ancient parish of Haworth in Yorkshire, a post he would retain until his death in 1861. He was not the stereotypical stodgy churchman but instead wrote novels and accounts of rural life, poems and newspaper articles.

He also took a great interest in the raising and educating of his six children, whose mother died after just nine years of marriage, leaving Patrick a life-long widower, despite his apparent attempts to re-marry. However, he spent a lot of time away from home ministering to the sick, poor, and dying, so that his children were mainly brought up by their mother's sister, Elizabeth, known as 'Aunt Branwell' and the family maid, Tabby.

The oldest daughters died in childhood, leaving three sisters - Charlotte, Emily, and Anne – to grow up with their brother, Branwell.

In this time before state-funded education, finding a satisfactory but affordable school for someone on the minimal income of a clergyman was difficult. Horror stories of malnutrition and mistreatment were widespread (think Dicken's Dotheboys Hall!), but Patrick Brontë tried hard and sent his children to Cowan Bridge School, which proved a disaster. The cruel mistress and tyrannical headmaster were to be immortalized in the girls' future literary efforts, and more seriously, all the children were infected with tuberculosis while there, the oldest daughters coming home to die when just 10 and 11 years old. The other girls were also infected.

More successful was their time at Miss. Wooler's School, where the eponymous Miss. Wooler was much kinder, and where the girls received a far better education. Charlotte was happy and made many friends, and after she left the school, she was soon invited back to work as an assistant teacher. She does not seem to have been an enthusiastic or particularly involved one.

Charlotte and Emily also spent six months at a boarding school in Brussels, learning German, French, and piano. They were fortunate to have an enthusiastic and brilliant schoolmaster – Monsieur Heger, who introduced them to literary analysis and philosophy and invited them to remain at the school as instructors, which they accepted. Neither sister seemed to make much impression on their pupils.

For girls of the lower-middle class in the early 19th century, there were few options in life. If they did not marry young, they could become teachers or governesses. Charlotte had several stints at both with her time at Miss Wooler's and in Brussels with Emily, while Anne spent time as a governess in two different homes of the wealthy. She had the longest period of single employment of all the sisters, spending five years with the Robinson family at Thorp Green Hall near the city of York.

The direst final option of being a companion to an elderly

woman of wealth was one they all managed to avoid.

Towards the end of their time in Brussels, which was in 1842, Aunt Branwell died, an event that brought the sisters home and which did not please Charlotte, perhaps because she had developed a 'certain passion' for Monsieur Heger sufficient to bring her into the confessional in a local Catholic church. She continued to write very personal letters to him after her return to Yorkshire, which he tried to destroy, but which his wife retrieved and later made public. They are currently held by the British Museum.

However, the return to Yorkshire was not without benefits. The Branwell family had been wealthy grocers, and the sisters received a small inheritance which allowed them to clear all the family debts and still have a small sum for security left over. On the negative side, their father had recently had cataract surgery, and their brother increasingly suffered from drunkenness and mental illness.

During all this time, the sisters had been cultivating their literary talents, encouraged by the steady influx into the house of subscription magazines, books, and daily newspapers. Their first ventures into literature involved elaborate match-book-sized handmade books for a set of 12 toy soldiers belonging to Branwell. These books featured imaginary adventures and explorations of the soldiers, complete with maps and diagrams. Lord Byron, who had died in 1824 while they were still children, became an object of passion, representing all the adventure and freedom that was denied them in real life.

Their first publication was a joint collection of poems written by all three sisters. It was published in 1846 as Poems by Currer, Ellis, and Acton Bell. The masculine pseudonyms were chosen to reflect their initials, but more to overcome the persistent prejudice against women as poets. It sold three copies and attracted no attention at all.

Undeterred, the sisters continued to write. After a year spent circulating manuscripts to publishers, all three sisters had their first novels published in 1847, still under their pseudonyms. Charlotte released Jane Eyre to generally good reviews and large sales; Emily's Wuthering Heights was praised for originality but widely condemned for its violence and immorality; Anne's Agnes Grey garnered little interest.

The following year, Anne Brontë had The Tenant of Wildfell Hall published, her last novel before her death in 1849. Today it is widely considered one of the first feminist novels. The story is what we would now describe as a woman's entrapment in an abusive relationship with an alcoholic husband and enjoyed significant popularity, outselling Wuthering Heights. However, it was considered inappropriate even by her sister Charlotte, who suppressed its publication after Anne's death.

Emily was as wild and untamed as her characters in Wuthering Heights and is regarded today as a literary giant among women writers. Cripplingly timid around others and uninterested in fame, she spent her days roaming the moors around Haworth, encouraging the tuberculosis she refused treatment for and dying at the end of 1848 when just thirty years old.

The success of Jane Eyre resulted in Charlotte being invited to London to meet the literary community. Despite acute shyness, she went and seemed to have enjoyed her time there, meeting literary figures such as Thackeray and visiting the Great Exhibition and the Crystal Palace. Other less well-known novels followed, and in 1854, after a protracted and difficult courtship, she succumbed to convention and married a curate from her father's church, Arthur Bell Nicholls. Her feelings for Arthur seem to have been uncertain, although she adopted all the trappings and behavior of a conventional wife. The following year she died from a combination of her tuberculosis, a bout of typhoid fever, and the early stages of pregnancy. She was thirty-eight.

Branwell Brontë, considered by his family a genius, but mired in failure, alcohol, and laudanum, died, also of tuberculosis, in 1848.

Their Legacy

The Brontë sisters developed their talents in the isolation of the wilds of Yorkshire, alone and unique. Although they influenced other 19th century novelists such as Thomas Hardy and George Elliot, they created no 'school' of literature or style to be emulated. A biography of Charlotte published in 1860 by her friend Elizabeth

Gaskell caused friction between Patrick Brontë, Arthur Bell Nicholls, and another of Charlotte's friends, Ellen Nussey. The uproar and scandal only heightened the fame of the family, and the house in Haworth became a pilgrimage site for thousands as the sisters entered a state of near-sainthood for their adoring fans. Today it remains one of the most visited literary sites in the world.

Sites to Visit

- The family home in Haworth is now the Brontë Parsonage Museum, run by the charity Brontë Society. It contains a wide range of artifacts and materials, including Charlotte's writing desk. The museum is open from April to October between 10 am, and 5.30 pm, and from November to March between 10 am and 5 pm.
- Emily and Charlotte are buried in the family vault at St. Michael and All Angels' Church, Haworth.
- Anne's grave is in St. Mary's churchyard, Scarborough, Yorkshire.

Further Research

There are numerous biographies available, including:

- The Brontës: Wild Genius on the Moors: The Story of a Literary Family, by Juliet Barker
- The Brontë Sisters: The Brief Lives of Charlotte, Emily, and Anne, by Catherine Reef
- Brontë: A Biography of the Literary Family, by Paul Brody
- The Brontes at Haworth, by Ann Dinsdale
- The Life of Charlotte Brontë, by Elizabeth Gaskell (1860)
- Emily Brontë: A Biography, by Mary F. Robinson and John H. Ingram

Most, if not all, of their books, remain in print or readily available free online.

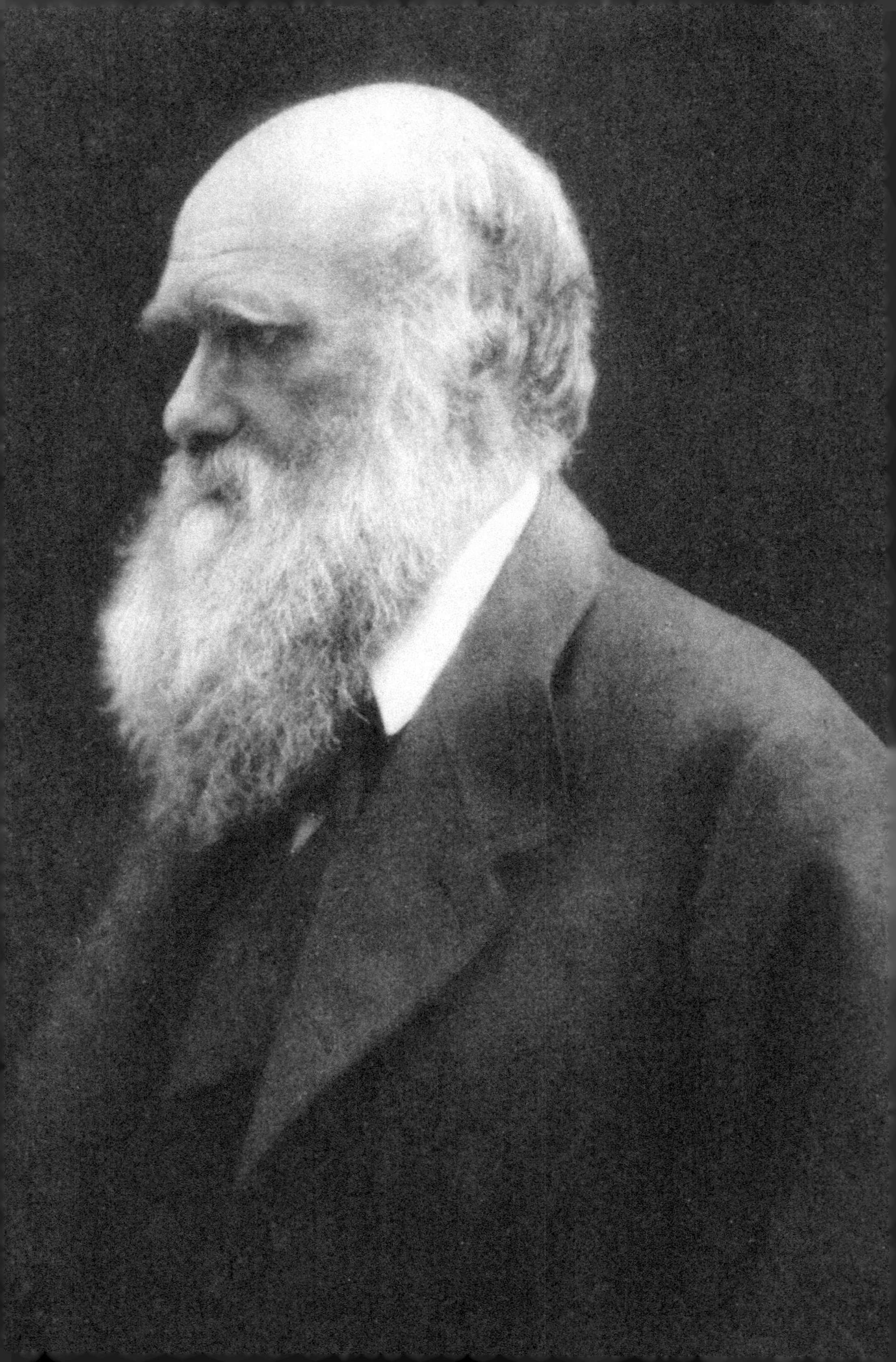

CHARLES DARWIN
Father of Evolutionary Theory

Key Facts

- Born 1802, died 1882
- The world's most famous naturalist
- Established the principles of evolution and man's place in nature

Charles Darwin was born on February 12, 1802, in the town of Shrewsbury, to comfortably well-off parents. His father was a doctor and financier and his mother Susannah was the daughter of the pottery magnate and anti-slavery campaigner Josiah Wedgewood. His paternal grandfather, Erasmus Darwin, a doctor, and prominent naturalist, had also been an opponent of slavery. His interest in natural history was apparent from an early age. Following the death of his mother when he was eight, Charles was sent to a boarding school. Although later enrolled at the University of Edinburgh Medical School, at the time the best medical school in the UK, he had little interest in medicine and far more in natural history, studying plant taxonomy and marine invertebrates.

His lack of interest in medicine bothered his father, who sent him to Christ's College, Cambridge, to prepare to be a parson, a typical choice for a desperate parent. Darwin continued with his natural history studies and began to excel in entomology, which was a 'fashionable' pursuit of the time. He graduated 10th out of 178 candidates.

His botany professor, John Stevens Henslow, arranged for

Darwin to be offered a place as a naturalist and companion to Captain Robert FitzRoy, about to sail on HMS Beagle. FitzRoy's remit was to create the first accurate charts of the coast of South America. The voyage was planned for two years, but in the end, it lasted almost five and became a voyage around the world.

The Beagle sailed on December 27, 1831, and the 29-year-old Darwin quickly discovered that he was prone to acute sea-sickness. To avoid him spending more time than necessary at sea, FitzRoy arranged for him to be dropped off at one port-of-call and picked up at a later one, traveling overland to meet the ship. This was fortuitous as it allowed him many opportunities to study the local geology, fossils, plant life and animals, and to make collections. FitzRoy had arranged for his collections and notes to be shipped back to England periodically.

Questions on the diversity of life and the changes which had taken place during the geological past were highly debated among natural scientists. Issues such as the use of deductive reasoning from observation as a method of scientific investigation: whether the adaptions of organisms to their environments were due to 'divine design'; the significance of fossil remains; Lamarck's theories of the inheritance of acquired characteristics; and catastrophic versus gradualist changes in the Earth's geology were all 'hot topics' for Darwin. In his carefully written journals, he assembled evidence for his ideas on the formation of coral atolls, reefs, and major movements of land-forms over time. On the Galapagos Islands, he collected bird specimens that he realized were probably related to species he had seen in Chile.

On his return to England towards the end of 1836, Darwin found himself already a celebrity in scientific circles for his collections and notes. Finally convinced, his father organized investments to support Darwin as a gentleman scientist, necessary at a time when public funding for science was virtually non-existent. Darwin was caught up in a whirlwind of presentations of his work and meetings to interest other scientists in examining his new specimens. He moved to Cambridge to organize his material and work on a final draft of his Journal and then later returned to London to be near the other scientists working with his specimens. When he learned that his bird specimens from the Galapagos were 12 distinct species, he began to consider the biggest question of all – did one species change into another, and if so, how?

This idea of the 'transmutation of species' was already a popular subject with political radicals who immediately saw the connection with overturning the prevailing social status quo, but Darwin pushed on with his deductions, comparing man-made changes through domestication to changes in wild species and already speculating on man's relationship to primates.

The stress and work began to take their toll on his health, and Darwin developed symptoms of distress such as heart palpitations, stomach pains, vomiting, and trembling, which recurred throughout his life at times of stress, such as important presentations of his work. In 1838 he read Malthus's An Essay on the Principle of Population and realized how environmental pressure would eliminate poorly adapted individuals and enable better-adapted individuals to survive in changing environments – an idea often translated as survival of the fittest but more accurately as survival of the best adapted.

On January 24, 1839, he was elected a Fellow of the Royal Society, and five days later, he married his cousin Emma Wedgwood, despite differences in their religious affiliations and her personal rejection of his theories. They were to go on to have ten children, who, despite Darwin's fears about inbreeding, became eminent in a variety of fields.

Several books on geology followed as he gradually assembled his ideas on the transmutation of species, but by 1858 fellow he became aware that fellow naturalist Alfred Russel Wallace was thinking along the same lines as himself. Wallace sent Darwin a private paper outlining his ideas, and this prompted the idea of a joint presentation which in the end, due to the sudden death of his young son, Darwin did not attend. The presentation caused little interest in the scientific audience.

Finally, on November 22, 1859, On the Origin of Species was published in an initial run of 1,250 copies. These sold quickly and started the debate on evolution and on what particularly interested the general public, the Descent of Man, the title of one of Darwin's later works. He continued to experiment, study, write and publish books on many related subjects, all of which supported and expanded the principles of evolution and placed mankind firmly among the other species of animals. His health continued to deteriorate, and shortly before his death, he was diagnosed with heart disease. On April 19, 1882, he died at home, surrounded by his family.

His Legacy

Although illness kept Darwin away from most of the debates, the supporters of Darwinism worked actively to promote his ideas, which fitted well with the generally 'evolutionary' attitudes to social change popular at the time. It was to be more than 50 years before genetics caught up with Darwin's ideas and provided scientifically plausible mechanisms for natural variation to produce the modern synthesis that characterizes evolutionary thinking today. Despite initial ridicule, few people today find anything disturbing about these theories, and all main-stream religions have incorporated evolution into their doctrines.

There are very few thinkers who have had such a profound impact on society as the shy but determined naturalist who found the key to the diversity of life and simultaneously re-drew the map of Man's place in the universe. After 150 years, Charles Darwin's enunciation of evolution is so deeply entrenched that it is almost impossible to imagine a world where it is not a basic paradigm, just as before it no other world-view than Creation seemed possible.

Sites to Visit

- Down House in Downe, Kent was Darwin's home for much of his life. It is now a museum to his life and work.
- Darwin had planned to be buried in the local churchyard at Downe, but after pressure and petitions, he was buried in Westminster Abbey, where his memorial can be seen near that of Isaac Newton.
- There are statues of Darwin in the main hall of the Natural History Museum in London and in front of Shrewsbury

Library, which used to house Shrewsbury School, attended by Darwin as a boy.

Further Research

- Darwin's books are all still in print or available online, and major works such as The Voyage of the Beagle, On the Origin of Species, The Descent of Man, and The Expression of the Emotions in Man and Animals are all highly readable today.
- The Autobiography of Charles Darwin, by Charles Darwin (1887 and unexpurgated, 1958), tells his life story in his own words.
- Recent biographies include: Charles Darwin: A Biography (vols. 1 and 2), by Janet Browne (1998, 2003) and Darwin by Adrian Desmond & James R Moore (1992)
- Films about Darwin include The Genius of Darwin, a 3-part documentary by Richard Dawkins, and The Voyage of Charles Darwin, a 7-part BBC documentary of his life. The partly fictionalized Creation (2009) was never released in the USA.

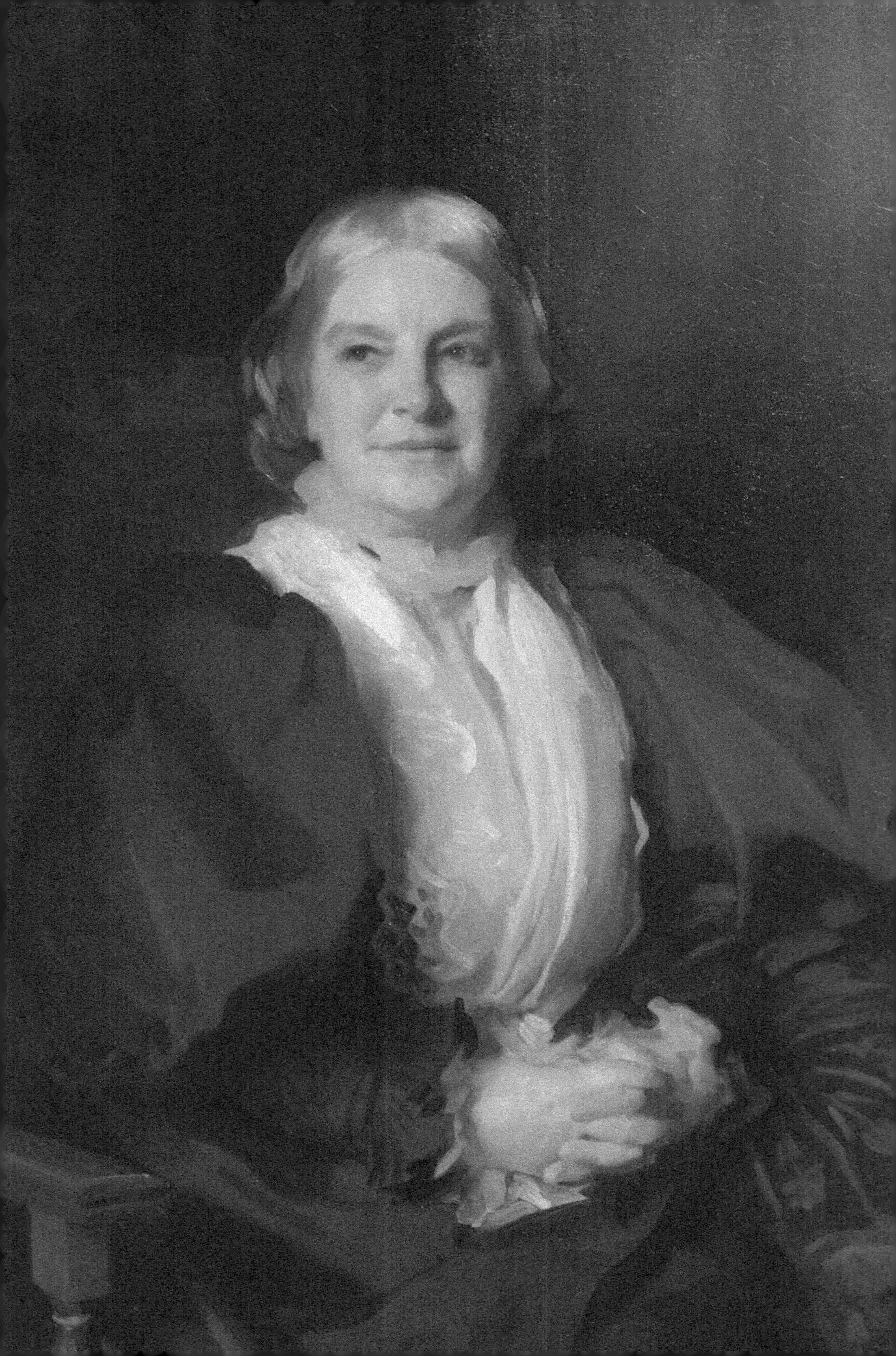

OCTAVIA HILL
Social Reformer and National Trust Co-Founder

Key Facts

- Born 1838, died 1912
- Fought for improvements in urban living standards for the poor
- Created a widely-adopted model of urban development
- Championed the creation of open spaces for cities and helped found the National Trust
- Encouraged women to enter professional work

The Industrial Revolution is generally seen as a major step forward in history, but for those caught up in it, there were many negatives. For those who migrated from rural life to the cities to provide the huge labor forces needed for the early factories, both working conditions and living conditions were often appalling. From the modern perspective of unions, social housing, and welfare systems, it can often be hard to imagine what life was like in the urban slums and also to appreciate the work that was done by social reformers in their attempts to alleviate these problems. A key figure in the development of both social housing and support for the poor was Octavia Hill.

Octavia Hill was born on December 3rd, 1838. Her father was a quite prosperous corn merchant and banker who had been widowed twice and had married Caroline Southwood Smith in 1835. Caroline was no ordinary mother. Her father, Thomas Southwood Smith, was a social reformer and a pioneer in public health. Caroline had written on education, and it was her writing that had attracted James Hill to hire her as a governess for his children, an appointment that led to their eventual marriage.

Life for Octavia and her eight siblings did not continue for very long in a comfortable way, however. Her father got into financial difficulties, suffered a mental collapse, and in 1840 became bankrupt. Caroline's father stepped in to support his daughter and the children both financially and as a surrogate father. The family moved to a small cottage in what was then the village of Finchley outside London. Octavia was educated at home and was greatly influenced by the activism of her mother and grandfather, who both worked on social issues of the time, such as child labor in mining, housing for the poor, education, and public health.

As a child, Octavia was already carrying out secretarial duties for women's classes at the Working Men's College in Bloomsbury and making toys for the Ragged School Movement. These were schools, often established by churches, which provided free education for children of the slums who otherwise would have had no education at all. The conditions in these schools were often very poor, and they attracted the attention of social reformers, including Charles Dickens, who wrote A Christmas Carol in response to the plight of these children. These schools ultimately provided the impetus for the state education system.

At the age of 13, Octavia found employment at a co-operative established to provide income for what at that time were referred to as "distressed gentlewomen," that is to say, members of the middle-class who lacked the normal support structure of their class and background. When the co-operative started a workshop so that children from Ragged Schools could come and make their own toys, Octavia, now just 14, was placed in charge of the workshop. She developed strong views on the need to foster self-reliance rather than charity and joined the Charity Organization Society, which had a reputation for taking a strong stance on the poor who simply took hand-outs.

Although Parliament had begun to tackle the problems of urban housing, the poorest – unskilled laborers – were still neglected, and Octavia found the behavior of landlords who rented to the poor so exploitive and indifferent that she decided that the only solution was to become a landlord herself. She was by this time known to John Ruskin, someone famous for his work in promoting artists like

Turner and the Pre-Raphaelites but who was also a philanthropist for social issues. In 1865 he paid £750 to buy three run-down cottages in Paradise Place, Marylebone, which he placed under Octavia's management, telling her she needed to demonstrate a 5% annual return on the investment to make the concept attractive to other investors. The following year he purchased a further five houses nearby.

By strict management, Octavia not only generated the required 5% return but had an excess to re-invest in improving the properties. Her success attracted further investors, and by 1874 she had 15 such schemes with a total of 3,000 tenants. She believed in direct contact between landlords and tenants with both sides sharing in the upkeep. She also believed in the importance of open spaces and developed small parks adjacent to her properties whenever possible. In addition, she used other women, first as volunteers and then as paid professionals, to manage her properties, thus creating opportunities for women to enter the workforce in non-traditional roles.

Octavia Hill was a passionate speaker, short in stature, with little regard for her appearance and so outspoken in her demands for action by the wealthy, that the Bishop of London said that after listening to her speak for half-an-hour he had 'never had such a beating' in his life. She also developed a concept of 'cultural philanthropy,' believing that exposure to art and beauty could improve the life of the poor. She founded the Kyrle Society in 1875 as a society 'for the diffusion of beauty' and was strongly supported by William Morris. The Society planted trees and flowers in urban areas and promoted aesthetics in the architecture and decoration of houses.

Because of her belief in the value of open spaces, she campaigned for the preservation of parks close to the center of London, arguing that it was very difficult for poor working people to go to more remote places, such as the Epping Forest, which had recently been preserved. Largely because of her efforts, Hampstead Heath and Parliament Hill Fields were preserved from development, and in fact, she was the first person to use the term Green Belt. She also worked with Canon Hardwicke Rawnsley and John Ruskin to create the National Trust.

As she became older, her work was largely taken over by the growth of state-funded housing – which she opposed. She also opposed the vote for women, welfare payments, and old-age pensions, and she became increasingly isolated. She died in her home in Marylebone on August 13th, 1912.

Her Legacy

Her concept of Housing Trusts became a model for many others, and her original trust still exists as Octavia Housing. The concept of social housing flowed directly from her work. Her pioneering work in housing integrating different income levels became the Settlement Movement. Her ideas on urban housing were adopted across Europe and influenced the development of North American cities too.

The women she employed eventually became the Chartered Institute of Housing, the professional body in the UK for workers in the housing field.

Her Charity Organization Society became a model for the profession of social work and still exists today as the charity Family Action.

The National Trust became the key player in the preservation of homes, gardens, and countryside in the UK.

Sites to Visit

- The house in which Octavia was born, at 7 South Brink, Wisbech, Cambridgeshire, is now a listed building and a museum to her work.
- There is a large stone seat erected in 1915 as a monument to Octavia Hill on Hydon Ball, a hill in Surrey owned by the National Trust.
- There is an English Heritage Blue Plaque at Garbutt Place (previously Paradise Place), Marylebone, London, Octavia's first cottages.

- Other Octavia Hill housing can be seen at St Christopher's Place, W1.
- Her style of low-rise cottages can also be seen at Ranston Street, NW1, and her concept of urban planning in the Red Cross Cottages, hall, and gardens at Redcross Way, Southwark.

Further Research

- Her work in her own words can be read in Homes of the London Poor (1875) and in the Life of Octavia Hill: As Told in her Letters edited by C. Edmund Maurice (2010)
- Biographies include: Octavia Hill, by Gillian Darley (1990) and Octavia Hill: a Biography by E. Moberley Bell (1986)

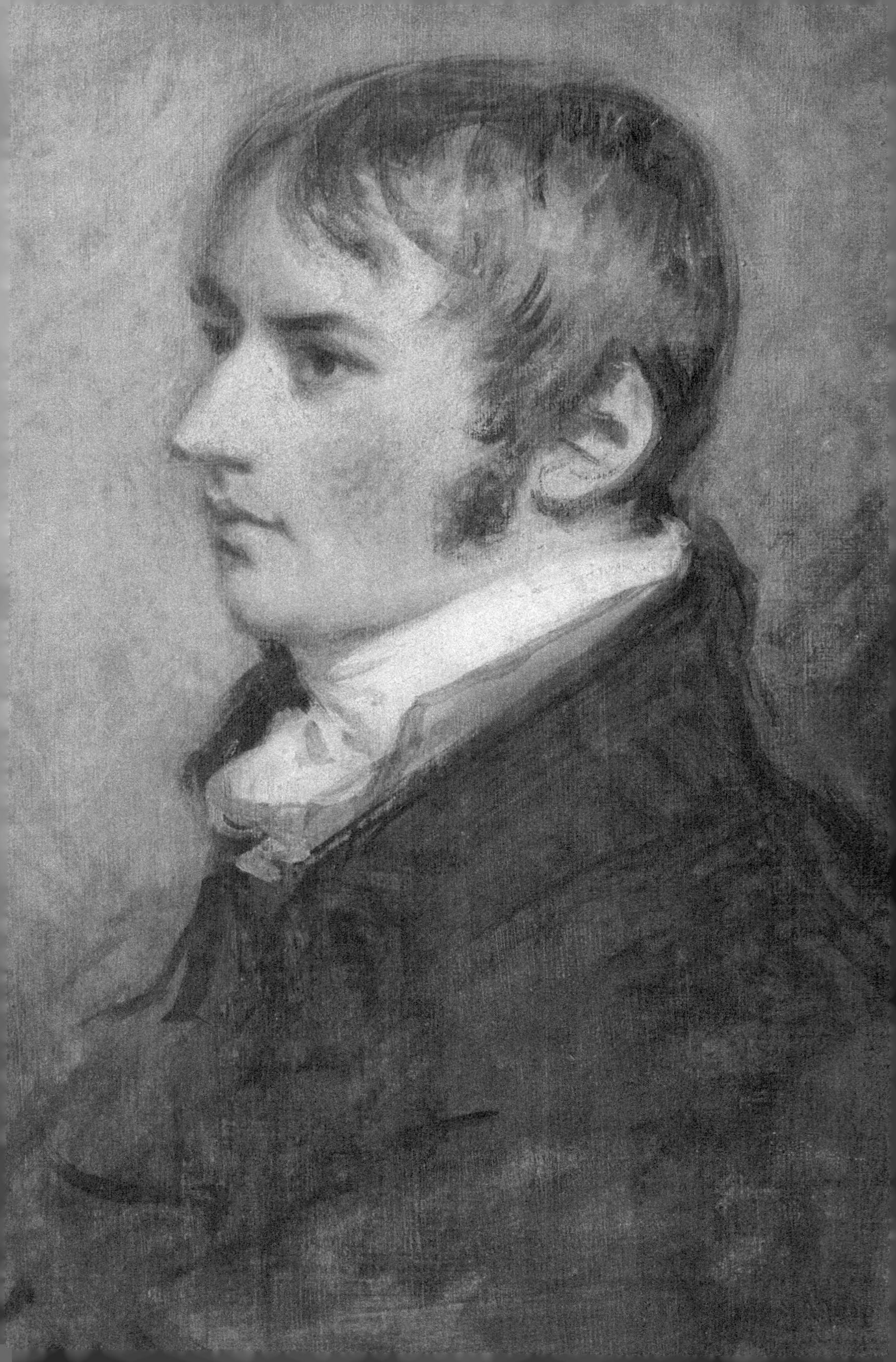

JOHN CONSTABLE
English Landscape Painter

Key Facts

- Born 1776 – died 1837
- One of England's greatest landscape painters
- Painted from nature rather than imagination
- Remained in England for his entire life

The painter John Constable was an English landscape artist noted for his use of light and shade, an emphasis on the sky, and for painting exactly what he saw. His career was slow to develop, and he never achieved significant fame during his lifetime, although he enjoyed greater popularity in France, which he never visited. He painted primarily in the area around his birth-place in West Suffolk, creating a lasting vision of a rural idyll that is still sought-out in the English countryside today.

John Constable was born on the 11th of June, 1776, into the family of a prosperous farmer and miller, Golding Constable, who worked a watermill on the banks of the Stour River, in the village of East Bergholt, Suffolk. The area was an idyllic rural district, to become famous in the paintings Constable would later make of the area. Although the middle son, his father planned for him to take over the business after a brief period of schooling, but in the end, it was his youngest brother who took over the mill.

Even as a boy, Constable loved to roam the countryside around his home village, sketching and painting. Even though he was advised by a professional artist, the antiquarian engraver John Thomas Smith, to enjoy painting but to stay in his father's business, when he was 23, he persuaded his father to let him train as an artist. He was already painting in oils and had exhibited some of his rural landscapes in London.

With his father's approval and a small allowance, he entered the school of the Royal Academy at the lowest level and began attending drawing classes and copying old masters, the standard approach to learning to paint at that time. He was inspired by French and Dutch painters like Jacob van Ruisdael and Claude Lorrain, as well as English artists like Thomas Gainsborough, who was already the official Court artist. Within a few years, he was exhibiting at the Academy, but his work was unconventional since he painted ordinary scenes of rural life and landscapes, lacking the allegorical references of historical or mythological landscapes that were considered the highest form of landscape art at the time.

As a result, his early career was difficult, and he had to rely on commissions for portraits of minor local dignitaries to survive. He turned down a position as an art teacher at the Great Marlow Military College, which would have given him financial security but no possibility of a professional career as a painter. He was fortunate to have Dr. John Fisher, who became bishop of Salisbury Cathedral, as a patron, and he commissioned numerous studies and completed paintings of the Gothic Cathedral under a variety of weather conditions.

Constable had a long childhood friendship with Maria Elizabeth Bicknell, the granddaughter of the local rector of East Bergholt, but her father was a wealthy and powerful solicitor to King George IV, and Maria's grandfather considered the Constables to be social inferiors and John, a totally unsuitable match for his daughter. Although her father was more sympathetic, it was only when both Constable's parents died, and he inherited part of the business that he was financially able to propose marriage. They were married in 1816 when Constable was already 40. Their honeymoon on the English south coast proved an artistic inspiration to Constable, who began to paint with more vigor, color, and emotion.

However, it was not until 1819 that he made his first significant sale, The White Horse, and also began to paint on a much larger scale. It was in the same year that he was made an Associate of the Royal Academy and began to exhibit at the Academy. During the early years of the 1820's he began to paint cloud and sky pictures, meticulously dated and evenly timed, but these were never shown until after his death, although today they are some of his most celebrated works.

His big breakthrough came in 1821 when the French artist Théodore Géricault (painter of The Raft of the Medusa) saw and arranged for the purchase of The Hay Wain when it was shown at an Academy exhibition. The painting was subsequently exhibited at the 1824 Paris Salon and won a gold medal. He became celebrated in France, selling 20 paintings in a few years – as much as he sold in a lifetime in England. Eugène Delacroix modified his style and even re-painted one of his works after seeing Constable's art. However, Constable resisted calls to travel to 'the Continent,' saying he would "rather be a poor man in England than a rich man abroad." He quarreled with his French dealer and lost that outlet for his work by 1825.

In 1828, Maria fell ill with tuberculosis and died, leaving Constable, now in his 50's, bereft with grief and sick with worry for the future of his seven children. He raised the children himself and dressed in mourning black for the rest of his life. The following year he was elected a full Fellow of the Royal Academy.

He had inherited £20,000 from his wife, left to her on her father's death, but his attempts to increase that small fortune by selling sets of mezzotint engravings of his landscapes ended in financial disaster, floundering on his indecision, uncertainty, and obsessive perfectionism.

He became a lecturer at the Royal Institution, known more for science than art, proposing a scientific approach to painting and encouraging painting from nature rather than the imagination. He also spoke out against the then newly-fashionable Gothic Revival.

He died in his home of a heart attack on the 31st of March, 1837.

His Legacy

Just as his artistic peer, the eccentric J.M.W. Turner, had struggled to paint pure light, so Constable wanted to paint the sky, which he considered the 'chief organ of sentiment' of landscape, that is, the place where emotion was expressed. He and Turner are considered to be the greatest English landscape painters, and Constable's vision of the English countryside has become a bucolic paradigm of how it should be perceived.

His emphasis on naturalism inspired the Pre-Raphaelites and other artists in the Romantic tradition. Although his mezzotints were a financial disaster, they stand today as emblematic of his work and his emphasis on chiaroscuro, the interplay of light and dark, in the emotional impact of art.

Sites to Visit

- Constable is buried in a small family vault, alongside his wife and two of their children, in the graveyard of St John-at-Hampstead church, Hampstead.

- Bridge Cottage is a 16th-century thatched cottage owned by the National Trust in East Bergholt, Suffolk. Although not lived in by Constable, it is in the heart of 'his' countryside, surrounded by landscapes he painted.
- Flatford Mill, the watermill owned by Constable's father, is a listed building close to Bridge Cottage.
- There is a blue plaque on one of his London homes at 40; Well Walk, in Hampstead.
- There is another blue plaque in Brighton at 11, Sillwood Road, formerly known as 9, Mrs. Sober's Gardens, where Constable lived in the 1820s.
- There is a statue of Constable on the Cromwell Road frontage of the Victoria & Albert Museum, South Kensington, London. It is part of a series of 32 statues of artists, craftsmen, and architects built into the façade of the building.

Further Research

There are several biographies of Constable and his art, including:

- John Constable: The Man and His Art, by Ronald Parkinson
- John Constable: The Making of a Master, by Mark Evans and Stephen Calloway
- Constable: Great Art and Artists Series, by Peter D. Smith and Madeleine Ledivelec-Gloeckner
- John Constable, by William Vaughan
- John Constable: A Kingdom of his Own, by Anthony Bailey
- England's Constable: The life and letters of John Constable, by Joseph Darracott

Most of his works can be seen in high-resolution on the Internet.

There is also a film documentary on his work:

- Constable: The Changing Face of Nature

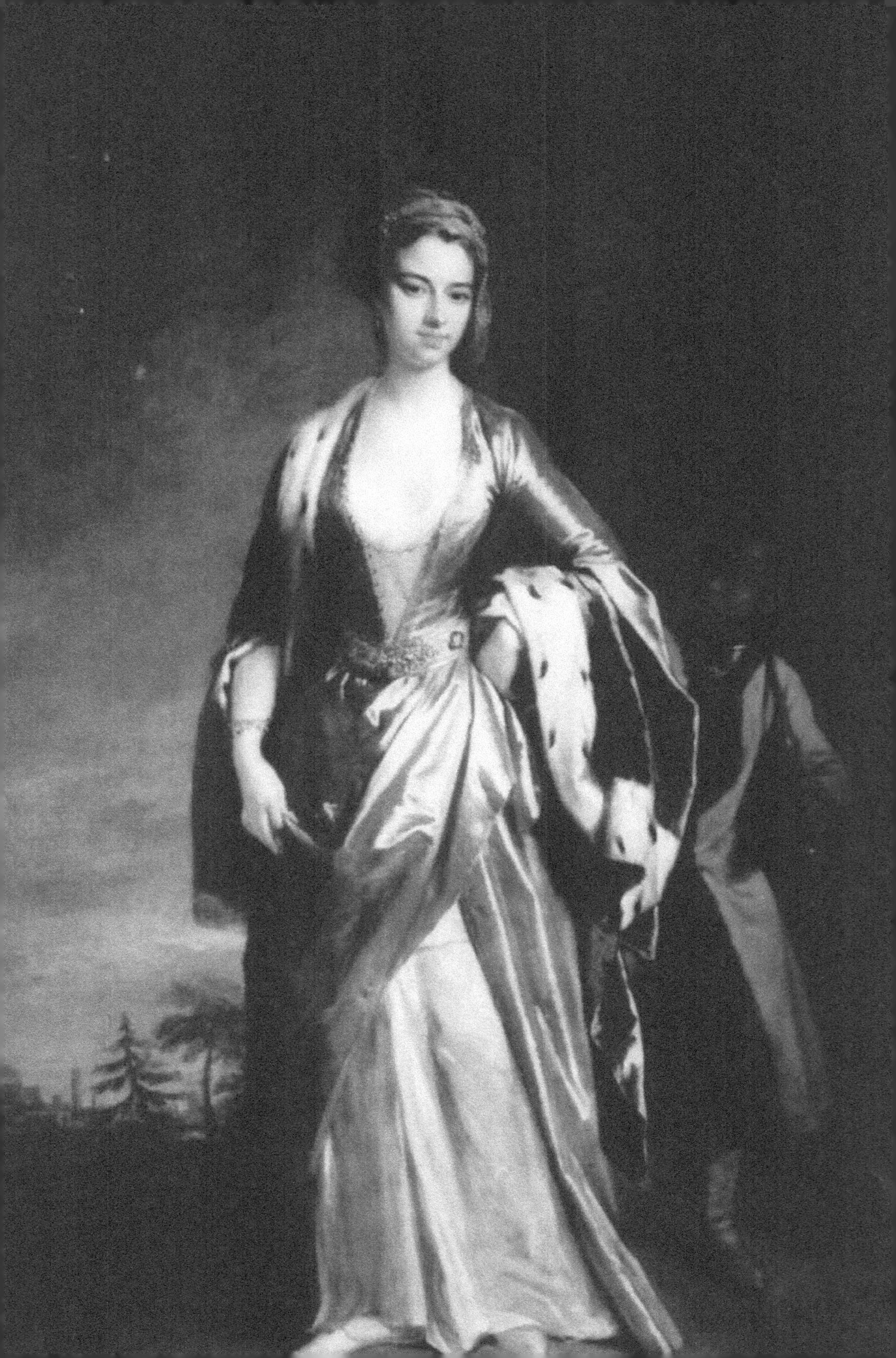

LADY MARY WORTLEY MONTAGU
Important Diarist and Letter Writer

Key Facts

- Born 1689 – died 1762
- Prolific letter writer of her travels and opinions
- Early promoter of smallpox inoculation
- Increased knowledge and interest in the lives of Ottoman women

Letter writing was a major occupation of the wealthy classes in the 18th and 19th centuries. Few wrote as many as Lady Mary Wortley Montagu, who described in detail her travels and insights on life in the Ottoman Empire. The beautiful daughter of a member of the Court of Charles I, she was disfigured by smallpox. Later she pioneered inoculation with live smallpox as a protection, having both of her children inoculated, and introducing the practice to the Court. By affecting Turkish dress and disseminating information of life in the Ottoman Empire, especially that of women, she contributed to the later Orientalism fashion in Europe. She spent the latter part of her life living in Italy. Her letters were published posthumously. Her son Edward went on to be a notable traveler and eccentric, also affecting Turkish dress, and converting to Islam.

Instead of travel forum posts, tweets and selfies, travelers of the past – and indeed everyone literate – wrote letters. Long, extensive and frequent letters. If you were rich, you most probably spent every morning, after your toilette and breakfast, doing your 'correspondence' for several hours. Carefully hand-written letters passed back and forth between family members, friends and professional colleagues, and contained factual information as well as personal opinions and news. So important was letter writing that the first novels were written as a fictitious exchange of letters, most famously perhaps in Tobias Smollett's, The Expedition of Humphry Clinker. This book is generally considered one of the finest early English novels. It was published in 1771, and it takes the form of correspondence of a trip around England.

This was surely a novel that would have appealed to Lady Mary Wortley Montagu – had she not died nine years earlier. Lady Montagu was a prolific letter writer, and she is remembered mostly for her letters written while traveling in the Ottoman Empire, a significant accomplishment at such an early time.

Lady Mary was born into a position of prestige. He father was Evelyn Pierrepont, 1st Duke of Kingston-upon-Hull. He had risen from the position of a lowly MP through the peerage to become a Duke in 1715 and was the Lord President of the Council, one of the most powerful positions in the country, and head of the King's Privy Council. Mary had been born in May 1689, when her father was still an MP, and grew up as her family ascended the social and political ladder.

At the tender age of seven, she came to the attention of the Kit-Kat Club. This was a society of prominent literary and political figures who met at the Fountain Tavern on The Strand, among other venues. The main activity of the members was the toasting of beautiful women, in glasses especially engraved with those women's names. These were often wives or mistresses of members, so the addition of Lady Mary at such a young age is suggestive of her great beauty. Highly intelligent too, she chafed under the restrictions of a girl's limited home education, and she taught herself Latin from her father's libraries. By 14 she had already written two albums of poetry, a brief novel, and a prose-and-verse romantic play.

When twenty Mary was being courted by two men - Edward Wortley Montagu and Clotworthy Skeffington. Her father favored Skeffington, who was going to inherit an Irish peerage. He rejected Montagu because he refused to entail his estate – that is, ensure it would only go to a male heir. Mary, however, would have none of this, and chose to scandalously elope with Edward Montagu, grandson of

Edward Montagu, 1st Earl of Sandwich, a lawyer at the Inner Temple, and clearly a much more effective letter writer. (Courtship in those circles was mainly conducted by correspondence). The couple were married in August 1712, and in May of the following year a son was born, also called Edward. Her joy must have been shattered by the death from smallpox of her brother just a few weeks later.

In 1714 Edward was made Junior Commissioner of Treasury, and the family moved from the country to London, becoming members of the Court of Charles I. Mary soon became a prominent figure at the Court, but at the end of 1715, she too contracted smallpox. Although she survived, her beauty was permanently damaged by the disfiguring scars which this terrible disease invariably left in its wake. Voltaire wrote that at the time, 60% of the population would catch smallpox, and only 20%, or one in three of those infected, would survive it.

In 1716, Edward was appointed Ambassador to the Ottoman Empire, and they traveled, via Austria, to Istanbul, remaining there until the end of 1718. They had a daughter while there, called Mary. Lady Mary corresponded extensively while traveling, and while living in Istanbul. Her letters were later edited by her and eventually published as The Turkish Embassy Letters. As a woman, she had special access to women's living quarters and their lives, and her letters provide a unique insight into the customs and practices of Moslem women of that time. She tended to take a position that in many ways, their lives were superior to that of women in Europe. Her letters in their original forms were read by many influential friends back home. Lady Mary is depicted in several portraits dressed in Turkish dress, and her influence may have contributed to the latter wave of Orientalism that would become very fashionable in art, decorating and costume in the late 18th and early 19th centuries.

While in Turkey, Lady Mary encountered the practice of inoculation for smallpox, or variolation as it was called. This was widespread among the Turks, who are said to have learned it in turn from the Circassians, an Islamic people who lived near present-day Georgia. Mary saw that they took pus from a person infected with a mild case of smallpox and placed it on a scratch in the arm of another person, giving them a mild infection, which protected them from further infection. The procedure was risky since it used live smallpox. The person inoculated still had a risk of dying, although that was slight compared to the risk from a full infection. Variolation had been reported to Europe a few years earlier, in letters to the Royal Society of London, but it had received little publicity. Lady Mary was to change all that.

Because of her own damaged looks, she wanted to protect her children. In March 1718 she had the embassy surgeon, Charles Maitland, inoculate her 5-year-old son, Edward. She described the procedure extensively and enthusiastically in letters to friends. Back in London, she had Maitland inoculate her daughter, in the presence of the Court physicians. Interest spread among members of the Court. In 1721 Maitland was given permission for a trial on six inmates of Newgate prison, observed by Royal Society members. All the prisoners survived, and Maitland would go on to inoculate the two children of the Prince of Wales the following year. This led to widespread acceptance of variolation. It would be the end of the century before Edward Jenner would develop the vaccination process, using cowpox, that overcame the problems of vaccination and ultimately eradicated the dreaded disease.

In England, Lady Mary continued the life of an aristocrat, raising her children, editing her letters and corresponding. She had a one-way romance with the poet Alexander Pope, who she rejected, much to his humiliation and later anger. He children were difficult. Her daughter copied her mother and eloped with the 3rd Earl of Bute, against the wishes of her mother. Edward ran away regularly as a boy and had to be placed with a strict tutor and sent traveling around the world. He spent time in the military and even served as an MP, but he resumed traveling and became a well-known eccentric, converting first to Catholicism and then to Islam, wearing Turkish dress and affecting Turkish manners. His mother left him one guinea in her will.

In 1736 Lady Mary began a full-blown affair with Francesco Algarotti, an Italian man of letters and an art collector. When he left England, she followed him to Venice in 1739, pretending to be taking a winter break in the south of France for her health. For the next two decades, she traveled throughout Italy, staying in all the major cities, as well as spending four years in Avignon, France. During all this time she continued to correspond with friends and family, especially her daughter, who she had forgiven for her elopement.

In 1762, while living in Venice, she received news of her husband's death and returned to London. On route, she left her Turkish Embassy Letters with a certain Reverend Benjamin Sowden of Rotterdam, for safe-keeping, and to be dispos'd of as he thinks proper. After her return to England, she died, just a few months later, on the 21st of August 1762.

Sites to Visit

- Simpson's-in-the-Strand Restaurant, 100 Strand, London WC2, stands on the site of the Fountain Tavern, a haunt of the Kit-Kat Club.
- Wortley Hall, the residence of Lady Mary and later of her daughter, is in the South Yorkshire village of Wortley, south of Barnsley. It is today used as a meetings venue and for weddings. The extensive grounds are open to visitors.

Further Research

- The complete letters of Lady Mary Wortley Montagu, 3 volumes, ed. Robert Halsband, 1965-67
- The Turkish Embassy Letters, ed. Teresa Heffernan & Daniel O'Quinn, 2012
- Letters of Lady Mary Wortley Montague: Written During Her Travels in Europe, Asia, and Africa, to Which Are Added Poems by the Same Author, by Lady Mary Wortley Montagu, 2017
- Lady Mary Wortley Montagu: Comet of the Enlightenment, by Isobel Grundy, 2001
- Lady Mary Wortley Montagu and the Eighteenth-Century Familiar Letter, by Cynthia Lowenthal, 1994
- The Toast of the Kit-Cat Club: A life of Lady Mary Wortley Montagu, by Linda France, 2005

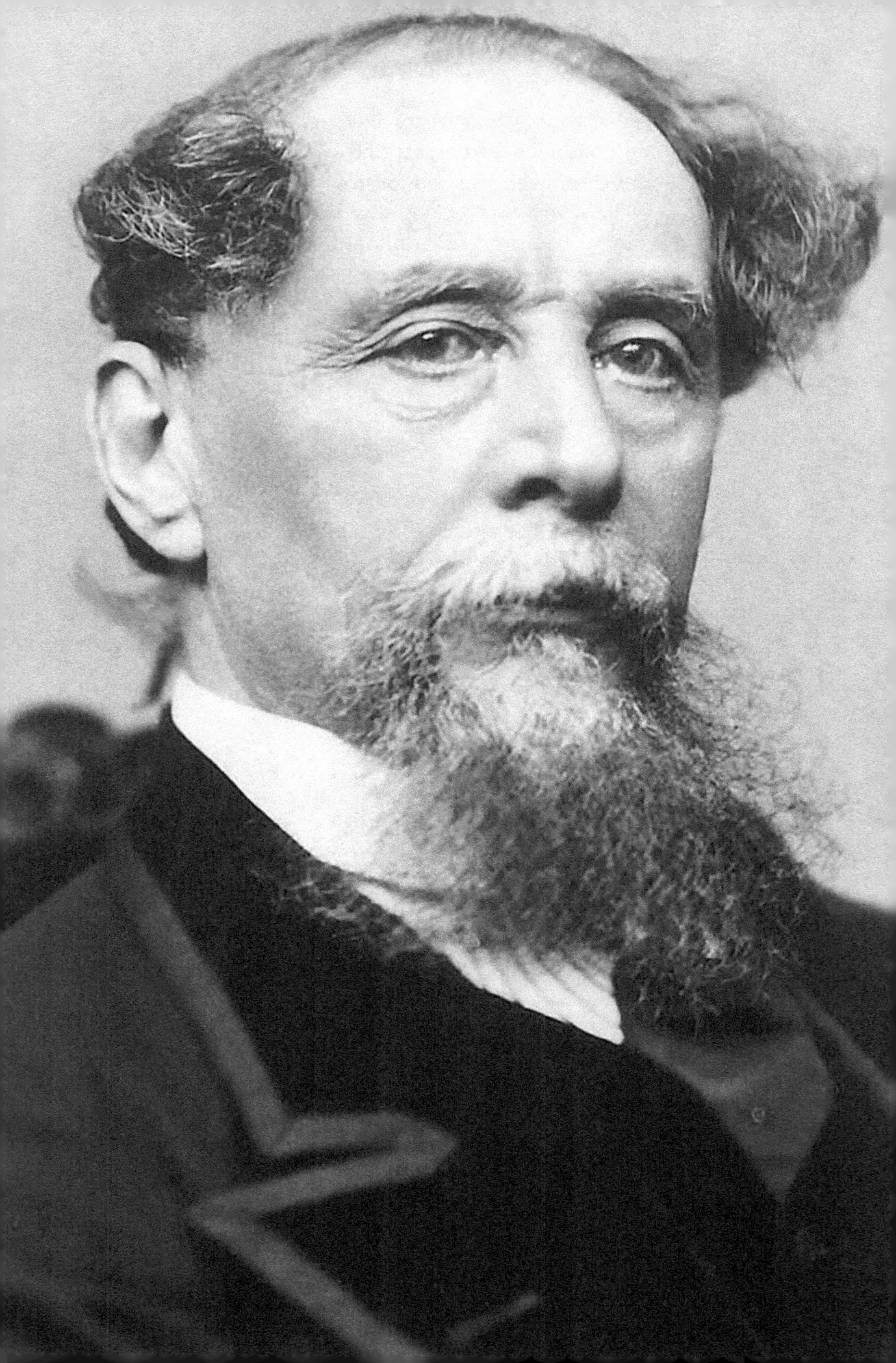

CHARLES DICKENS
Victorian Literary Giant

Key Facts

- Born 1812, died 1870
- Best known and most-read of English authors
- His books have never been out of print
- Used his writing and lectures to campaign for social reform and to improve the lives of the poor

The population of the UK grew from 13 million to 41 million over the course of the 19th century. When one realizes that there was also large-scale emigration occurring at the same time, that extraordinary tripling of the population contrasts sharply with the mere 50% increase of the 20th century, it was the result of the Industrial Revolution, but it caused massive social upheaval and disruption on a scale not seen before or since. Yet, the number of people who steered the country through those changes is quite small, and 19th-century social reformers formed a close network as they struggled to create a compassionate society from a brutal one. A pivotal figure whose huge influence with the public created awareness not only of the problems but also of the need for reform was Charles Dickens.

Dickens was born on February 7th, 1812, to John and Elizabeth Dickens in what is now Portsmouth. A short while later, the family moved to Bloomsbury, London, and then to Chatham, Kent. The young Charles spent some time in school and became a voracious reader of early novels, such as those by Tobias Smollett and Henry Fielding.

John Dickens was a Pay Clerk with the Royal Navy but had a poor head for his own personal finances, forcing the family to move to Camden Town and then, when Charles was just 12, placing him in Debtor's Prison. As was normal at the time, Elizabeth and her children had to join him there, while Charles was left to board with a family friend and was put to work at Warren's Blacking Factory labeling jars of shoe polish. The old factory, near the present-day Charing Cross railway station, was decrepit and rat infected. After a few months, his father inherited sufficient money to repay his debts, and the family left the prison and moved into the house Charles had been boarding at - 112 College Place, Camden Town. However, to Charles' horror, his mother forced him to continue working at the Blacking Factory, which caused permanent psychological scars and a distrust of women, which would continue throughout Dickens' life. It also built the deep wells of anger and resentment that were to fuel his social activism. Although he was soon removed from the factory and sent to the nearby Wellington House Academy, he found the school 'haphazard, desultory and sadistic'.

He became a clerk at a law office in 1827, just 15 years old, but the following year, having taught himself an early system of shorthand, left to become a freelance court reporter. He rapidly moved on to Parliamentary reporting and then newspaper reporting, where he enjoyed some success. When his father again fell into debtor's prison, he was resentfully forced to help out, and this was to be a recurrent event during his life.

After some early writing attempts, he found himself with the opportunity to write a series of humorous pieces for a periodical which resulted in the successful Pickwick Papers. The final episode sold a remarkable 40,000 copies. He began work as a magazine editor and simultaneously began work on Oliver Twist, which was published in 1838 and became a great success. It was the first Victorian novel with a child as the main character.

Meanwhile, in his private life, Dickens had become engaged, and in 1836 he married Catherine Hogarth, the daughter of the editor of the newspaper, the Evening Chronicle. Within a year, the first of their ten children was born. Now a successful novelist, Dickens began the prolific output that would continue for his entire life. Many of the characters of his novels were drawn from family members: his father became Mr. Micawber; his mother, Mrs. Nickleby; a sister who had died young Little Nell; his landlady while at the Blacking Factory Mrs. Pipchin; and so on. His school became Mr. Creakle's Establishment, and his experiences of poverty and exposure to the court system fueled his righteous anger at and exposure to the social inequalities of Victorian England. A Christmas Carol was inspired by a visit to a school for poor children.

In 1842, leaving their children in the care of Catherine's sister Georgina, Charles and Catherine set out on a journey to America, where he visited Virginia, Washington, St Louis, New York City, Niagara Falls, Montreal, and Quebec City. His trip was plagued with asthma, which he relieved with opium, a common cure of the time. In New York, he argued unsuccessfully against the pirating of his works by American publishers. In his travel journal, he wrote a scathing condemnation of slavery and was critical of several American ways, including the chewing of tobacco.

In 1842 he was encouraged to set up a home for 'fallen women' with the novel goal of reform rather than retribution and continued to take an active part in its running for the next ten years. Most of his social attitudes were inspired by a deeply Christian worldview, and he was an active Anglican during his life, condemning both Roman Catholicism and Evangelicalism.

In 1857, now wealthy, he purchased a country house called Gads Hill Place in Higham, Kent, which he had passed as a child and dreamed of living in. It was there he and the mystery writer Wilkie Collins started a theatrical company and hired professional actors to perform one of their plays. In that way, he met and fell in love with the 18-year-old actress Ellen Ternan. A year later, the 45-year-old Dickens did the then unspeakable and divorced his wife. She left Gads Hill with one of their children, but his sister Georgina stayed to care for the remaining children. Divorce was one thing, but re-marriage was impossible under church law, and although both Dickens and Ternan destroyed all their correspondence, it is likely that they lived together secretly for the next 13 years. They may also have had a son who died in his infancy. Certainly, when Dickens died, he left an annuity to Ternan, which made her financially independent.

Despite the scandal, Dickens discovered that in that age before radio or television, there was a lucrative market for him to read his novels at public lectures. He used these at first to raise money for his philanthropy but soon embarked on reading tours, giving hundreds of readings that netted thousands of pounds and simultaneously gave him an outlet for his theatrical ambitions. In 1867, following the end of the Civil War, he undertook a grueling reading tour of the United States during which he saw great improvements in the society and even publicly promised never to denounce America again. He left in the spring of 1868, barely escaping a Federal Tax Lien on the proceeds from his lectures.

Although his health was failing, he continued with a schedule of readings which sometimes had to be canceled because of his health. He also worked on his final novel, The Mystery of Edwin Drood, which was to remain unfinished. On June 8th, 1870, he suffered a stroke and died the following day without gaining consciousness. He was just 58 years old.

His Legacy

Charles Dickens left behind an enduring body of work that has never been out of print. His portrayals of Victorian England painted a picture that is still the vision of 'The English' for many both inside and outside the country. His blend of story-telling and social criticism became a model for generations of future writers and rallied popular support for a wide variety of reforms that created modern society and a sense of social fairness.

Sites to Visit

- The house where he was born is now the Charles Dickens Birthplace Museum in Portsmouth.
- 2 Ordnance Terrace, Chatham, Dickens's home from 1817–1822 also still exists.
- Gads Hill Place in Higham, Kent, is now an independent

school.
- Despite his request for "an inexpensive, unostentatious, and strictly private" burial, he was buried in Poets Corner, Westminster Abbey, with much pomp, where his memorial can be seen.
- There are statues of Dickens in Portsmouth near his birthplace, in the Spruce Hill district of Philadelphia, and another in Centennial Park, Sydney, Australia.

Further Research

- Dickens complete works are still in print and available in numerous editions and as downloads.
- The original manuscripts, many first editions, and original illustrations are held at the Victoria and Albert Museum.
- Recent biographies include: Charles Dickens: A Life by Claire Tomalin (2012) and Becoming Dickens: The Invention of a Novelist by Robert Douglas-Fairhurst (2012)
- Most of his stories have been turned into films and plays in multiple versions and formats.
- The Invisible Woman (2013), starring Ralph Fiennes, is a speculative biographic account of his relationship with Ellen Ternan. Charles Dickens: A Tale of Ambition and Genius (1995) is an episode of the Biography TV series.

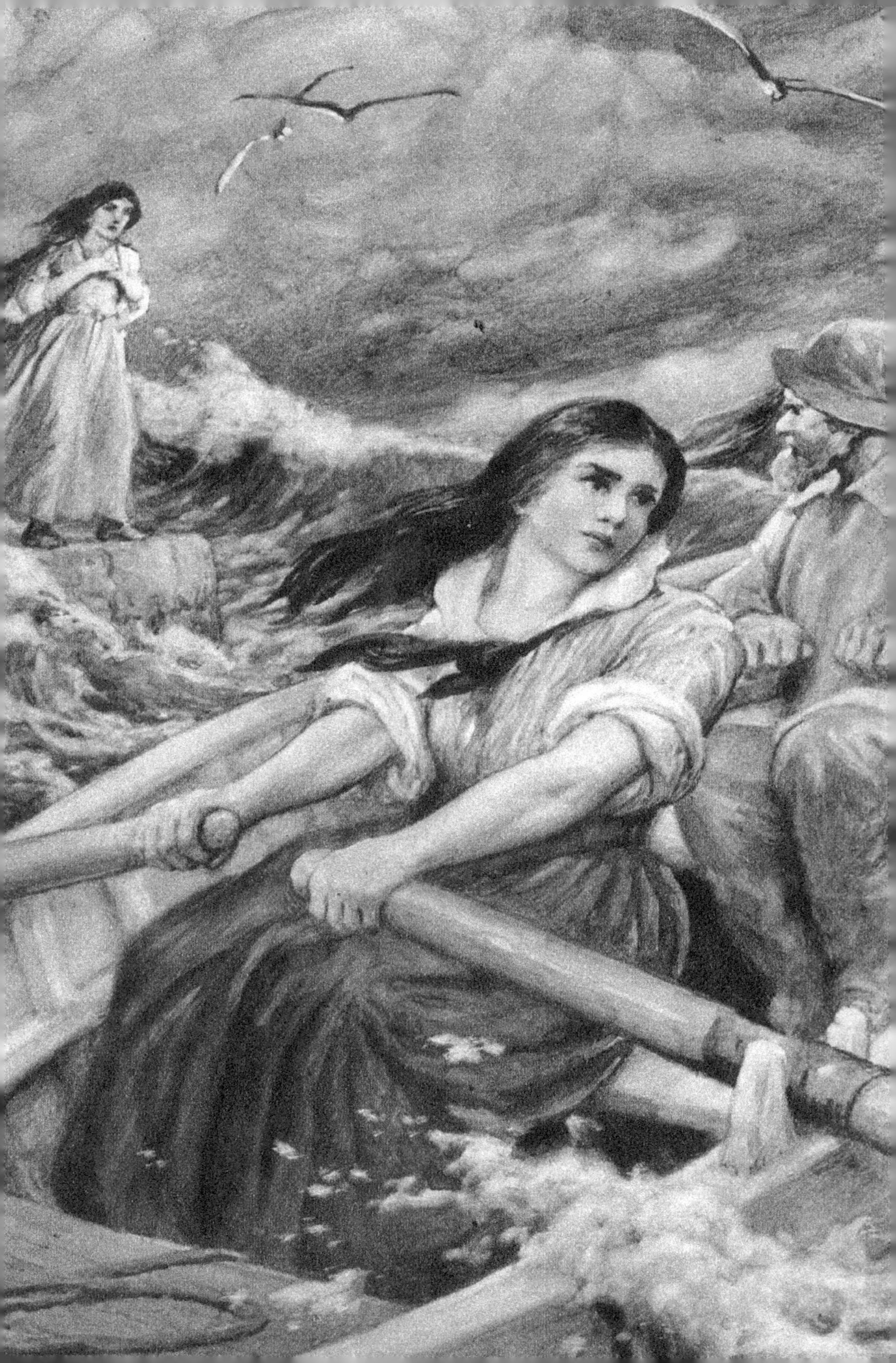

GRACE DARLING
The Hero Who Saved Seaman

Key Facts

- Born 1815 – Died 1842
- Lighthouse keeper's daughter on the Farne Islands
- Saw a wreck and helped rescue the survivors
- Became a Victorian media superstar

From time to time, someone does something extraordinary that catches the popular imagination. Often it is an obscure person who steps up in a crisis. Grace Darling did just that in 1838 and became a media star, the subject of books, poems, and artworks. From the lighthouse on the remote Farne Islands where she lived with her father, 23-year-old Grace spotted a wreck in a storm, and she persuaded her father to venture out in a howling gale in their rowboat. They rescued nine survivors from the original 61 passengers and crew of the paddle steamer Forfarshire, which had hit rocks after its engines failed. She was hailed as a heroine and became wealthy from the generosity of an adoring public. She died of consumption (tuberculosis) when only 26.

Off the coast of Northumberland, the most northerly county of England, just below the Scottish border, lie a group of 15 to 20 low islands called the Farne Islands. Their exact number depends on the state of the tide. These islands were once the homes of Culdees, ascetic Christian monks who favored remote islands for withdrawal and meditation. St Cuthbert, patron saint of northern England, retreated thereafter his missionary work in the 7th century.

For centuries the remote, desolate islands were favored by monks and hermits until eventually they were bought by William George Armstrong, 1st Baron Armstrong, the inventor of modern artillery and owner of Armstrong Whitworth, the armaments company.

The outermost islands, lying rocky and low in the water almost 5 miles off the shore, were always shipping hazards, especially during storms. Fires had been placed on such places for centuries to warn ships, and Trinity House, the body responsible for lighthouses, was founded in 1514 to regulate their placement. But the first lights were only placed on the Farnes in 1776 when Trinity House gave their permission to a certain Captain John Blackett, the lessee of the Farnes at the time. He put fire baskets on the top of a 15th century stone tower and also built a new light on another island, but that was destroyed in a storm a few years later.

In 1795 a square stone tower for fire baskets, with a cottage, was built on Brownsman Island. These fire towers needed manning and lighthouse keepers – perhaps the most romantic, and at the same time desolate and lonely, occupation in the world was created.

Shipping was by now a major means of transport around the coast – canals were used inland, but paved roads capable of carrying heavy loads were still a long way off. Many boats plied up and down the coast of Britain. Much more attention was paid to shipping safety, placing lights in dangerous locations, and improving the technology behind them. In 1810 a new lighthouse, designed by Daniel Alexander and built by Joseph Nelson, was placed on Brownsman Island and another on Inner Farne Island. These lights used rotating reflectors and paraffin lights instead of the fire baskets and were much more our image of what a lighthouse should look like.

The lighthouse keeper on Brownsman Island for the new light was called William Darling. In 1815 his wife Thomasin gave birth to their seventh child – a daughter they called Grace. Conditions on the island were primitive, and so Thomasin had gone to her father's house in the pretty coastal village of Bamburgh. When Grace was still a baby, Thomasin returned to Brownsman Island with her to rejoin her husband and her other children. Two more were to follow, bringing the family to four boys and five girls.

The lighthouse still did not stop ships running onto the rocks, as it was not ideally located. Consequently, in 1826 the Brownsman light was extinguished, and a new light was placed further out on Longstone Island. This was a more desolate island, and when the tide was high, little more than the lighthouse itself stood above the water. So the Darlings would go back and forth to Brownsman, tending a vegetable garden, and some animals, probably cows, they had there. They were largely self-sufficient, with the addition of fish they caught. The children grew up with seals, puffins, terns, and many other sea birds, that still attract bird-watchers today.

There were three bedrooms on the upper floor of the house, connected to the living areas below by a spiral staircase. Rising at dawn of the 7th of September 1838, Grace looked out of her window at a howling gale and saw a wreck on the rocks of Big Harcar, a low rocky island about 600 yards away. The ship was the Forfarshire.

Two days earlier, the Forfarshire had left Kingston-on-Hull, in Yorkshire, heading for the Scottish town of Dundee. This 400-ton paddle steamer was powered by two 90 horsepower steam engines, and it was also rigged for sails if needed. She carried a cargo of cotton for the mills and 61 passengers and crew. From the beginning, the voyage went badly. First, the pumps supplying water to the boilers began to fail, and then the boilers began to leak, flooding the bilges and pulling the ship lower into the water. Around 10 pm on the 6th, the boilers failed completely. Despite the gale-force winds, the captain had the sails put up and continued on. Around 3 am the ship struck Big Harcar. Eight sailors and a passenger immediately lowered a lifeboat and rowed away. They were picked up by a passing schooner and taken to safety.

The storm snapped the boat in two, leaving just the bow and fore-section wedged on the rocks – the rest of the boat quickly sank below the sea, taking many people with it. The surviving passengers clung to the railings all night, and at first, light struggled onto the rocks of the island. This was the sight that Grace, 23 years old, saw that stormy morning. She counted 13 people huddled on the rocks. Running to her father, she begged him to take out their boat and rescue them. At first, he said the seas were too rough to venture out with just the two of them. She pleaded with him, and after a hasty meal, they set out in their boat, a traditional flat-bottomed rowboat called a Cobble. The boat was 21 feet long and designed to be rowed by at least three strong sailors, but they were just an older man and a young woman. They could not take the direct route because of the turbulent and dangerous seas. Instead, they had to row around the back of the rocks, a distance of 1,700 yards, to reach the wreck.

By the time they arrived, only nine people were left – the sea had swept away four of the original survivors. The most distraught passenger was Mrs. Dawson, who had spent the night clinging to the bodies of her two dead sons, only to have them finally torn from her arms by the sea. Grace and her father got the mother into the boat, along with three crew members, two of them strong rowers. Grace's father and the two sailors rowed back to Longstone, and leaving the two women there, the three men returned to the wreck for the remaining five survivors. The official lifeboat arrived after all the survivors had been rescued, and when the weather deteriorated further, everyone was trapped on Longstone for the next three days.

Culturally, this was the beginning of the Dickensian era (Oliver Twist first appeared as a serial from 1837 to 1839), and there was a large public appetite for drama and heroics. The quiet, isolated and simple lighthouse keepers found themselves the center of a media frenzy, and the compelling story of the heroic young woman facing the raging sea was published widely. Many felt that her extraordinary bravery should be rewarded.

Queen Victoria sent a gift of £50, and many others followed, totaling around £700. Considering that William was paid £70 a year, this was a huge sum for them. The Royal National Lifeboat Institution gave them each a new award – the Silver Medal; the Royal Humane Society gave Grace its Gold Medallion; and she received awards from the Glasgow, Edinburgh, and Leith Humane Societies too. More than a dozen artists came to the island to paint portraits of the heroine. Others painted the rescue itself. Writers created fictionalized accounts of 'the girl with windswept hair', and the poet William Wordsworth commemorated here in verse. She was swamped with gifts, letters of praise, and even marriage proposals.

The Duke of Northumberland stepped in, creating a trust fund for the money, as well as making personal gifts to Grace.

Life on the island was harsh, and in 1842 she fell ill with the scourge of the 19th century, consumption (tuberculosis). The Duchess and Duke of Northumberland heard of her illness and sent their personal physician, as well as providing good accommodation near Alnwick Castle, the family seat. Her condition worsened, and she asked to be taken to her birth-place, Bamburgh. In October, she died and was buried in a local churchyard.

Sites to Visit

- The Farne Islands are today owned by the National Trust. They can be visited by boat from Seahouses, Northumberland, and are popular with bird-watchers.
- Grace Darling's grave is in St. Aidan's churchyard, Bamburgh, where she rests with her parents. The original, worn headstone has been replaced with a replica, and the original moved to the Royal National Lifeboat Institution Grace Darling Museum, Bamburgh. There is a large cenotaph in the churchyard dedicated to her memory.
- There is a monument in St. Cuthbert's Chapel, Great Farne Island (erected 1848).
- There is a painting by William Bell Scott of Grace's rescue mission at Wallington Hall, Cambo, Northumberland.
- There are three paintings by Thomas Musgrave Joy, depicting the rescue at The McManus Galleries, Albert Square, Meadowside, Dundee, Scotland.

Further Research

- Grace Darling, or the Maid of the Isles, by Jerrold Vernon, 1839
- Grace Darling, Her True Story: From Unpublished Papers in Possession of Her Family, by T. Darling
- Grace Darling: Maid and Myth, by Richard Armstrong, 1965

- Grace Had an English Heart: The Story of Grace Darling, Heroine and Victorian Superstar, by Jessica Mitford, 1989
- Grace Darling: Victorian Heroine, by Hugh Cunningham, 2007
- Grace Darling - Heroine of the Farne Islands, by Eva Hope, 2015
- Grace Darling, by Marianne Farningham, 2015

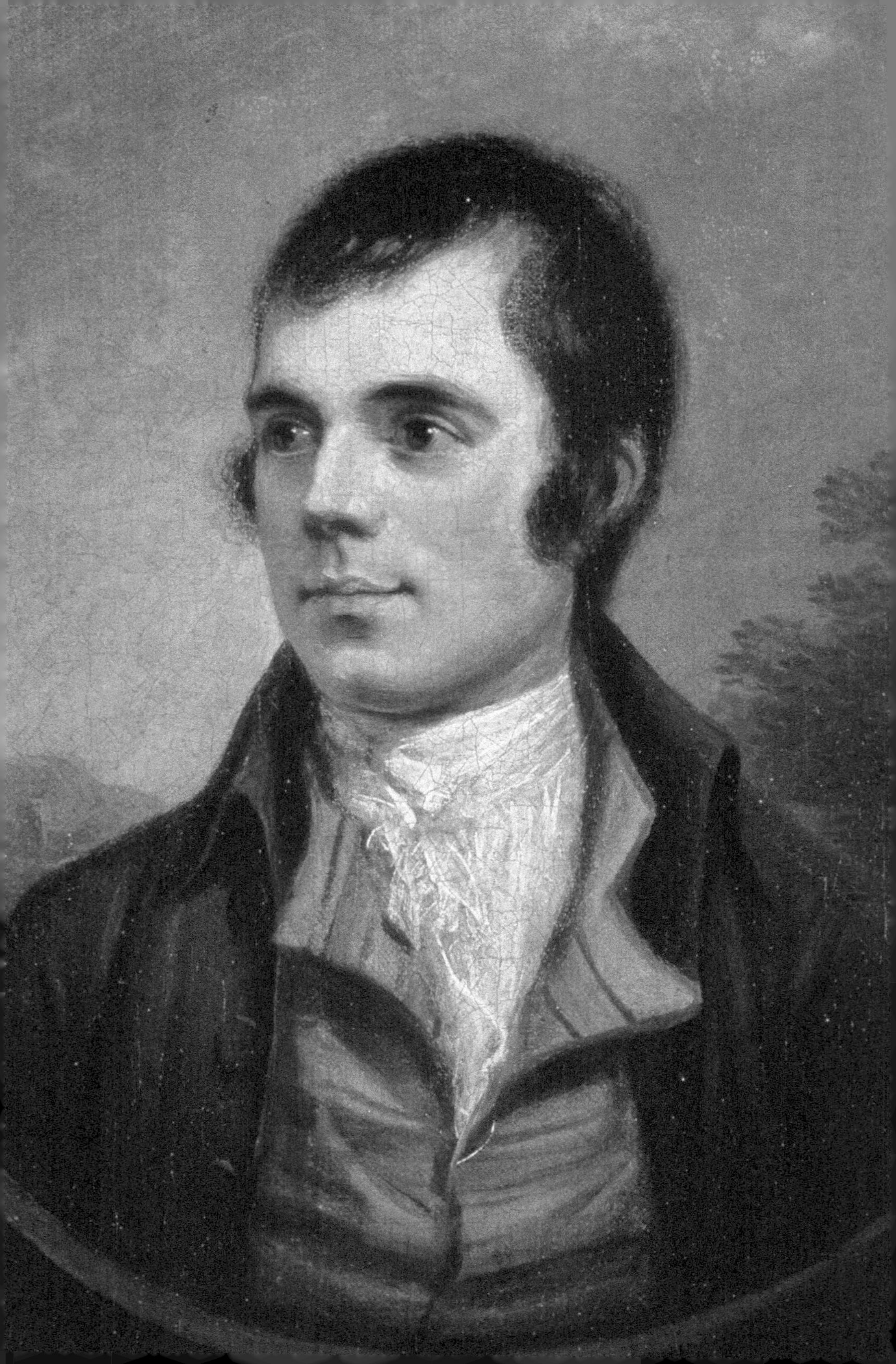

ROBBIE BURNS
Scotland's National Bard

Key Facts

- Born 1759, died 1796
- The greatest Scottish poet ever born
- Most famous for Auld Land Syne
- Voted the Greatest Scot of all time, narrowly beating William Wallace

Robert Burns was a Scottish poet most remembered for writing "Auld Lang Syne", but who wrote many poems and songs loved by Scots around the world. In his 37 years, he loved and lost on numerous occasions, always accompanied by a poem or three, and he advocated freedom and liberty in politics and life.

William Burns was a second-generation private gardener to the rich when his first son, Robert, was born on the 25th of January, 1759, into the small cottage he had built on some land he owned in Alloway, a few miles south of the town of Ayr, on the Scottish west coast. His wife, Agnes Broun, was a farmer's daughter and 11 years younger than William. Robert was followed by six more children over the next 12 years. The cottage became too small before that time, and William had ambitions to become a farmer, so in 1765 he leased Mount Oliphant, a farm two miles away.

Robert was seven at the time and was already being educated at home by his father, who had educated himself in the three R's and passed that on to his children, as well as the Christian virtues in a small book he wrote for them. He also learned Latin and French at a local school developed as part of the growing Scottish education-system. Robert's father was probably a Jacobite, a supporter of the restoration of the Stuart kings to the throne of England and Scotland, and his Scottish nationalism rubbed-off on young Robbie. William's farming at Mount Oliphant was not successful, so in 1777 the family moved to a larger farm at Lochlea, near Tarbolton, where William lived with Agnes until his death.

As for Robert, he already showed a taste both for writing and women, taking up dancing and writing four songs in a failed attempt to woo a wife. He also joined the local Masonic Lodge, which had strong Jacobite leanings. When he was 22, he moved to the nearby town of Irvine to become a flax-dresser. Flax was used in weaving to make linen and tapestries. While there, he met a sea-captain called Richard Brown, who Burns always credited with encouraging him to become a poet. Sadly, his shop caught fire during New Year's celebrations, and Robert had to return home to Lochlea.

After his father's death in 1784, Robert and his brother Gilbert tried to keep the farm going but failed and moved again to another nearby town called Mauchline, where he met and began to court Jean Amour. During that time, he also got his mother's servant girl pregnant, and she bore his first child, Elizabeth, in 1785. Not deterred, Jean also became pregnant and was sent away in disgrace by her parents to an uncle for the confinement.

Like so many in Scotland, Burns was unable to earn enough to keep his growing family, so around 1785, he decided to take a position as a bookkeeper on a sugar plantation in Jamaica. Unfortunately, he didn't have the money to get there, so he published two collections of his work - Scotch Poems and Poems, chiefly in the Scottish dialect, usually called the Kilmarnock Volume, to raise it. Some of the poems were written for another girlfriend, Mary Campbell, who he may have been planning to take to Jamaica with him. However, Mary died of typhus in 1786.

His poems proved popular, and he went to Edinburgh, where he was fêted by the top literary circles as a new and fresh voice. He made a favorable impression, and his poems were published in a new edition in Edinburgh, for which he received the enormous sum of £400. While in Edinburgh, he became involved in a protracted and complex relationship with Agnes "Nancy" McLehose, who was separated from her husband. When no physical side developed from it, he had an affair with her servant girl, who became pregnant, and with another servant girl as well. His courtship of these various women was always accompanied by splendid love-poems. He never did get to Jamaica.

As well as a poet Burns was a collector of traditional songs and contributed a large number to several volumes of The Scots Musical Museum, which was completed only after his death. Others occur in his collection, The Merry Muses of Caledonia. Often expressed indirectly in his work, Burns continued to hold Jacobite and revolutionary principles.

In 1788 he finally married Jean, and they moved to Dumfries, first farming and then working as a tax collector. He continued to write and had more songs and poems published in newspapers and collections. However, his excesses and drinking-habit, coupled with rejection by friends for his revolutionary views, combined with a rheumatic heart condition caused rapid aging in Burns. Following a tooth extraction, he died on the 21st of July, 1796, aged just 37, at home in Dumfries. Jean eventually managed to secure the future of his 12 children with the publication of a four-volume collection of his poems and an official biography.

His Legacy

Robbie Burns, or The Bard, as he is often known to Scots, is regarded as the national poet of Scotland. His works unite expatriate Scots around the world, and at least one, Auld Lang Syne, is known to everyone. He is considered an early Romantic and admired by socialists and liberals for such poems of equality and freedom as A Man's a Man for A' That and Scots Wha Hae.

Lines like O my Luve's like a red, red rose / That's newly sprung in June, or The best-laid schemes o' mice an' men / Gang aft agley are instantly recognized by all.

There are Burns Clubs globally fostering his work and bringing together lovers of his poetry and songs. His birthday, Burns Day, is widely celebrated around the work as an unofficial Scottish National

Day. He also enjoyed special popularity in Imperial, Communist and modern Russia.

Sites to Visit

- Burns' house in Dumfries, where he died, can be visited and is a small museum.
- His Mausoleum is in St. Michael's churchyard in Dumfries, and there is a Robert Burns Centre in the town as well. There is also a statue in Dumfries town center.
- The house he was born in, Burns Cottage, is now at the center of a theme-park, the Robert Burns Birthplace Museum, in Alloway. One wonders what he would make of it.
- There is a replica of Burns Cottage in Atlanta, Georgia.

Further Research

Biographies of Scott include:

- The Bard: Robert Burns, A Biography, by Robert Crawford (2009)
- Life of Robert Burns, by Thomas Carlyle (also available as a free e-book)
- Robert Burns in Your Pocket: A Biography, and Selected Poems and Songs, of Scotland's National Poet, by Robert Burns (2009)
- Red Rose (2004) is a film about his romantic life. A new biographic film is in the making.

Burns' literary works are also readily available as free e-books or in numerous hard-copy collections.

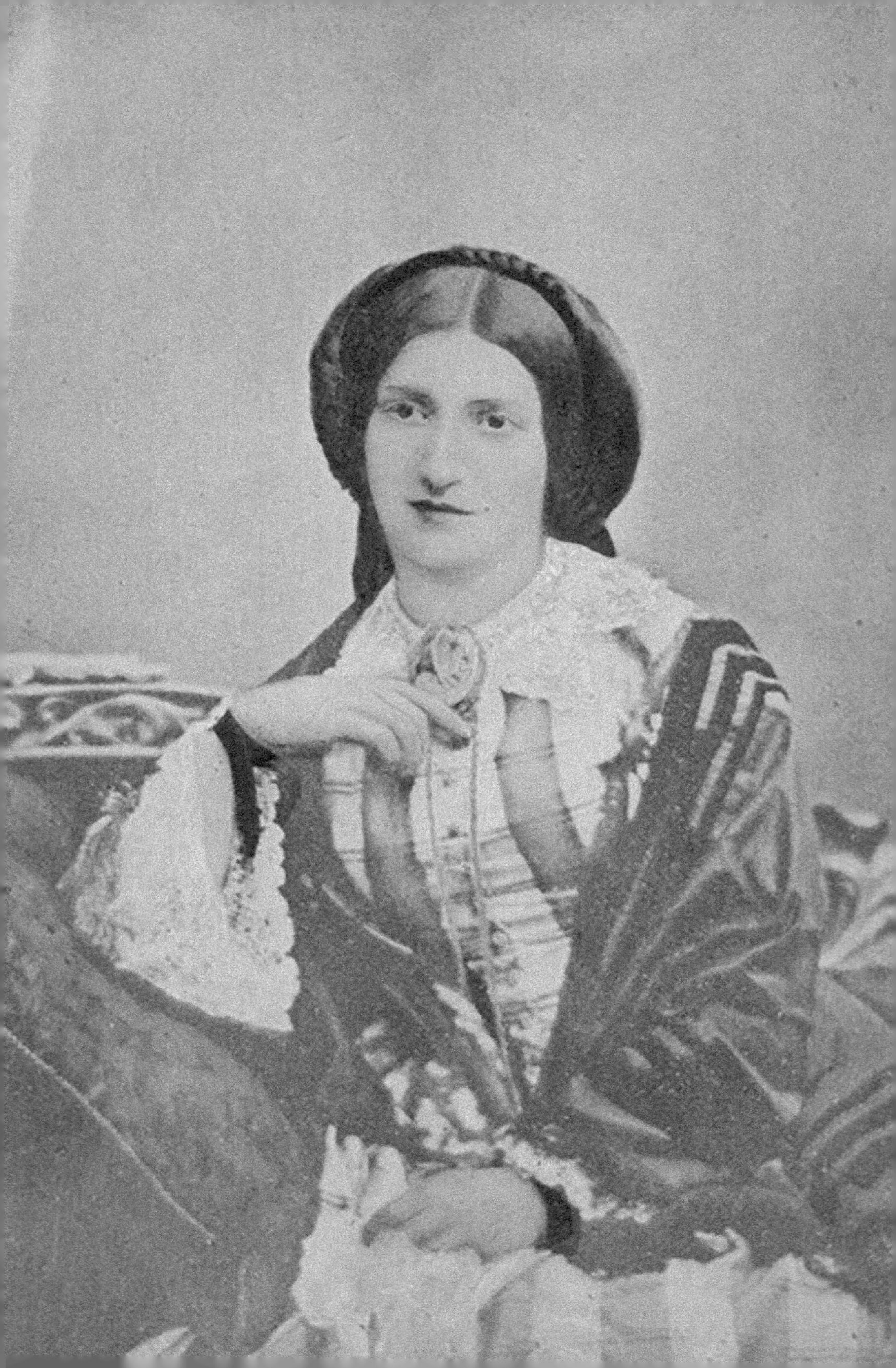

MRS. BEETON
The Victorian Martha Stewart

Key Facts

- Born March 12, 1836, died February 6, 1865
- One of the very first cook-book writers
- Set the standard for domestic life

The 19th Century was a time of great social change in Britain. By defeating Napoleon, it became the dominant naval power, and it used that power to consolidate the Empire, both as a source of raw materials and as a market for the products of its rapidly-developing industries at home. The nation became richer, and for the first time, this wealth, through manufacturing and trade, was spread across a larger segment of the society, greatly expanding the middle-class.

This growing middle-class wanted to emulate the fashions and manners of the upper-class as they moved into their family villas, still seen lining the streets of London. Although now usually multi-family dwellings, these houses originally contained a single-family, with servants working in basement kitchens and sleeping on the top floor, while the family lived on the ground and first floors, with bedrooms above.

The upper-classes had for centuries perfected the organization of households and the small army of servants necessary to run their stately homes. For the women of this new middle-class, with just a few servants for their grand new houses, organizing a household did not come naturally – help and guidance was needed. Into this knowledge-vacuum stepped Mrs. Beeton.

Isabella Mary Mason was born in Cheapside, London, just a few months before Queen Victoria took the throne. Her father died when she was young, and her mother remarried. The family settled in Epsom, Surrey, where her step-father ran the Epsom Racecourse. Isabella spent two years in Germany studying piano – she became an excellent pianist and then returned to her family home.

As was normal at that time for unmarried daughters, she remained with her family and helped raise the younger children. Since her family now numbered twenty-one children, including her four step-sisters from her step-father's first marriage, that was a challenging task. Even by Victorian standards, the family was exceptionally large.

During a visit back to her childhood home on Cheapside, her mother visited an old friend, a Mrs. Beeton, who she had kept in touch with by mail while living in Epsom. Isabella was introduced to Samuel, one of Mrs. Beeton's sons. The two became friendly and wrote to each other after Isabella returned home.

On July 10, 1856, Samuel Orchart Beeton married 'Fatty' (the nickname Isabella used to sign her letters to Samuel), and the newly-weds moved to a large new house, built in the fashionable Italianate style, at 2 Chandos Villas, Hatch End in north-west London.

Samuel Beeton was a successful publisher of books and magazines, for which there was a rapidly-growing market among the new middle-class. One of his magazines was The Englishwoman's Domestic Magazine which he had started in 1851. The magazine combined articles on household matters, fashion, and fiction. Beginning in 1859, Isabella began to write material on cooking and household management as supplements to the main magazine.

These were well-received, and in 1861 Beeton published them in a single volume under the title of:

The Book of Household Management, comprising information for the Mistress, Housekeeper, Cook, Kitchen-Maid, Butler, Footman, Coachman, Valet, Upper and Under House-Maids, Lady's-Maid, Maid-of-all-Work, Laundry-Maid, Nurse and Nurse-Maid, Monthly Wet and Sick Nurses, etc., etc.—also Sanitary, Medical, & Legal

Memoranda: with a History of the Origin, Properties, and Uses of all Things Connected with Home Life and Comfort.

The book, which quickly became known as Mrs. Beeton's Book of Household Management, sold 60,000 copies in its first year, and by 1868 it had sold over two million copies. The concept of having all knowledge in a single source was a popular Victorian ideal and is found in many fields at that time, the Encyclopædia Britannica, which had begun in 1768, being the supreme example.

Her book included sections on child-care, animal husbandry, fashion, managing servants, and even religion, but most popular were the recipes, which were on almost every page of the 1,112 page epic. Each one had an engraved color illustration, and they were written in a new format which was to become the standard still used today. The recipes were drawn from many earlier sources, and some sections of the book were simply copied from un-credited sources, but never-the-less the book set a standard for British cooking, which lasted for over a hundred years.

Mrs. Beeton, as she now became known, had given birth to her first child, a boy named after his father, in 1857, but he died within a few months. A second son, also named Samuel Orchart, was born in 1859, but he too died when just over a year old. She had two more sons, born in 1863 and 1865, both of whom survived into adult life.

However, immediately after the birth of her last son, Isabella contracted a puerperal fever. This serious infection of the reproductive system was a common killer of women after childbirth, at a time when the germ-theory of disease was very new, medical hygiene poor or non-existent, and antibiotics a distant dream. Isabella died a week later at the young age of twenty-eight.

She is buried beside her husband in West Norwood Cemetery, London.

Her Legacy

The enormous cooking, fashion, and home-decorating industries of today are all the result of Mrs. Beeton.

She raised women to the level of household managers on the industrial model, bringing them closer to the rank of men and giving domestic work a new status that set the stage for middle-class women to move into work outside the home.

Sites to Visit

- Her grave in West Norwood Cemetery, which is near the tube station of West Norwood, London, can still be found. The original Victorian monument became dilapidated and was replaced by a headstone in the 1930s.
- Although the house in Chandos Villas was destroyed during the Blitz in World War II, a plaque can be found at the original site.

Further Research

- The full edition of Mrs. Beeton's Book of Household Management can be found on the internet.
- Biographies include The Short Life and Long Times of Mrs. Beeton, by Kathryn Hughes (2005); Isabella and Sam: The Story of Mrs. Beeton, by Sarah Freeman (1977) and Mr. and Mrs. Beeton, by H. Montgomery Hyde (1951).
- A TV biography, The Secret Life of Mrs. Beeton (2006), caused some controversy by suggesting that she had contracted syphilis from her husband, which led to her own death and that of her first two children. There is no evidence for this theory, which was first proposed in Kathryn Hughes' biography.

WREN.
General of
Buildings.
1723, aged 91.

SIR CHRISTOPHER WREN
Builder of St Paul's Cathedral

Key Facts

- Born 1632, died 1723
- Supervised the rebuilding of London after the Great Fire of 1666
- Renowned architect whose buildings and style dominate traditional architecture

Sir Christopher Wren was born on October 20th, 1632, in the village of East Knoyle in Wiltshire. His family had some wealth through Christopher's mother, who died when he was about two years old. His father was the local rector, and he later became the Dean of Windsor, responsible for the Chapel at Windsor Palace. Christopher was educated at home by his father and another local clergyman. He was a sickly child and seems to have had an unhappy childhood since he began to drink heavily and smoke at an early age and was often caught stealing cakes from the bins behind a neighboring bakery.

He went to Oxford and graduated M.A. in mathematics in 1653 when just 21 years old. He continued to work at Oxford for a while and was then appointed Professor of Astronomy at Gresham College in London. While at Oxford, he had come under the influence of John Wilkins, the Warden of his College, who, along with old friends from Oxford, would travel to London to attend the weekly lectures that were part of Wren's duties. Other meetings with the members of Wilkins' circle gradually became the Royal Society, Britain's first and preeminent scientific organization. The Society received a

Royal Charter in 1662 after Charles II had returned to the throne following the Civil War and the Cromwell era. Isaac Newton was a contemporary of Wren, although ten years younger.

In 1665 he traveled to Paris and studied the architecture of that city, as well as being able to see drawings by the Italian artist and architect, Bernini, who was responsible for, among other things, the Piazza in front of St Peter's. Bernini was in Paris at the same time as a guest of Louis XIV, but it is not known if they met.

A week after Wren returned from Paris in 1666, the Great Fire of London broke out. The whole medieval City of London inside the original Roman Wall was destroyed, including the original St Paul's Cathedral and 87 other churches. Only the outlying areas of Westminster, Whitehall, and the surrounding slums remained. Of the City of London's 80,000 inhabitants, it is estimated that 70,000 lost their homes. The total population of London at that time was only around 500,000, and the fire followed a plague in 1665 that had already killed 80,000 people. Fearing a rebellion, Charles II dispersed much of the population to other parts of the country.

At the invitation of the King, Wren, and others, including John Evelyn, submitted plans to rebuild the City. In the end, due to shortages of labor and legal disputes, rather than creating a new, grand Baroque city, it was basically rebuilt on the old street plan, but with wider streets, the implementation of some safety measures, and most importantly, construction in brick and stone rather than in wood. In 1669 Wren was appointed King's Surveyor of Works, which gave him oversight of the rebuilding rather than a direct part in the actual reconstruction of individual buildings. His particular mandate was St Paul's and the other churches.

With this appointment, Wren felt sufficiently secure to attend to his personal life, and later the same year, he married Faith Coghill, a neighbor from his childhood. Judging from his letters to her, he was deeply in love. However, in 1675 Faith died of smallpox, and their surviving child, Christopher, was taken by Wren's mother-in-law to be raised by her. Just seventeen months later, Wren re-married. This marriage seems to have come out of nowhere, and Wren's friends had never heard of his new bride, who was the daughter of the 2nd Baron Fitzwilliam. This too was a brief marriage, and in

September of 1680, Jane Wren died of tuberculosis. They had two daughters. Wren never married again.

Wren had already begun work on St Paul's before the Great Fire and continued to work on the building until 1711, when it was finally completed. It went through several designs, and Wren was happy with the final design except for the balustrade around the dome, which was added against his wishes. The work on the other churches also proceeded slowly, and although Wren is popularly considered as their architect, it is likely he did not prepare the final plans for very many of them. He did, however, design numerous other buildings that are landmarks of London. In 1673 Wren was knighted for his work in the reconstruction of the City.

Towards the end of his life, Wren's style began to be criticized, and in the end, he was dismissed as Surveyor of Works in 1718. Since he was 87 years old by then, he probably was ready to go. He died while taking a nap in his house in St James's Street on February 25th, 1723.

His Legacy

Some great historical figures leave their mark in laws and institutions. Others do so in our bookshelves or music collections. Yet others change the physical structure of our daily environment – as Christopher Wren did. Not only are the buildings associated with him landmarks of London, but his style influenced buildings around the world and a copy of the dome of St Paul's can be seen, for example, on the U.S. Capitol Building in Washington D.C. His style continued to influence future architects right up to the development of modernism in the 20th century.

He was also a great physicist and astronomer, carrying out numerous studies in these fields and in optics, surveying, methods to measure longitude at sea, microscopy, medicine, and meteorology, to name a few of his many interests. He even asked the questions that inspired Newton to develop his laws of motion.

Sites to Visit

- A tour of Wren's buildings is a tour around London. Besides St Paul's and the numerous churches associated with him, he designed the monument to the Great Fire, which can be seen outside Monument Tube station, Chelsea Hospital, the Royal Observatory, Kensington Palace, Greenwich Naval Hospital, as well as parts of Whitehall and Hampton Court. Numerous other buildings can be seen in Oxford and Cambridge, and other locations in Britain.
- There is an English Heritage blue plaque on The Old Court House, Hampton Court Green, East Molesey, where Wren lived on occasions. Other plaques in Windsor and near the Globe Theatre in London are disputed.

Further Research

- Recent biographies include: On a Grander Scale: The Outstanding Life of Sir Christopher Wren, by Lisa Jardine

(2003); His Invention So Fertile: A Life of Christopher Wren, by Adrian Tinniswood (2001); and Christopher Wren, by James Chambers (2013).
- Wren's City of London Churches, by John Christopher, is a guide to visiting some of his buildings.

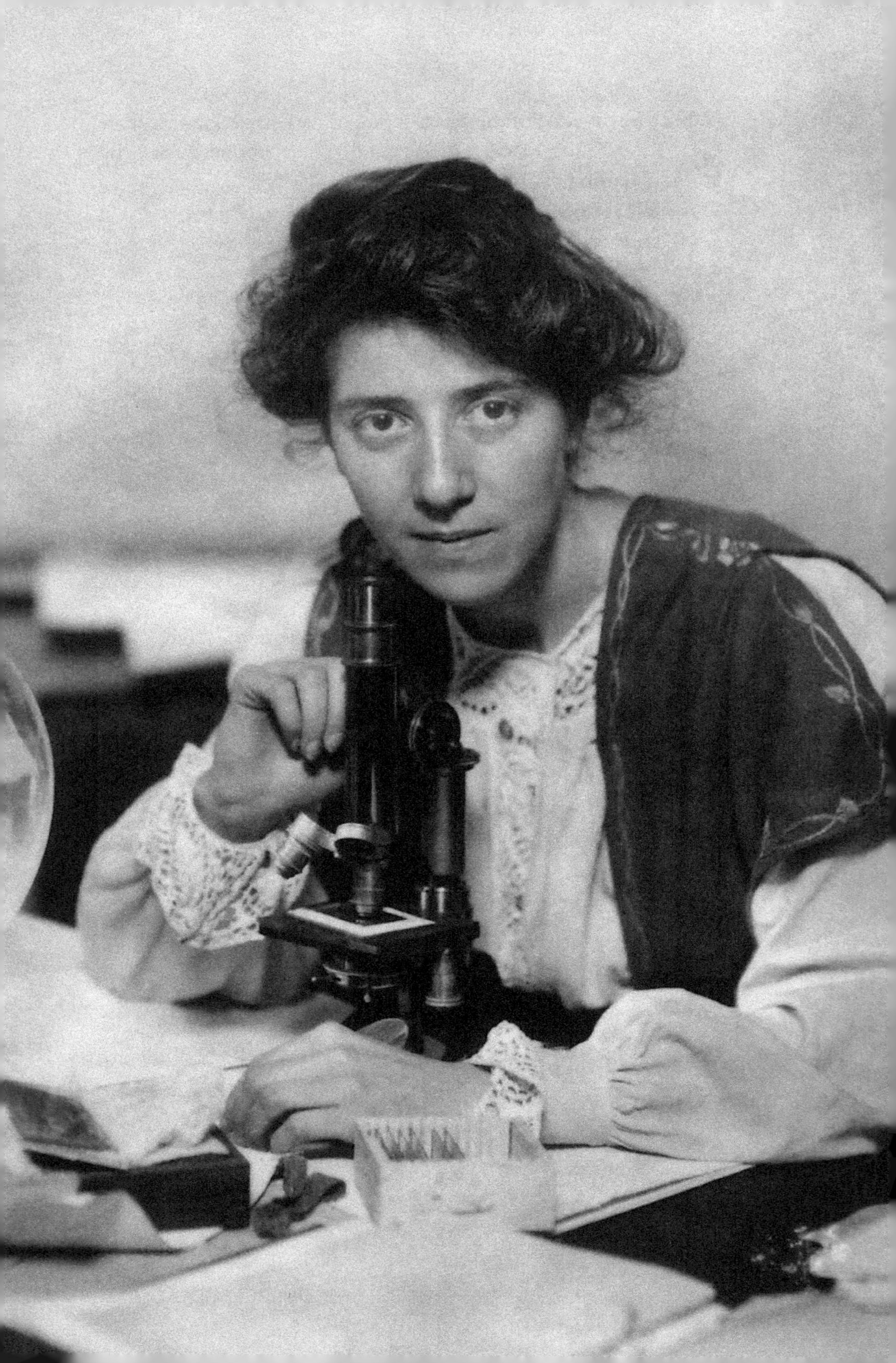

MARIE STOPES
Birth Control Pioneer

Key Facts

- Born 1880, died 1958
- Wrote some of the earliest books advocating birth-control
- Opened the first birth-control clinic in England
- Advocated for women's control over their own reproduction

The commonly held view that the late 19th century in England was an era of Victorian respectability and stuffiness, populated by narrow-minded people with limited horizons, is really quite false. There was, in fact, a great deal of social turmoil, and just like today, people had widely-ranging interests and beliefs that formed many of the features of the later centuries that we now take as 'normal.' Progressive social ideas were widespread, and the desire to improve society was common. So being born into a family where your father is both a businessman and a scientist and having a mother who is an academic and a suffragette, as Marie Stopes was on the 15th of October, 1880, was perhaps not as strange as it seems.

However, going on to obtain a bachelor's degree in two years, studying in Europe, and becoming one of the first female University Lecturers in England by the age of 24 was certainly exceptional for the times.

Stopes began as a palaeobotanist, studying plant fossils, an interest probably fostered by her father's own work with animal fossils. She spends her twenties as a scientist, traveling to Japan and Canada, working to prove the existence of the ancient supercontinent Gondwana, which led to our knowledge of continental drift and plate tectonics.

It was while working for the Geological Survey of Canada that she met Reginald Ruggles Gates, and in a whirlwind romance, they were engaged in two days and married within three months. The newlyweds returned to England in 1911, where Maria worked for the British Government and began what was to become her major scientific contribution - studies on the nature of coal and its different types.

While her career was proceeding well, in her private life, things were going badly. Her suffragette upbringing had led her to keep her maiden name at marriage, and clearly, her ideas on marriage did not fit with her husband's much more traditional ones. Within a few years, Maria was looking for a way to separate, and after just two years of marriage, she filed for divorce. It appears that Reginald Gates suffered from impotence, and he did not contest the divorce.

Disillusioned, Marie began working on a book describing her ideal of marriage. In 1915 she met the prominent American advocate of birth-control Margaret Sanger, who was soon to open America's first birth-control clinic – and be prosecuted for it. She asked Sanger's advice for the chapter on birth-control that she had written for her book. Although desired, practical and effective methods of birth-control were very limited at the time. By the end of the year, her book was finished, but Stopes could not find a publisher willing to be associated with her blunt and outspoken words on sex. She found support from a wealthy businessman and philanthropist with an interest in birth control, Humphrey Verdon Roe. With Roe's financial backing, her book – Married Love – was finally published in 1918. Her book was an instant success and sold five editions in the first year. She was now a national figure. Other books followed, some directed at working-class women rather than her initial audience of the middle-class, and others aimed at changing the Church's prohibition on birth control.

Two months after Married Love was published, Stopes and Roe were married. Although she briefly continued her academic career, her success led her to resign her lectureship, as did also her pregnancy, which sadly ended in 1919 with a stillbirth. The couple had an open marriage, and Stopes had numerous affairs with younger men, although she never advocated sex outside marriage.

Humphrey Roe had been interested in opening a birth-control clinic even before meeting Marie, and in 1921, in the North London district of Holloway, they opened the 'Mothers Clinic' with midwives and visiting doctors to give practical birth-control assistance. She was at that time, and remained, opposed to abortion and even had her nurses sign a declaration that they would not give advice on it. A strong part of the support for birth-control at that time was the desire to eliminate the injury and death caused by illegal 'back-street' abortions, which were often the only form of birth control available, especially to the poor. Further clinics were opened in other British cities in the 1930s and '40s.

Of course, there was strong opposition to her ideas, including the publication in 1922 of a book critical of her and her ideas. She responded with a libel case, which dragged through the courts for years with the verdict going both ways until in the House of Lords – England's highest court – she lost. Despite the huge legal costs, the trials generated massive publicity for her books and for her ideas, leading to much greater acceptance of birth-control by most of British society.

In 1924 she had a son, Harry, but she seems to have been a controlling mother, and in 1947 she strongly objected to his choice of fiancé, it would seem chiefly on the grounds that she needed to wear glasses. He went ahead with the marriage, and Marie disinherited him.

Her issues with Harry's choice of a 'defective' partner connected with her involvement in the Eugenics Movement. While never reaching the level of support it was to achieve in the USA; eugenic beliefs were promoted in Britain by a number of prominent social reformers prior to World War II. While most social reformers of the time believed that education and higher wages would produce a better society, eugenicists saw the solution as the compulsory sterilization of the insane, feeble-minded ... revolutionaries ... (and) half-castes' – to quote Marie Stopes. It seems that her beliefs in giving couples control over their reproduction had a dark side of elitism and racism, and her support for birth control for the poor was for her chiefly about social engineering. She also seems to have had anti-Semitic views, although her support for Hitler in the 1930s was tempered when he burned her books and closed down birth-control clinics in Germany.

Stopes died at her home in Dorking Surrey on the 2nd of October, 1958. She left her clinic to the Eugenic Society.

Her Legacy

Stopes' books and clinics opened up the taboo subject of sexuality and birth-control and led directly to today's liberal attitudes on the subject. Although eugenics is discredited, her role in reducing the sizes of families is directly responsible for the global growth of the middle-class and rising standards of living.

She still remains a target for anti-abortionists and those opposed to birth-control and greater sexual freedom, and her writings, viewed with hindsight, certainly provide plenty of ammunition. Like many social reformers, she had a complex character and was strongly convinced of the absolute correctness of her views.

Sites to Visit

There are English Heritage blue plaques at:

- 28, Cintra Park, Upper Norwood, in South-East London, which was Stopes' childhood home.
- 14, Well Walk, Hampstead, where she lived from 1909 to 1919.
- The Portland Museum, on the island of Portland in Dorset, was founded by Stopes, who had a house on the island, which is famous for its fossils. One of the buildings – the Marie Stopes Cottage, contains a small exhibition on her, along with artifacts of Dorset life. The museum is open daily during the summer months.
- Stopes was cremated, and her ashes scattered in the sea

around the Island of Portland.

Further Research

- Passionate Paradox, the Life of Marie Stopes, by Keith Briant (1962), is a biography of her life.
- Marie Stopes: Feminist, Eroticism, Eugenicist, by William Garrett (2008) is a collection of her writings and an analysis of her work.
- Many of Stopes' books are available as e-books.
- Although her clinics briefly closed down after her death, they were re-born as Marie Stopes International and operated in 38 countries.

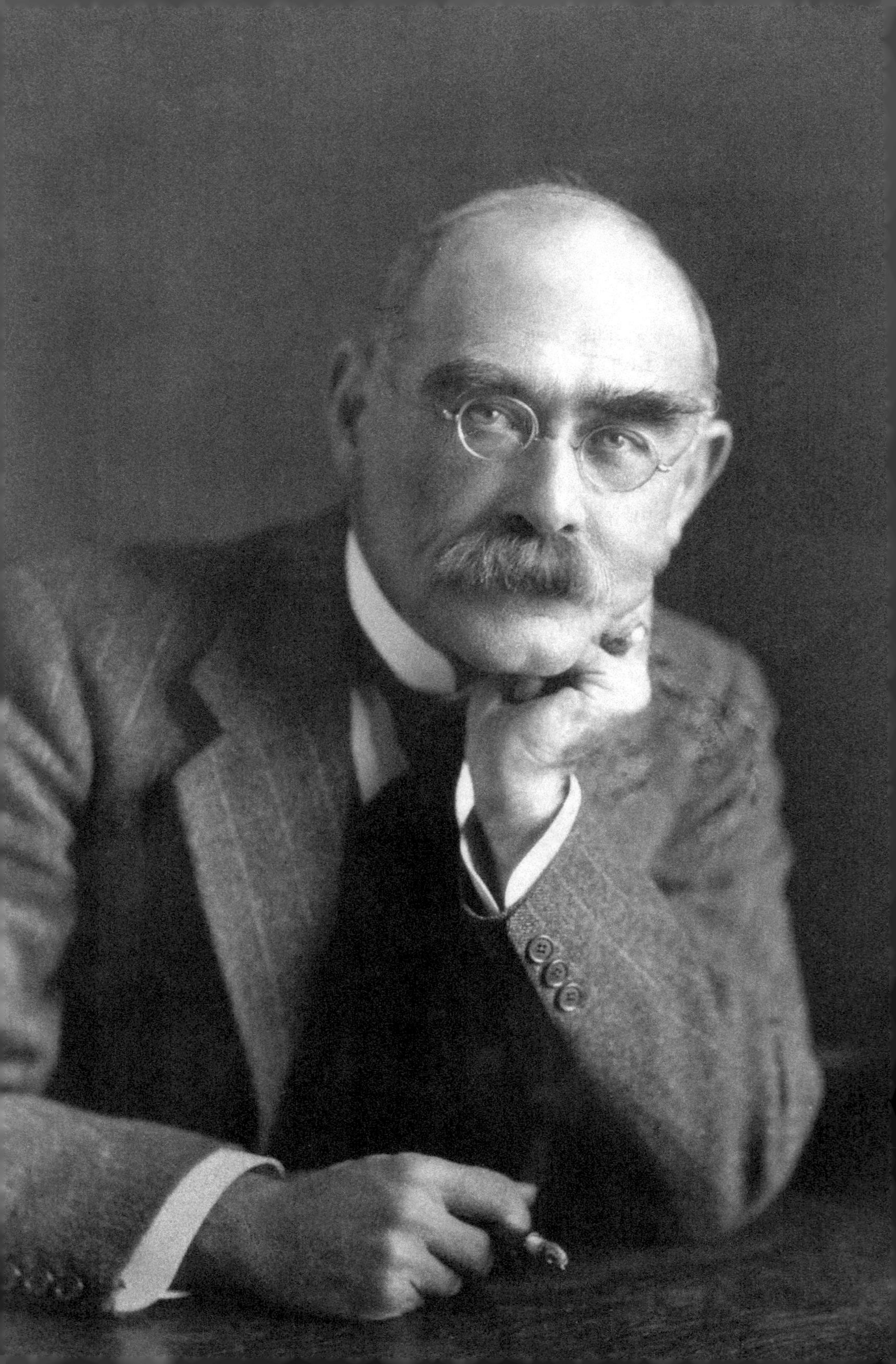

RUDYARD KIPLING
Novelist of the Empire

Key Facts

- Born 1865, died 1936
- Awarded the Nobel Prize for Literature in 1907
- Prolific writer of stories of life in India under the Raj

Rudyard Kipling was born on December 30th, 1865, in Bombay (now Mumbai), India, to Alice and Lockwood Kipling. His father was a professor at an art college, and his mother was a vivacious member of the Anglo-Indian community. He was brought up by Indian servants and so first spoke Hindi, but had to speak English when with his parents.

To ensure they grew up as English children, it was the habit at that time for Anglo-Indians to send their children back 'home' for their education. So when he was five, Rudyard and his three-year-old sister were sent to Portsmouth to live with an English family and go to school. Their surrogate parents were Captain and Mrs. Holloway, and Kipling was to recall with horror the six years he spent with them. He much later attributed his story-telling skills to having to learn to lie to avoid being punished. Eventually, his mother seems to have found out that he was being mistreated since she returned to England in 1877 and removed him from the care of the Holloways.

The following year Rudyard was sent to a Military college in Devon to prepare him for a career in the British Army, but his academic achievement was poor, and he was not able to obtain the scholarship that would have made it possible for him to go to Oxford University. His father had by now moved on to another Arts College in Lahore in the Punjab (now part of Pakistan), and he found Rudyard a job as an assistant editor at an English-language newspaper. So in 1882, he sailed back to India, where he experienced a strong sense of home-coming and a return to the mental security of his early childhood.

In his new job, Kipling wrote prolifically and was soon producing verse and short stories for the paper. As was the habit of the Anglo-English, he would spend the hottest part of the year in the cooler hill climate of Simla (or Shimla), which became each year the temporary capital of British India. In 1887 he was transferred to a much larger paper (The Pioneer) in Allahabad in what is now the northern area of Uttar Pradesh. Early in 1888, his first book of short stories was published in Calcutta, titled Plain Tales from the Hills. By the end of the year, he had published six more books of short stories, all based on his life in British India.

The next year, following a dispute with the paper, he was fired, although he continued to contribute material for publication. With the money he received and with money from selling his rights to his early books, Kipling decided to go to London, which he did via North America, where he traveled extensively in both the United States and Canada and met Mark Twain. He finally arrived in London towards the end of 1889, where he was greeted with acclaim for his writing.

Kipling took a room just off The Strand and continued to write. In 1892 he married Caroline Starr Balestier, the sister of a writer friend. At the wedding, she was given away by Henry James. The Balestier family was American, and the newly-weds moved to a small rented cottage on a farm near Carrie's family estate in Brattleboro, Vermont. Following the birth of their first child at the end of the year, they bought some land nearby and built a house inspired by Kipling's memories of Moghul architecture.

Kipling continued to write, and it was while living in Vermont that the Jungle Books were created. A second child was born early in 1896, but due to friction between Britain and the US over borders in Venezuela, and family scandals with his brother-in-law, in June of that year, the family returned to England. They settled in Torquay, Devon, with Kipling already a famous writer, and a third child was born in 1897. The family began a regular custom of wintering in South Africa where Kipling became involved in writing about the Boer War – Britain's battle to expand its colonies in Africa. In 1897 they bought Bateman's, a 17th-century house in Burwash, East Sussex, where Kipling was to spend the rest of his life.

His popularity as a writer continued to grow as his enormous output continued, including novels, short stories, poetry, and non-fictional writing on issues of the time. In 1907 he was awarded the Nobel Prize for Literature, but in his private life, there were tragedies. In 1899, while on a trip to the US, his oldest daughter Josephine died of pneumonia. At the outbreak of World War I, Kipling, like many others, became strongly anti-German and encouraged his youngest child, John, to enter the Army. Kipling had to use his contacts to get him in because he had poor eyesight, but by 1915 he had died in battle.

Kipling continued writing into the 1930s and became increasingly interested in politics, supporting the continued involvement of America in world affairs, the United Nations, an Anglo-French alliance, and opposing both Bolshevism and Fascism. He had always used the reverse swastika, which was a Hindu good-luck symbol, on his books, but ordered that to be stopped when the Nazis came to power. He died on January 18th, 1936, of a perforated ulcer.

His Legacy

When alive, Rudyard Kipling was one of England's most popular and prolific writers. Since his death and the end of the Empire he described so eloquently, his reputation has suffered from the changes in attitude to Britain's Empire building. Whether seen as an apologist for racism and jingoism or as an eloquent voice for the romance of Empire and far-away places, his story-telling remains to give us one of the most colorful and entertaining pictures of life when Britain was at its peak of power.

Sites to Visit

- There is a closed and locked cottage at the Jeejebhoy School of Art in Mumbai that has a plaque giving it as Kipling's birthplace, although the original cottage was actually torn-down and a new one erected.
- His Vermont house, Naulakha, can still be seen on Kipling Road, Dummerston, north of Brattleboro.
- Bateman's, Burwash, East Sussex, Kipling's home for 40 years, is now a National Trust property open to the public.
- Kipling is buried in Poets Corner, Westminster Abbey, where his memorial can be seen.

Further Research

- Kipling's books are all still in print and available on-line.
- His Autobiography, Something of Myself, is still available.
- Recent biographies include Rudyard Kipling: A Life, by Harry

Ricketts (2000) and The Long Recessional: The Imperial Life of Rudyard Kipling, by David Gilmour (2003).
- There are numerous film versions of many of his works, chiefly the Jungle Books, Kim, and Gunga Din.

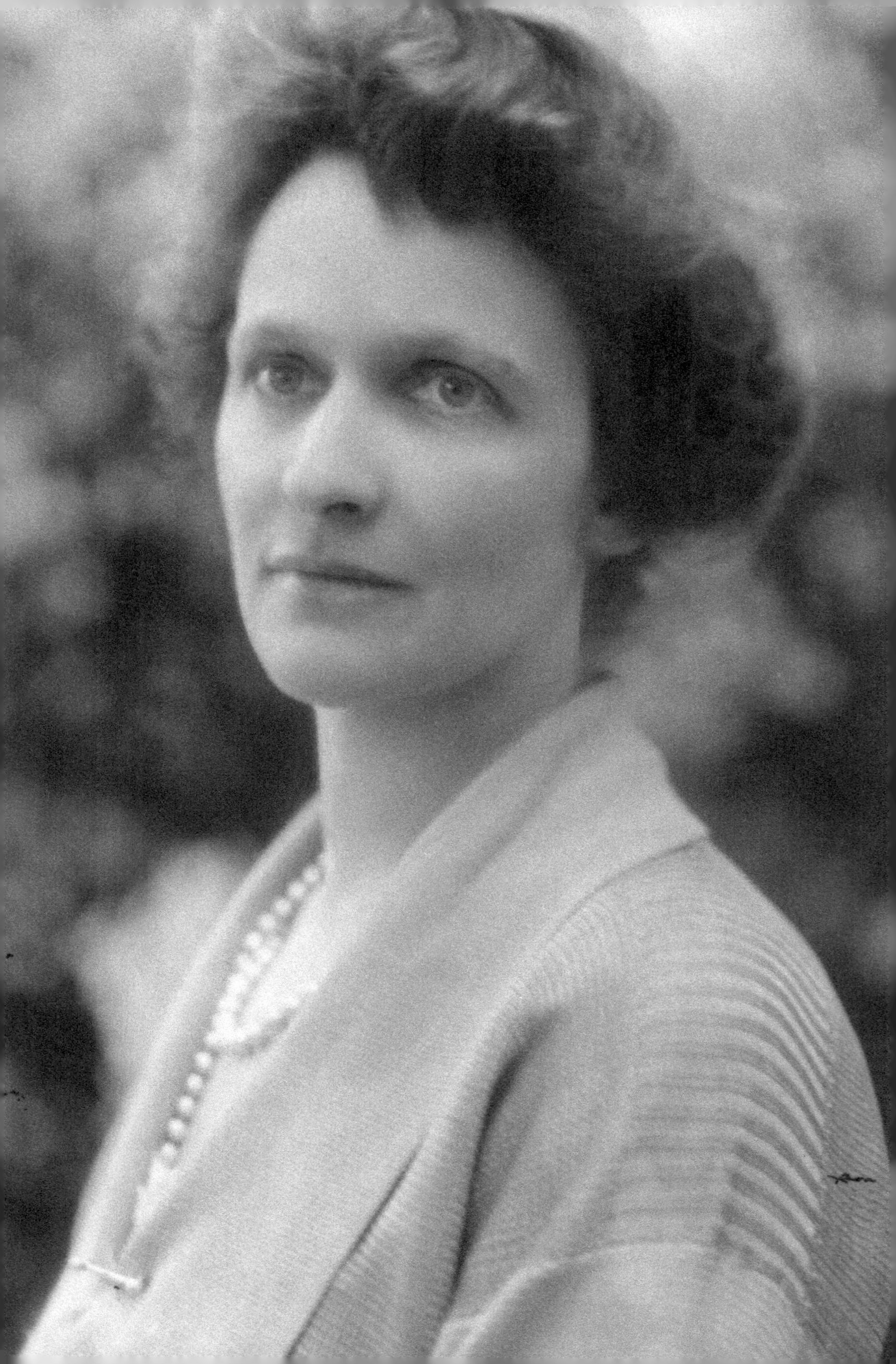

NANCY ASTOR
Socialite and MP

Key Facts

- Born 1879, died 1964
- First female MP in the House of Commons
- Controversial for her anti-Catholic, anti-Semitic, and racist views

Nancy Astor is a bit of a strange and controversial figure in British history. First, she's an American, but she became British later on and eventually was elected to the House of Commons as the first woman to take a seat. She served in Parliament for decades but became known for her anti-Semitism and Nazi sympathetic leanings. Sir Winston Churchill particularly loathed her. Her life, though, represents the growth of Anglo-American relations in the late Victorian era, and it was quite a life.

Following the American Civil War, prosperous Southerners who had relied on slavery fell on hard times. Such was the fate of Chiswell Dabney Langhorne, who had been a successful railroad businessman before the war. So when his eighth child was born on May 19th, 1879, he was still struggling to recover. However, by the time that daughter, who had been christened Nancy, was thirteen, he had re-established his fortune, and a few years later, he could send Nancy Langhorne and one of her sisters to a Finishing School in New York City.

She finished successfully, and on October 27th, 1897, when only eighteen, she married a wealthy socialite, Robert Gould Shaw

11. Or perhaps for Nancy, it was not such a success since she left her husband for the first time during their honeymoon, and after a turbulent and troubled four years and a son, they separated permanently.

In 1903 Nancy's mother died, and with the divorce finalized, she moved back to the family estate known as Mirador, in Albemarle County, Virginia. Following a trip to England, she was encouraged by her father to join the many other young American women living there and marrying into the nobility. She quickly developed a reputation for wit and charm and the ability to flirt with the young men while appearing proper to their parents.

While crossing the Atlantic to Britain, Nancy had met Waldorf Astor, the son of the American magnate William Waldorf Astor. Waldorf had been born in New York on the same day as Nancy, but when he was ten years old, his father had moved the family to Britain to raise his children as English aristocrats. Waldorf had been educated at Eton College and Oxford University. In May of 1906, Nancy and Waldorf were married and moved into their wedding gift – the 375 acre Cliveden Estate and its 400-foot-long mansion in Buckinghamshire, which Nancy modernized and had electrified. She proved herself to be a brilliant hostess, and socialite and Cliveden and the Astor's London home in St. James's Square were fashionable venues for the elite. She began to move in political circles and became involved with groups interested in preserving the unity of the English-speaking world and the British Empire.

Nancy encouraged Waldorf to enter politics, and he became a Member of Parliament in 1910 for the Conservative Party, although he broke ranks with his party and tended to vote for social reforms. When his Liberal friend David Lloyd George became Prime Minister of the wartime Coalition government in 1916, Waldorf became his parliamentary private secretary and part of his circle of advisors. In 1916 his father William was made a peer – Viscount Astor. When William died in 1919, Waldorf tried unsuccessfully to avoid taking the title but was forced to surrender his seat in Parliament and enter the House of Lords as the 2nd Viscount Astor. This triggered a by-election for his Plymouth seat, which Nancy contested and won.

She was actually the second woman to be elected a Member of Parliament, but the first - Constance Markievicz of the Irish Party Sinn Féin - had refused to take her seat as a protest over the situation in Ireland. So this left Nancy as the first woman to actually sit in the Houses of Parliament. Despite her political naiveté and opposition to alcohol, her wit, financial resources, and charity work won her the seat. Her American informal style was new to the British and seems to have charmed them in an age where campaigning was very much about personality.

After her election, she befriended other women who were subsequently elected, although political differences limited these friendships. Although she sat as a Conservative member through the governments of four Conservative Prime Ministers, she was never chosen as a minister or made much mark in Parliament. She did succeed in having a bill passed that raised the legal drinking age to eighteen. She justified her limited career by saying it left her freer to criticize government policies. She also worked outside Parliament to develop nursery schools for early childhood education.

In the years between the wars, she became increasingly anti-Catholic, anti-Bolshevik, and anti-Semitic and was sympathetic towards the rising Nazi party, which she considered a good solution to these 'world problems.' She exchanged anti-Semitic letters with the then American ambassador to Britain, Joseph P. Kennedy Sr. and entertained prominent members of the Nazi government. Her circle of friends became known as the Cliveden Set and was notorious for their sympathetic views towards Germany and their desire to avoid another war at all costs.

When World War II did break-out, Nancy admitted that she had made mistakes and supported the war effort, although still causing controversy by, for example, opposing the entry into Britain of Communist refugees at a time when Russia was an ally in the war. As her views became more extreme and eccentric, she became an embarrassment to the Conservative Party, and with them facing defeat by the Labour Party in the 1945 election, Waldorf Astor was persuaded to force her to step down. She did, but with anger and bitterness, which she continued to express for many years. She and Waldorf drifted apart, and his movement to the political left did not help their marriage. They began to live separate lives and travel apart, although there was a reconciliation before his death in 1952.

During the 1950's she added racism to her other views and became notorious for, among other statements, proudly announcing to the white minority Rhodesian government that she was the daughter of a slave owner and telling a group of Afro-American students that they should be more like the servants of her southern childhood. As her brothers and sisters died, and she became estranged from her children, loneliness took over. She died in 1964.

Her Legacy

Although she was the first sitting female MP in Britain, this is perhaps more a tribute to wealth and privilege than to skill or worth. Her sharp wit hid a cold, aggressive, paranoid, and illiberal personality.

Sites to Visit

- Her childhood home, Mirador, near Greenwood, Albemarle County, Virginia, is now a historic home open to the public.
- The Cliveden Estate and Mansion at Taplow, Buckinghamshire, is a National Trust property leased to a hotel company.
- The Astor's London house, 4 St. James's Square, is the Naval & Military Club and carries a commemorative blue plaque.

Further Research

- Lady Astor is a TV documentary made in 1962. There is a TV mini-series, Nancy Astor, made in 1982. She is also featured in The Astors: High Society, an episode of the Biography TV program made in 1996.
- Recent biographies include: Nancy: The Story of Lady Astor, by Adrian Fort (2013) and Nancy Astor: A Lady Unashamed, by John Grigg (1983).

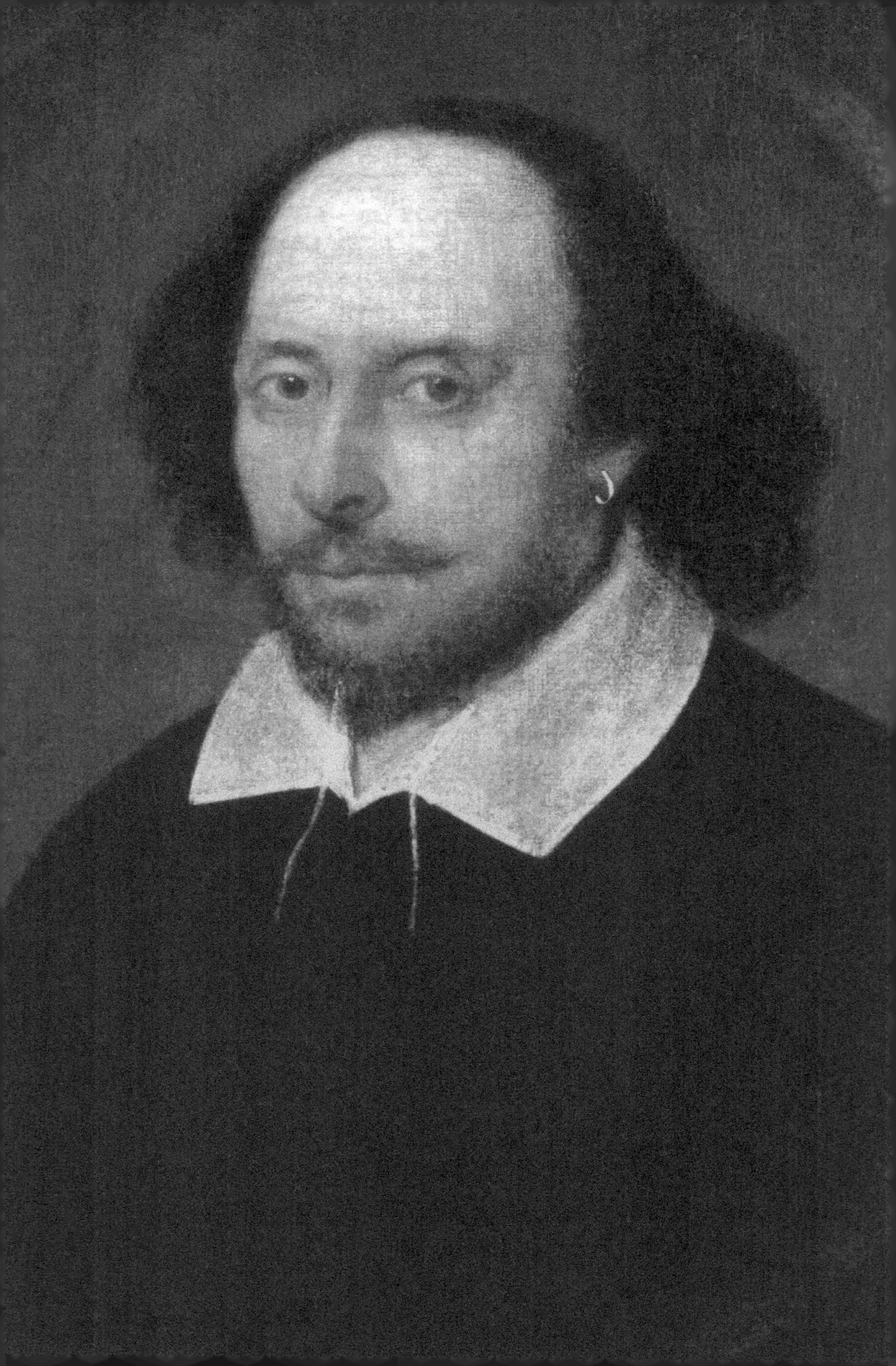

WILLIAM SHAKESPEARE
The Bard

Key Facts

- Born 1564, died 1616
- His plays and themes continue to be relevant to modern life
- Still the world's more widely performed playwright
- Speculation abounds of his 'true' identity in the absence of hard facts on his private life

William Shakespeare was born around April 23, 1564, into an England ruled by Queen Elizabeth I, and after Henry VIII's break with the Catholic Church was well established. England was about to embark on a period of expansion in trade and exploration in competition with its rival, Spain. This was a time of growing wealth and confidence and a period of creativity and novelty in art, literature, and social mores.

He was born and grew up in the small market town of Stratford-upon-Avon in south-central England, where his father John was a local alderman and a glove maker. William went to the local grammar school, where he would probably have learned Latin and read the classic Greek and Roman writers who, along with writers of the Italian Renaissance, were to provide the story-lines for many of his plays. At eighteen, his teenage romance with an older woman – the 26-year-old Anne Hathaway – led to the equivalent of a shotgun wedding, and their first daughter was born just six months after their hasty marriage. Two years later, Anne gave birth to twins, a boy, and a girl, but the son died when he was just eleven.

After the record of the twin's births in 1585, nothing is known of Shakespeare's life until he appears in the London theatre scene in 1592. This period, often referred to as his 'lost years', has been widely speculated about, but there is no concrete evidence of what he was doing during that time.

Certainly, by 1592, several of his plays were being performed, and he had developed a reputation as an upstart, perhaps rather self-important actor and playwright, so he may have been working in the theatre for several years by then. By 1594 he and a group of fellow actors had begun to work as a company under the name of the Lord Chamberlain's Men, which quickly became the leading theatrical company in London. In 1603, shortly after the ascension to the throne of James I following the death of Elizabeth, the company received a royal patent and changed their name to the King's Men. A royal patent was a license to perform plays, which limited the number of companies and allowed greater control over the content of the performances. In 1599 several members of the theatre company, including it would seem, Shakespeare, formed a company to build a new theatre on the south bank of the Thames, which was called The Globe. This became the preferred venue for Shakespeare's plays, and its popularity added to Shakespeare's growing wealth.

In 1597 he had purchased the second-largest house in Stratford, called New Place, and in 1605 invested in the Stratford tithes system, which was the collection of payments from poorer farmers as a form of rent. Starting in 1594, he began publishing his plays and the sale of these, with his name on the title page as a selling point, added further to his wealth. Full, definitive collections of his works would not, however, become available until after his death. He divided his time between Stratford and London, living in various parts of the city, including a suite of rooms rented in an upscale area of the city north of St. Paul's Cathedral. As well as writing, he continued to also act in his own and other plays, probably in supporting roles such as the ghost of Hamlet's father, although there is no clear evidence of the roles he actually played.

As he grew older, it seems he spent less time in London, probably encouraged to stay away by repeated outbreaks of bubonic plague, which led to the periodic closing of theatres. His last works were written by 1613 – some later works were collaborations with his successor as a playwright for the King's Men, a certain John Fletcher. He died on what was probably his 52nd birthday, April 23, 1616. He left the bulk of his wealth to his older daughter, Susanna, but her line, as well as that of her sister Judith, died out by 1670, leaving him with no direct heirs. He famously left his 'second-best bed' to his wife Anne, but scholars disagree on whether this was an insult or a significant gesture.

He was buried in the Holy Trinity Church in Stratford under a stone slab bearing a warning not to disturb his bones (they are still there presumably), and in 1623 a monument with a bust of him holding a quill pen was built into the wall of the church.

His Legacy

The little that is known of Shakespeare's life fades to insignificant against his influence. His work continued to be popular after his death and enjoyed a significant revival by the Romantic Movement in the 19th century when his status soared so much that George Bernard Shaw dismissed it as 'bardolatry.' His plays continue to be studied by British (and many other) schoolchildren and are regularly performed in traditional and modern versions of all varieties right up to the present time.

Shakespeare's works cover the gamut of possibilities from bawdy comedy to tragic drama. They vary from historical drama (Henry VI, Julius Caesar) to romantic comedy (Much Ado About Nothing, A Midsummer Night's Dream, The Merchant of Venice), tragic romance (Romeo and Juliet), and complete tragedy (Othello, Hamlet). He also wrote poems throughout his life, often on themes of the dangers of lust and with erotic content.

He also had a major influence on the development of the English language, adding many new words (e.g., courtship, impartial, luggage, obscene, radiant) and countless expressions (such as 'a foregone conclusion', 'with bated breath,' 'to be or not to be,' 'out damned spot'). His explorations of the full range of human emotions and limitations continue to speak to the human condition.

Sites to Visit

- Stratford-on-Avon is a major center for Shakespeare-themed visits. Besides his father's house, Anne Hathaway's cottage, statues, his tomb and funeral monument, and other properties associated with his life, there are numerous theme museums and activities.
- A reconstruction of the original Globe Theatre, called Shakespeare's Globe, opened in 1997 a few hundred yards from the original site in London. It stages traditional versions of his plays.
- There are additional funeral monuments in Poet's Corner, Westminster Abbey, London, and Southwark Cathedral also in London. There are also statues in Central Park (NYC), Chicago, Montgomery (Alabama), and the Library of Congress.
- As well as on monuments, his image appears on the British £20 note, and although there are numerous portraits that have been claimed to be of him, the best image is probably the one on his funeral monument in Stratford and the engraving widely printed on early editions of his plays, known as the Droeshout portrait.

Further Research

- There are literally hundreds of books about Shakespeare; recent ones considered among the best include Will in the World: How Shakespeare Became Shakespeare by Stephen Greenblatt; Shakespeare: The World as Stage by Bill Bryson; and Shakespeare: The Invention of the Human by Harold Bloom.
- Besides the frequent live performances still to be seen, there are over 400 film adaptions of his plays, including Taming of the Shrew with Elizabeth Taylor and Richard Burton; The Merchant of Venice with Al Pacino; A Midsummer Night's Dream with Michelle Pfeifer; and Hamlet directed by

Kenneth Branagh.
- There are also several speculative biographical films about his life, including Shakespeare in Love and a PBS series called In Search of Shakespeare.

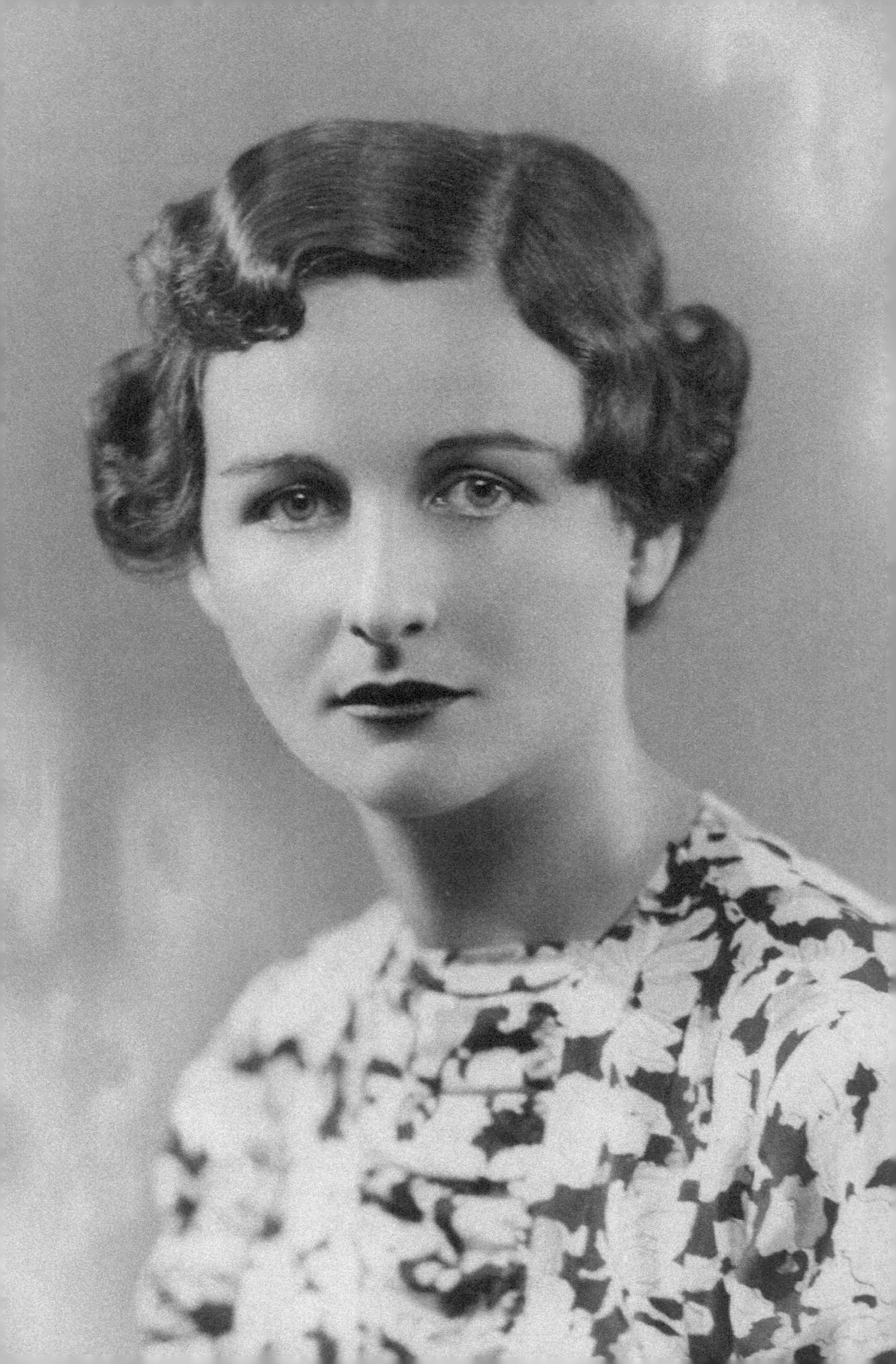

NANCY MITFORD
Chronicler of Aristocratic Decline

Key Facts

- Born 1904, died 1973
- Wrote numerous semi-autobiographical novels of aristocratic life
- Lived in France and wrote several biographies of French historical figures

Nancy Mitford was a British aristocrat who lived in the turbulent first half of the 20th century and chronicled through her novels the lives of her fellow aristocrats. She spent much of her adult life in France.

Nancy Mitford was born on the 28th of November, 1904, into a life of privilege. Her father, David Bertram Ogilvy Freeman-Mitford, was of noble British stock with a family that dated back to Norman times and was connected through marriages to the Royal Family, Winston Churchill, and the Dukes of Bedford. He had run a tea-plantation in Ceylon and fought in the Boer War but had returned seriously wounded and married Sydney Bowles, at the beginning of 1904. He was now the manager of The Lady, a magazine for the upper classes owned by his father-in-law, who also owned Vanity Fair. This dowry did not suit him, however, and at the outbreak of World War I, he returned to the military. After the war, on the death of his father, he became Lord Redesdale and took a seat in the House of Lords.

When Nancy was born, her mother proposed to raise her without being corrected or spoken to in anger, but of course, the responsibility for this rather bizarre notion fell to her nanny, who did all the actual raising. When Nancy's sister Pamela was born just before her third birthday, Nanny understandably began to favor the new baby, which created serious enmity towards Pamela from the now thoroughly spoiled Nancy, who was prone to red-faced rages whenever she was thwarted. She spent a few months at a day school, but the rest of her education was home-schooling with a series of governesses. Her childhood was spent in a manner typical of the time for her class, with summers in their country house at High Wycombe, Buckinghamshire, and the rest of the year in the family home in Kensington, London.

The family expanded rapidly to six daughters and a son. The girls were collectively referred to as the Mitford Sisters, and Nancy, as the oldest, seems to have ruled the nursery with a combination of violence and intimidation that went largely unchecked. In 1921, now 17, she boarded for almost a year at Hatherop Castle, a finishing school for future debutantes. While there, she traveled to Paris, Florence, and Venice and was stimulated by the experience and by the art she saw.

For her eighteenth birthday in 1922, she had a sumptuous 'coming-out' ball followed the next summer by a formal introduction to the court of King George V. These traditions marked her entry into adult society and allowed her to attend the numerous debutante balls and events of the London Season. She was part of the Bright Young Things, a devil-may-care group that included John Betjamin and Cecil Beaton and who were satirized in Evelyn Waugh's novel Vile Bodies. Nancy and Evelyn became friends for life, and it was Evelyn who advised her to 'catch a better man' than her first remarkably foppish boyfriend, Hamish St Clair Erskine. Nancy's father objected to all her male friends, but especially to Hamish.

In 1926 all the girls were sent to Paris for three months while a change in the family home took place, and this started for Nancy a life-long love affair with France. This would have seemed strange to her father, for whom Frogs were just one step above Huns.

In 1930 after writing some anonymous contributions to the society columns, Nancy was hired to write a regular column for The Lady, her father's old magazine. Her talent must have played a considerable part in her selection for the position. Her first novel, Highland Fling, was published to a muted reception in 1931. It, and her second novel Christmas Pudding, which was published the following year, used thinly-disguised versions of her friends to tell of the clash between the Bright Young Things and their parent's generation – so thinly disguised that her mother was outraged.

Despite several offers of marriage, Nancy remained true to her love for Hamish until in 1933 he told her he was marrying someone else. Within a month, she announced her engagement to Peter Rodd, and by the end of the year, they were married and living in a house in Strand-on-the-Green, Chiswick, West London.

In 1932 her sister Diana had deserted her husband to become the mistress of Sir Oswald Mosley, leader of the British Union of Fascists. In 1934 Nancy wrote Wigs on the Green, a satire of Mosley and his Blackshirts. Like her other sisters, Nancy had briefly flirted with fascism but rapidly turned against it. Her sister, Unity, appears in a very unflattering role in the novel as "Eugenia Malmains". The family split over fascism, with Nancy's father, her mother, sisters Diana and Unity all attended the Nuremberg Rally in 1938 and meeting Adolf Hitler, with who Diana and Unity were already friends. Lord Redesdale made speeches in the House of Lords in support of German demands and strongly in favor of Neville Chamberlain's policy of appeasement towards Germany.

In 1937 sister Jessica eloped with a communist who had fought in the Spanish Civil War. Although now married only in name to Peter Rodd, Nancy joined him in the south of France to work with refugees from the war in Spain, where what she saw strengthened her anti-fascist views.

At the outbreak of war, Lord Redesdale quickly reverted to his earlier anti-German position and became a patriot, but Nancy's mother stayed loyal to the fascists and on the day war was declared Unity, swearing her love for Hitler, attempted suicide, which left her permanently brain-damaged. Diana was imprisoned along with Mosley for the duration of the war. The family split into two factions, with Nancy, her sister Jessica and brother Thomas on one side with their father, and their mother, Unity, and Diana on the other. Thomas was killed in the war in 1945, and Lord Redesdale retreated to a remote property of the west coast of Scotland in a permanent state of grief.

Nancy's fourth novel, a comedy about spying called Pigeon Pie, published in 1940, was not well received by a public who saw nothing to laugh about in the war. 1940 was also the year Nancy suffered a second miscarriage. As the war came to a close, she wrote The Pursuit of Love, another thinly-disguised novel about her family, which finally hit the right note with the public and sold 200,000 copies in the first year. Its themes of upper-class life and romance provided an antidote to the harsh realities of a Britain crippled by a long and devastating war.

In 1946, her marriage now completely over, but still on amicable terms with her husband, Nancy moved to Paris to be with Gaston Palewski, with whom she had been having an affair since 1942 when she met him in London. Palewski was a French Colonel attached to General de Gaulle's London office, and for the rest of her life, she lived in Paris in her own apartment near Palewski. Her writing was interspersed with a busy social life, summers in Venice, and trips to England to see her family. Her next novel, Love in a Cold Climate, was published in 1948 as a sequel to The Pursuit of Love. It proved an even greater success. During this period, she also had a successful West End play with her translation of André Roussin's La petite hutte and started a regular column in the Sunday Times. Her next novel, in 1951, was a Parisian romance called The Blessing. She also wrote a non-fictional biography of Madame de Pompadour.

In an article on the British Aristocracy in 1955, Mitford used the terms "U" and "Non-U," which had been first used by a University of Birmingham professor of linguistics to describe the different speech patterns of the British classes. The term caught the public imagination and is widely associated with Mitford. Her writing on the subject was used in Noblesse Oblige, a compilation of several writers on the subject of snobbery, which was widely studied in England as the post-war society struggled to establish new, or re-establish old, social divisions.

Mitford continued writing through various personal upheavals. Her relationship with Palewski faded, at least for him, and they saw less and less of each other. Her mother died in 1963, and her friend

Evelyn Waugh died in 1966, causing her real grief. Her books during this period included Voltaire in Love and The Sun King, as well as another novel with some of her familiar characters, Don't Tell Alfred.

With her health failing, she moved from Paris to a house in Versailles, where she completed Frederick the Great in 1970. In 1972 she was made a Chevalier of the Légion d'Honneur, and a Commander of the Order of the British Empire. She died of cancer on the 30th of June, 1973.

Her Legacy

Still read today, Mitford's novels paint a vivid picture of the life of the British aristocracy when its influence was strong and before death-duties pushed most estates into the hands of the National Trust. Her non-fiction created a style of popular historical biography that remains popular.

Sites to Visit

- There is an English Heritage blue plaque at Heywood Hill bookshop in Curzon Street, where Nancy worked during World War II.

Further Research

All of her important novels and biographes are still in print.

Biographies of Mitford include:

- Nancy Mitford, by Selina Hastings (2012)
- Nancy Mitford: The Biography Edited from Nancy Mitford's Letters, by Nancy Mitford and Harold Acton (2012)
- The Sisters: The Saga of the Mitford Family, by Mary S. Lovell (2003)

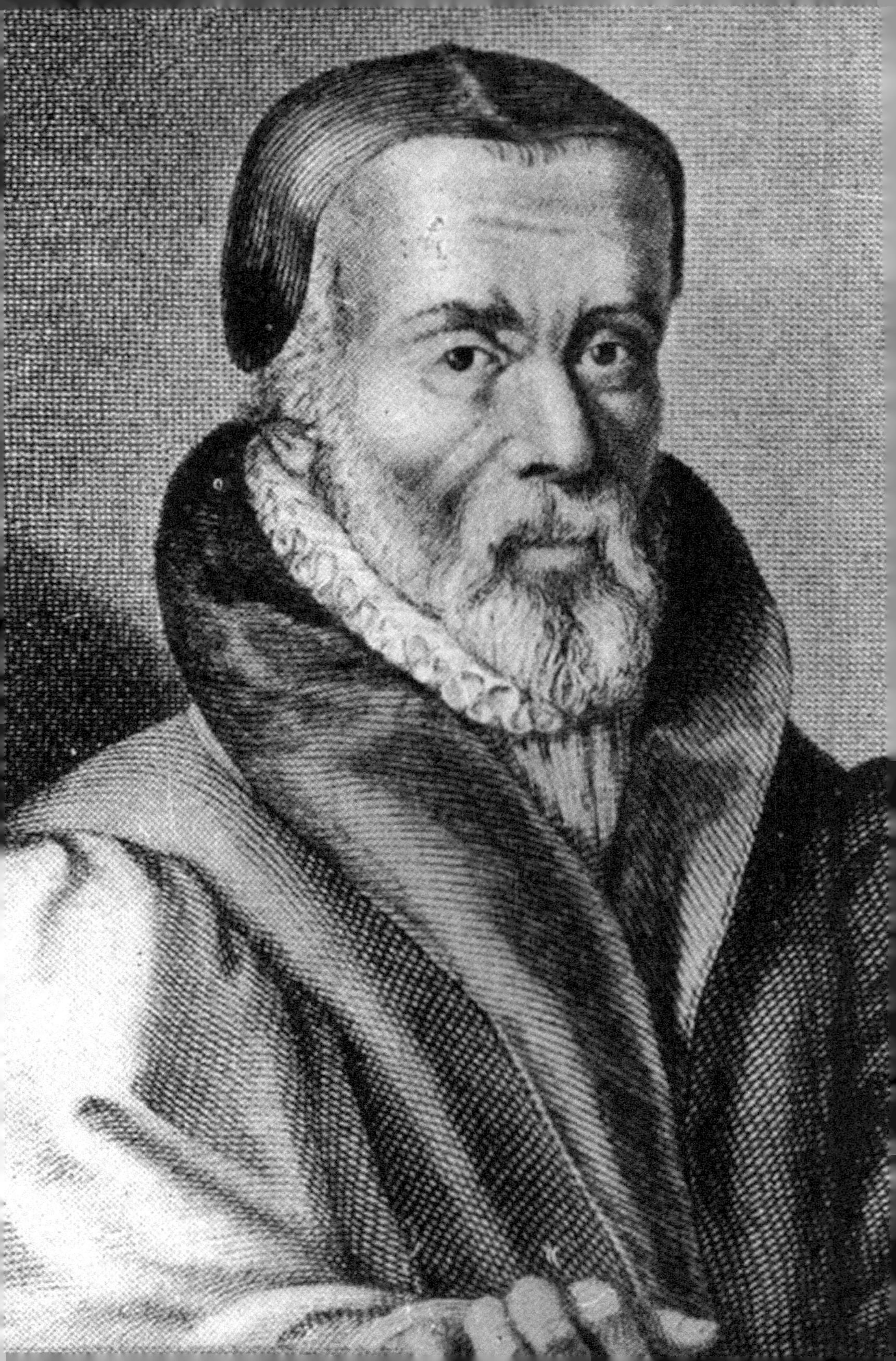

WILLIAM TYNDALE
Translator of the Bible

Key Facts

- Born 1494, died October 6, 1536
- The first person to translate the Bible into English
- Condemned as a heretic and burned at the stake

In the history of England, there has been a no more contentious issue than that of religion and its role in the state and the life of individuals. From the Christianization of Britain in the 7th century until the formation of the Anglican Church by Henry VIII in 1538, the country was entirely Catholic. The struggle between Catholics and Anglicans lasted from 1538 until the restoration of the Monarchy in 1660, with the bloody Civil War hardening the lines between those who broadly accepted the traditional teaching of the Church (minus the authority of the Pope in the case of Anglicans) and those who sought deeper reform.

A key issue was access to the Scriptures by ordinary people. For historic reasons, the Bible was written in Hebrew and Greek, and these languages were only understood by a small educated elite, chiefly in the priesthood. So all biblical knowledge passed through the filter of the Church, and dissidents became increasingly frustrated with this. With the development of Protestantism in Germany by Marin Luther at the beginning of the 16th century, pressure for direct vernacular access to the Scriptures grew.

As Protestantism took hold in Northern Europe, an Englishman called William Tyndall arrived in Wittenberg, Germany.

Tyndall had been born around 1492 in Gloucestershire to a family that seems to have been at the lower end of the nobility and the upper end of the gentry. William's brother had, for example, been knighted, and the family was probably descended from a Baron.

Tyndall had attended Oxford from 1506 to 1515, graduating with a Master of Arts. Although this qualified him to go on to study theology, Tyndale was unhappy that much of that study was of the Ancients such as Aristotle and Plato rather than direct Bible study. Since the Church had taken on the task of controlling all knowledge, this study was designed to continue the propagation of 'correct' views in Astronomy, Natural History, and so on, but Tyndale considered it inappropriate and irrelevant.

He spent 1517 to 1521 at Cambridge University, becoming a gifted linguist and fluent in French, German, Italian, Spanish, Latin, Greek, and Hebrew, as well as English.

He became private chaplain to a Sir John Walsh but quickly found himself in trouble with the Church for pressing the supremacy of the Biblical text over Papal edicts and for wishing to make it possible for, in his words, the boy that driveth the plough, to be able to directly learn Christianity from the Bible.

In 1523 he went to London to argue his case for an English-language version of the Bible but could find no support. So rejected, he headed for Germany, where he expected to meet a warmer reception. There he immediately began to translate the New Testament into English, completing the work by 1525.

These were turbulent times, and it was a year later before he was able to find a printer in the city of Worms, a free-city adopting Lutheranism and, therefore, free of Catholic interference. Copies of his translation were smuggled into England where they were quickly condemned; booksellers warned not to sell them and copies publicly burned. By 1529 Tyndale had been publicly declared a heretic by no less a figure than Cardinal Wolsey, a close religious adviser to the Royal Court and instrumental in forming the Church of England a few years later. Tyndale held several other heretical views, including not praying to saints and the mortality of the soul, which must have strengthened the case against him.

Tyndale moved to Antwerp and began work on a translation of the Old Testament. When he heard of Henry VIII's intention to divorce Catherine of Aragon and marry Anne Boleyn with the support of Cardinal Wolsey, he wrote a tract – The Practice of Prelates – condemning the King's decision as a violation of scripture.

Not known for a calm temperament, Henry VIII was furious and attempted to have Emperor Charles V, who had jurisdiction in Antwerp, extradite Tyndale back to England for trial. The Emperor declined. However, this respite was to be short-lived as a plot was developed – by whom we do not know, to ingratiate a man called Henry Phillips into Tyndale's confidence. Phillips seems to have been in need of money for gambling debts, so his motive seems clear. He was able to lure Tyndale out of his safe location, and in May 1535, he was seized by soldiers of the Emperor, imprisoned, and a trial for heresy planned.

Tyndale had been transferred to the Castle of Vilvorde in present-day Belgium, which was the main prison for the area. Finally, in August 1536, his trial began. He was found guilty and executed. The official date of his execution is October 6, 1536, but there is some dispute that it may have been some weeks earlier. He was strangled with a noose - which was actually considered an act of mercy - and then burned at the stake.

Ironically, four years later, Henry VIII published versions of the Bible in English, including his Great Bible, which was to be read aloud in the newly-formed churches of the Church of England. These translations followed those of Tyndale closely. Of course, the King had not forgiven Tyndale, merely done what was expedient to create the new Church he needed to sanction his divorce and re-marriage.

His Legacy

Tyndale's New Testament formed the basis of numerous future translations, the most famous being the King James Version of 1611, which owes much to Tyndale for phrases it used.

Such everyday expressions as a moment in time; in the twinkling of an eye; eat, drink and be merry; let there be light; the spirit is willing, but the flesh is weak; signs of the times; the powers that be, and many others widely used, were all first coined by Tyndale.

Tyndale is considered a martyr by Protestants, and it was the reading of the Bible in English perhaps more than anything else that produced the multitude of Puritan sects that led to the English Civil War and the settlement of America.

Sites to Visit

- In Vilvoorde, Belgium, there is a memorial and a small museum to Tyndale.
- There is a statue of Tyndale in the Victoria Embankment Gardens in London and another in Millennium Square, Bristol.
- There is a stained-glass window in the chapel of Hertford College, Oxford.
- There is a monument on a hill above North Nibley, Gloucestershire, where Tyndale is reputed to have been born.

Further Research

- Tyndale's Bible can be read on-line.
- There is a film, God's Outlaw: The Story of William Tyndale (1986) and another in cartoon form. Torch-lighters: The William Tyndale Story, (2005).
- There are documentaries about Tyndale, including William Tyndale: Man with a Mission (2005), William Tyndale: His Life, His Legacy (2003), and The Most Dangerous Man in Tudor England (2013).

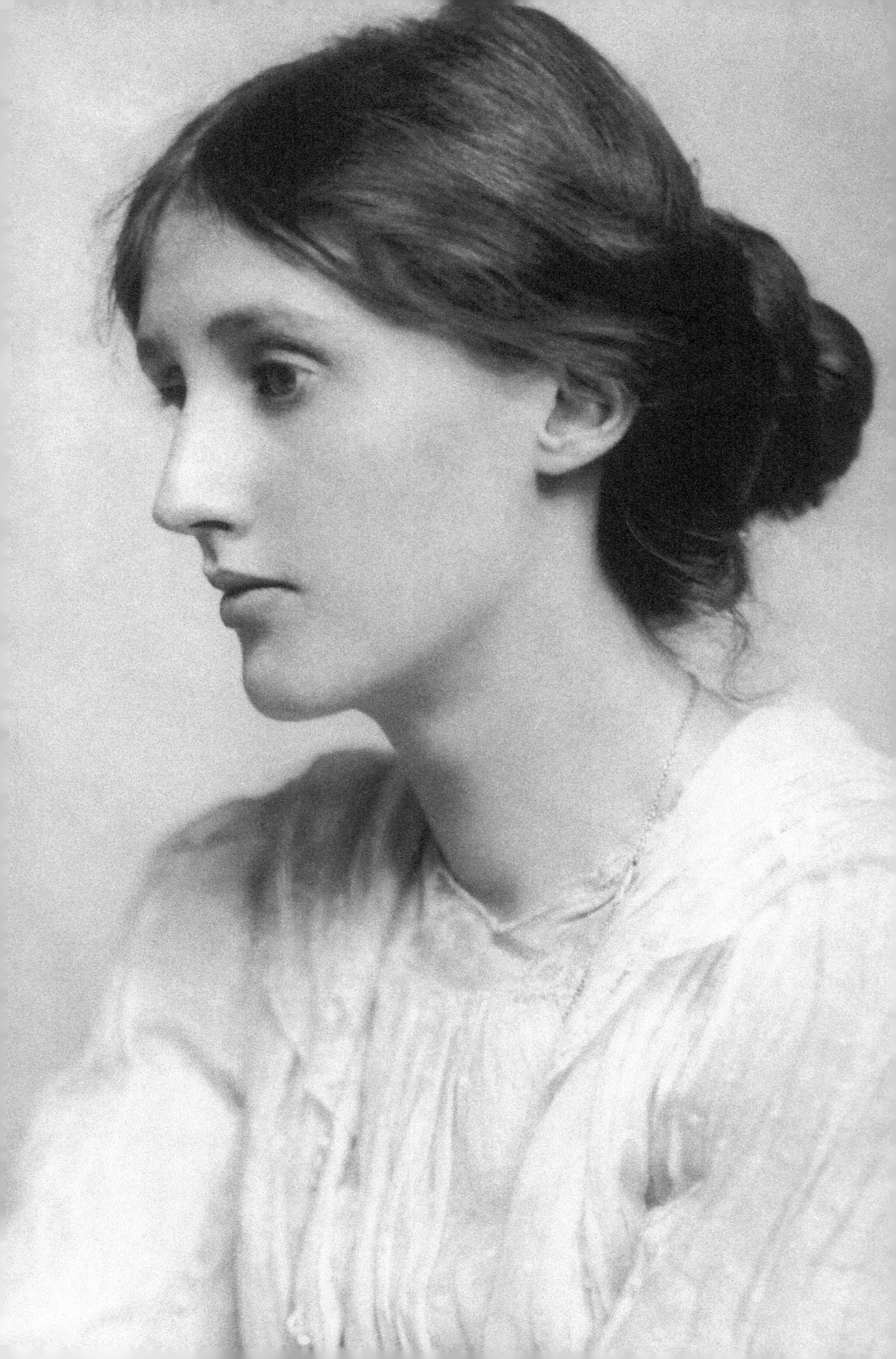

VIRGINIA WOOLF
Pioneering Feminist Writer

Key Facts

- Born 1882 – died 1941
- Early writer of 'stream of consciousness' novels
- Founded the Hogarth Press
- Supporter of feminism and female authors

The end of the 19th century, and the early decades of the 20th, were times of great social upheaval. Virginia Woolf lived her life during those times, and her writing helped bring the modern world into existence. Sufficiently privileged to almost always have the 'money and a room of her own' to write, Virginia Woolf is often credited with conceiving the modern novel, with its emphasis on interior processes, rather than narrative. Since the 1970s, she has been embraced as a founder of feminism, and she has been taken as a role-model by many. Widely admired but also condemned as a snob and elitist, she remains influential far beyond her literary output.

Adeline Virginia Woolf was born on the 25th of January 1882 into the upper echelons of British intellectual society. While country lords had held sway in earlier times, as the Victorian era drew to a close, a wealthy class, connected to, but not part of, the aristocracy had developed. Funded by industry and the colonies, many members of this elite were of literary persuasion. Virginia's family was certainly so. Her mother, Julia's family, were Anglo-Indian – British expatriates who lived and built their fortunes in colonial

India – but she had numerous relatives connected with the art world, including a great-aunt who modeled for the Pre-Raphaelite painter Edward Burns-Jones. Others were early photographers or held fashionable salons for artists and writers. Her father, Leslie Stephen, was also an intellectual and had married the daughter of the writer William Makepeace Thackeray.

Julia's barrister husband died after just three years of marriage, leaving her with three children. Before his death, they had been friends with the Stephens family, and Julia was present when Leslie Stephen's wife Minnie died in childbirth. Julia invited Leslie to live next door to her so that his baby daughter could have the companionship of her own children. They were united in a shared agnosticism, a relatively rare lack of belief for the times, born from the bitterness of loss. After several years of close friendship, they married in 1879 and had four children, including Virginia. The family lived in Julia's house, 22 Hyde Park Gate, a quiet street a short distance from the recently-built Royal Albert Hall.

Virginia's childhood was occupied with the usual trappings of the Victorian middle-class, with frequent walks in nearby Hyde Park and summer trips to Cornwall, including visits to the Godrevy Lighthouse. Those trips would form the basis for novels such as To the Lighthouse, written in 1927. The production of an 'in-house' journal called Hyde Park Gate News also occupied the time for young Virginia and her sister Vanessa. With literary parents, and her father's connections to the Thackeray family, visits by notable writers of the time were common, and all the children were exposed to an intense literary and intellectual upbringing. Both parents disapproved of formal education for girls, so they educated their daughters in a dedicated space at the back of the drawing room.

In 1895 Julia Stephen died of influenza, and on the Isle of Wight, where the family went for the summer to avoid the memories of Cornwall, Virginia suffered her first nervous breakdown. After her mother's death, Virginia and Vanessa were enrolled in the Ladies' Department of King's College London, learning Greek, Latin, German, and history. Several of the teachers were politically active, and she was exposed to ideas of women's suffrage and the movement for higher education for women. In 1902 her father became ill, spending two years as an invalid before passing away, leaving Virginia bereft again. University was barred to her as a woman, but the attendance at Cambridge by her half-brother Thoby would become life-changing for Virginia. At Trinity College, he befriended a group of young intellectuals, who formed a reading group. Virginia was introduced to his circle at the Trinity May Ball in 1900.

After the death of their father, the children wanted to escape the oppressive atmosphere of Hyde Park Gate, filled with relatives and the memories of their parents. They traveled first to Wales and then to France and Italy. It was during this time that Virginia began to see her destiny as a writer, but in May 1904, she suffered another nervous breakdown and attempted suicide.

22 Hyde Park Gate was sold, as it was the principal family asset at this time, and the Stephen's children, now in their early 20s, moved to 46 Gordon Square in Bloomsbury, a bohemian neighborhood a considerable social distance from bourgeois South Kensington. They immediately began to entertain Thoby's Cambridge circle, which had expanded to include numerous artists and writers of the period, as well as the economist John Maynard Keynes. At Gordon Square, they were called the 'Thursday Club,' but as the circle grew, it became the Bloomsbury Group, an influential network of the Edwardian avant-garde. Members included Clive Bell, Lytton Strachey, Leonard Woolf, Rupert Brooke, E. M. Forster, Saxon Sydney-Turner, Duncan Grant, David Garnett, and Roger Fry, A roll call of British art and literature greats of the early 20th century.

Virginia began to teach at Morley College, an adult-education and theatre school for working people, but tragedy was waiting in the wings again. Thoby died, just 26, of typhoid fever. Her sister Vanessa married Clive Bell, and Virginia and her brother Adrian moved to a new house in the adjacent neighborhood of Fitzrovia. The house, 29 Fitzroy Square, had been occupied previously by George Bernard Shaw. The Thursday Club moved with them. Virginia began writing her first novel, called 'Melymbrosia' but published as The Voyage Out (1915). Rivalry with Vanessa emerged, and her flirtation with Clive Bell, reciprocated by him, led to the breakdown of the marriage.

In 1911 Virginia and Adrian, with John Maynard Keynes, Duncan Grant, and Leonard Woolf, took a house together at 38 Brunswick

Square, back in Bloomsbury. The next year Leonard Woolf and Virginia married, and since Woolf was basically 'a penniless Jew', in Virginia's words, they moved into a small flat. Several moves followed over the years; first to Richmond, then back to Bloomsbury, settling for a time at 52 Tavistock Square. Looking for a source of income, and with an interest in bookbinding that had begun when she was 19, Virginia and Leonard founded 'Hogarth Press,' starting with the printing press in their dining room. They used the company to publish Virginia's novels, as well as other new and unconventional authors such as T.S. Eliot and Laurens van der Post, and contemporary artists, including Dora Carrington and Vanessa Bell. Virginia dreamt of the Press becoming a community of women writers. She and Leonard had an international outlook and introduced Maxim Gorky to British readers. Politically they were pacifists and Fabian socialists.

Virginia met the gardener and successful writer Vita Sackville-West in 1922. Vita built a still-famous garden at Sissinghurst. They became very close, with Vita, more successful at the time, encouraging Virginia in her work and trying to build her self-confidence. Vita was well-known for her female lovers, although she only rarely bedded Virginia, who, in turn, boasted of relationships with other women over the years. None of this took away Leonard's boundless support, which continued long after her death, with him defending her as her fame grew.

More practically, Vita gave her books to Hogarth Press for publication, and their success took the company into the black and provided financial stability. Even before she married, Virginia had rented a cottage in Sussex as a retreat, and she and Leonard used it, and another rented house, Asham House, to escape London and for Virginia to write. With more financial stability, they bought the Round House in Lewes but soon sold it to buy Monk's House in the village of Rodmell. In 1940, after their London house was bombed in the Blitz, they moved permanently to Sussex.

Throughout her life, Vita suffered breakdowns and depressions of varying intensities. It has been suggested that these were the result of sexual abuse by her half-brothers, and she may have been bipolar. Sometimes she was institutionalized, and one doctor diagnosed 'excessive education' as the cause of her illness. In 1941, after completing her last novel, Between the Acts, she fell into a deep depression. When Leonard joined the Home Guard, she felt he was betraying their pacifist principles. On the morning of the 28th of March 1941, she filled her coat pockets with stones and walked into the River Ouse, which ran near their home. Her body was not recovered for three weeks, and Leonard buried her ashes beneath a tree in the garden.

Sites to Visit

There are Blue Plaques marking houses at:

- 22 Hyde Park Gate, South Kensington, London
- 29 Fitzroy Square, Fitzrovia, London
- Hogarth House, 34 Paradise Road, Richmond, London
- Round House, Pipe Passage, Lewes, East Sussex
- Monk's House, Rodmell, East Sussex
- There is a bust of Virginia Woolf in Tavistock Square, London.
- There is a plaque on the Virginia Woolf Building, King's College, Queensway, London.

Further Research

Selected Novels

- The Voyage Out (1915)
- Mrs. Dalloway (1925)
- To the Lighthouse (1927)
- Orlando (1928)
- The Waves (1931)
- Between the Acts (1941)
- Non-Fiction
- A Room of One's Own (1933) – feminist literary criticism
- Three Guineas (1938) – an indictment of fascism
- A Writer's Diary (1953, ed. Leonard Woolf)

Collections of Virginia Woolf's diaries and letters are also available.

Biographies

- Virginia Woolf: A Biography, by Quentin Bell, 1974
- Virginia Woolf, by Hermione Lee 1999
- Virginia Woolf: An Inner Life, by Julia Briggs, 2005
- Virginia Woolf, by Alexandra Harris, 2011

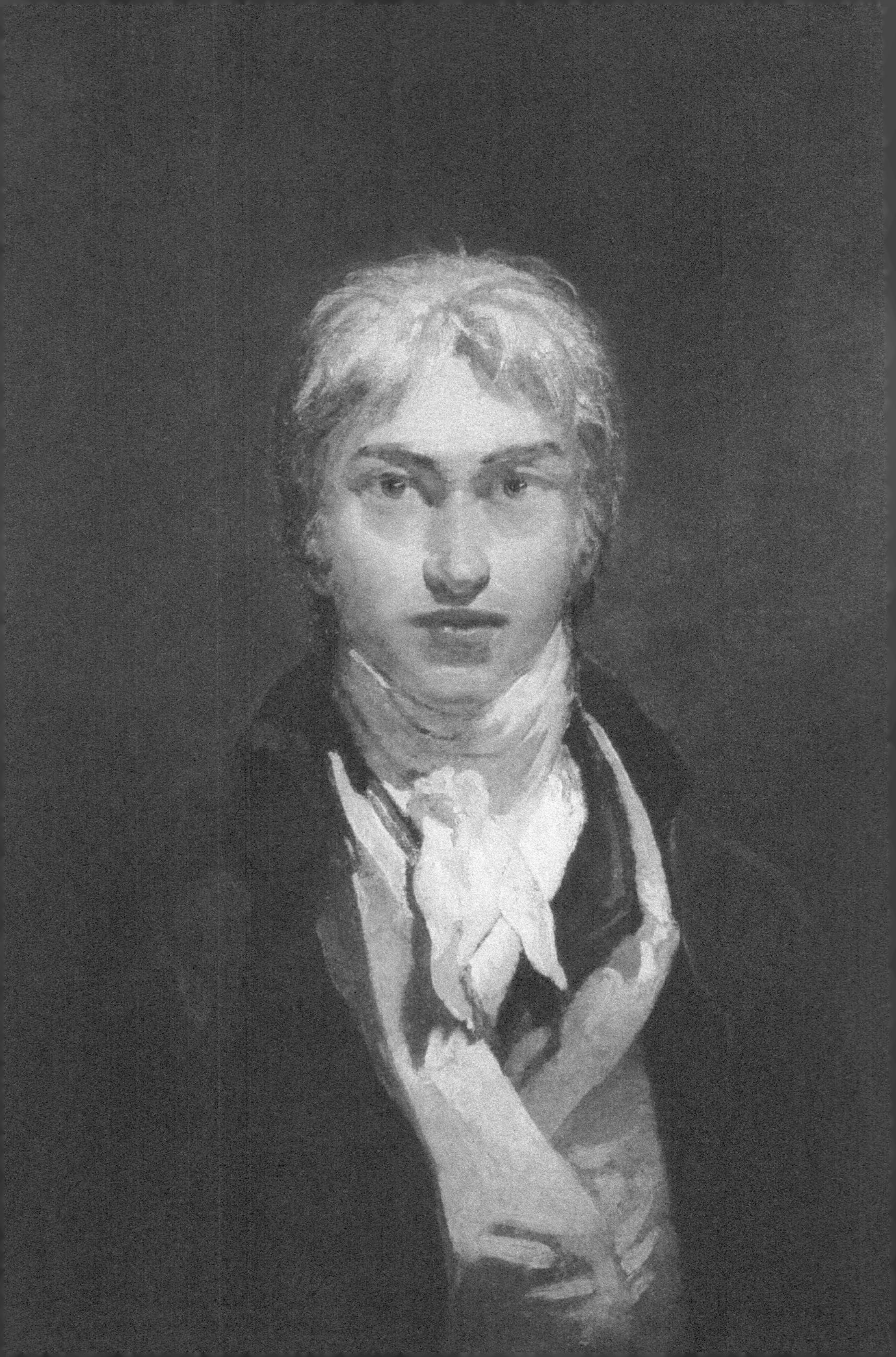

J. M. W. TURNER
Painter of Light

Key Facts

- Born 1775, died 1851
- A prolific artist, leaving 550 oils and 2,000 watercolors
- Became wealthy because or in spite of creating revolutionary art
- Considered Britain's greatest artist
- Presaged the Impressionists and even abstract art

The painter J.M.W. Turner was a prolific and brilliant artist, often called the 'painter of light,' who revolutionized landscape painting and set the stage for Impressionism and the development of abstract art. He became very wealthy from his work and increasingly eccentric. He never married but had two daughters from one lover and lived for many years with another.

There is a strong belief that revolutionary artists are 'outsiders,' battling the Establishment and dying in poverty, only to have their work finally appreciated by future generations. So the life of Joseph Mallord William Turner may seem a little abnormal since he was revolutionary and generations ahead of his times, while a favorite of the Establishment, enjoying the patronage of the rich and accumulating a large personal fortune.

Turner was probably born on the 23rd of April, 1775, he always claimed so, but there are no official records until his baptism on the 14th of May. His father was a wigmaker and barber in the modern sense – the traditional right to also be a doctor had been lost to barbers in 1745 in the UK. His mother came from a family of butchers. His only sibling died in infancy, leaving the young Joseph an only-child. His mother suffered from mental illness, so Turner was sent to live with the family of an uncle, in Brentford, a small town west of London, and from there to Margate, in coastal Kent. His uncle then moved to Sunningwell, just south of Oxford.

As a child, he was already drawing, and painting and his father was proudly selling his work in his shop. His works from this time were primarily drawings of buildings, and his father took him to Thomas Malton, the younger, an eminent architectural draftsman, to learn perspective. Turner always referred to Malton as his "real master." He was also taught and encouraged by Dr. Thomas Monro, the head doctor of Bethlem Royal Hospital ('Bedlam') and also a gifted amateur water-colorist and pupil of the landscape painter John Laporte. Monro supported several artists in his 'Monro circle,' who gathered at his home every Tuesday evening. Turner's mother was to later become a resident of Bedlam.

When he was 14, he went to study at the Royal Academy of Art, and a year later, he was accepted as a probationary member. He studied in the manner of the time by drawing first from plaster casts of famous pieces of sculpture and then from life-models. He continued to work for architects and was interested in continuing in architecture. The eminent architect Thomas Hardwick was an early employer, and it was Hardwick who advised him to focus on painting and made the point by purchasing some of his early works.

In 1790, still only 15, Turner had his first piece exhibited – a watercolor at the Royal Academy Summer Exhibition, an event that continues today. During his student years, he developed a working pattern that would continue for his life. In summer, he would travel, chiefly on foot and at that time mostly to Wales, doing pencil sketches for works he would then do in the studio during the winter. His watercolor The Rising Squall - Hot Wells from St Vincent's Rock, Bristol, from 1793, shows the first inkling of the dramatic use of light that was to characterize his future work. His early work caused a sensation, and by the age of 26, he was elected a full member of the Royal Academy.

He traveled in Europe, painting, and received patronage, which generally consisted of a combination of commissions and status as a semi-permanent house-guest from wealthy families across the country. His work sold well, and he became wealthy enough to purchase several homes, his chief one on Harley Street in London, with a special top-floor studio added and another for his mistress, Sophia Caroline Booth, on Cheney Walk, Chelsea. He had met the widow Sophia in 1820 while staying at her boarding house in Margate, Kent.

Turner had few friends or intimates, and his only other relationship besides Sophia had been an earlier one with Hannah Danby, his housekeeper and the daughter of a widow called Sarah Danby, who was for many years assumed to be the mother of Turner's two daughters. It seems more likely that the children, born in 1801 and 1811, were, in fact, Hannah's.

As he became older, he became more depressed, eccentric, and isolated, living mostly at Sophia's house in Chelsea, where he died on the 19th of December, 1851.

His Legacy

From an early time, Turner had fallen under the philosophical influence of Sir Joshua Reynolds, founder of the Royal Academy. Reynolds taught that art was akin to poetry and should attempt to transcend form and capture the essence of things, in the tradition of Plato's Theory of Forms as revived during the Renaissance. Turner's concentration on light at the expense of form was not simply abstraction but an attempt to capture on canvas the metaphysical, supported by his dying words that "the Sun is God." He freely altered scenes to capture the essence of his vision, and many of his pictures have little resemblance to the places they are named after.

His work presaged the Impressionists by decades, and he is still today considered to be the greatest British artist ever. The important art prize – the Turner Prize, has been organized by the Tate Gallery since 1984.

Sites to Visit

- There is a plaque at his birthplace, 21 Maiden Lane, Covent Garden.
- His house on 64 Harley Street was destroyed during the Blitz, but Sophia's house and the place of his death, now 118 and 119, Cheyne Walk, Chelsea, can still be seen.
- Statues of Turner can be seen at St Paul's Cathedral, the Royal Academy of Arts, and the Victoria & Albert Museum.

Further Research

Biographies of J.M.W. Turner include:

- Standing in the Sun: A Life of J.M.W. Turner, by Anthony Bailey (2014)
- Turner in His Time, Revised and Updated Edition, by Andrew Wilton (2007)
- J.M.W. Turner: Painting Set Free, by David Blayney Brown

and Amy Concannon (2014)
- J.M.W. Turner: A Biography, by Howard Brinkley (2014)

Other Media:

There was a biographic play, The Painter, by Rebecca Lenkiewicz, performed in London in 2011.

There is a film, Mr. Turner, released in 2014, depicting his later life.

Where to see his work:

- When Turner died, he left his works to the Nation to be displayed in one place, but that wish was never carried out. Today the bulk of his work is split between the Tate Gallery and the National Gallery, both in London.
- Turner's works in the US can be seen at the Frick Collection, The New York Public Library and the Metropolitan Museum of Art in New York City, the National Gallery in Washington, the Art Institute of Chicago, and the Yale Centre for British Art.
- The vast majority of his works can also be seen on-line in high-definition images.

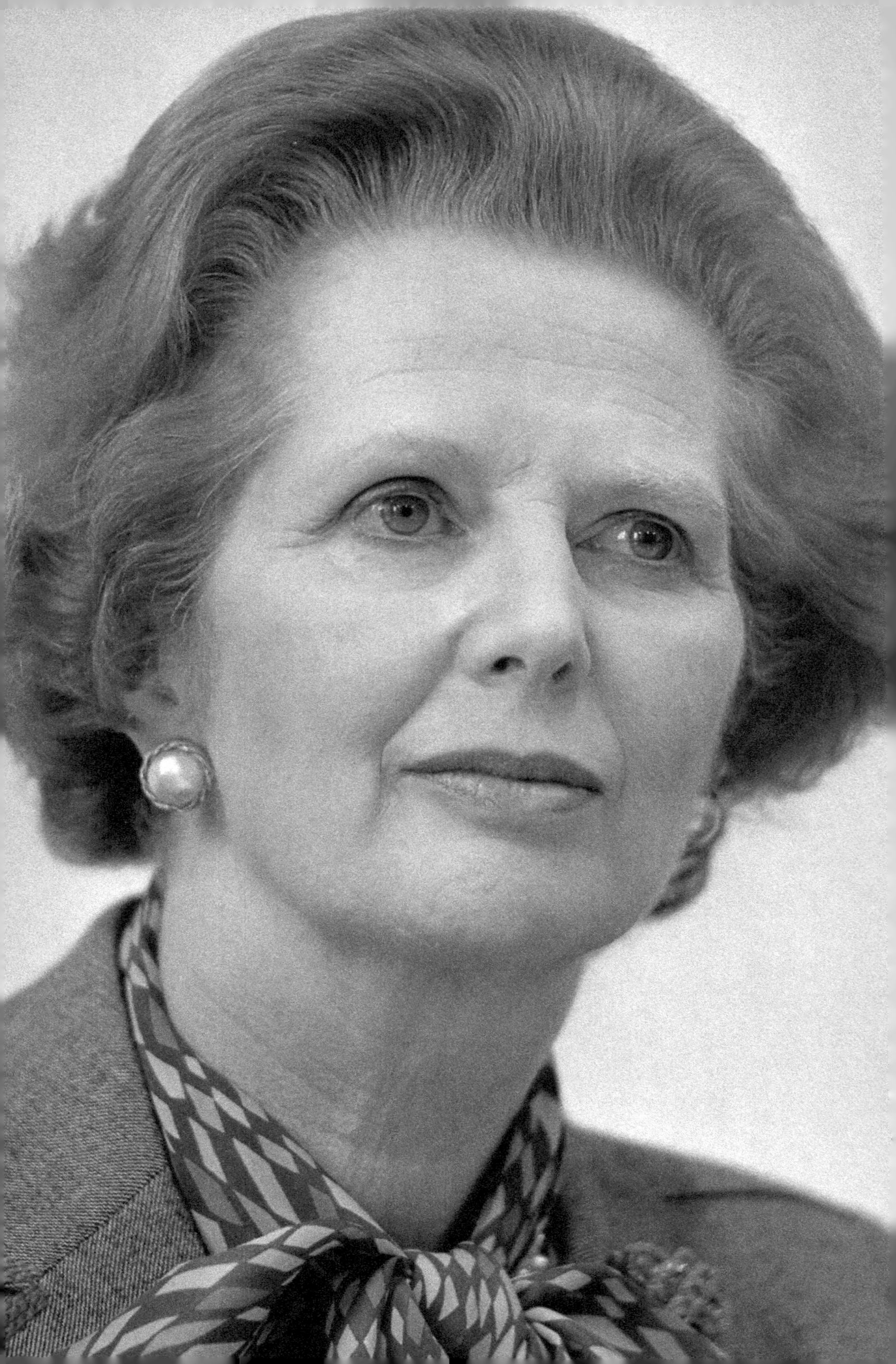

MARGARET THATCHER
The Iron Lady

Key Facts

- Born 1925 – died 2013
- Britain's first and only female Prime Minister
- Transformed the political landscape of Britain with her policies of 'Thatcherism'
- Attracted both strong support and opposition

Margaret Thatcher was the first and only female British Prime Minister, from 1979 to 1990, and leader of the Conservative Party from 1975. She undertook a radical reform of the British economy and society, dismantling many of the social programs introduced after World War II and introducing neo-liberal economic practices. She weakened the power of organized labor and dramatically increased home ownership by selling social housing. Her policies and political style were highly divisive, ultimately even in her own party, which turned against her to retain power when her popularity declined. The Iron Lady, as she was often called, increased nationalist sentiments in the UK and re-established its position as a world power. She was the most transformative leader in the second half of the 20th century, and her legacy still affects British politics and opinion today.

Margaret Hilda Roberts was born on the 13th of October, 1925, in Grantham, a market town set in the rolling countryside of Lincolnshire. Her father Alfred had two successful grocery shops in the town, and the family lived above one of them. As was typical at that time for clever children of the middle-class, Margaret won a scholarship to the local grammar school and from there won another scholarship to Somerville College, Oxford. This was a women's college founded in the late 19th century, and Margaret studied chemistry, graduating with second-class honors in 1947. Besides science, she had already developed an interest in politics and was President of the Oxford University Conservative Association during her final year. She was strongly influenced by the writings of the Austrian liberal economist F.A. Hayek, who was living in Britain at the time. Hayek was an opponent of government intervention in the economy at a time when the socialist Labour Party had just swept to power in the UK, displacing, among many others, Margaret's father from his position as Mayor of Grantham.

After graduation, and while working as a chemist, she remained active in Conservative politics, and in 1951, through political connections she had made at Oxford, she was invited to become the Conservative Party candidate for the seat of Dartford, Kent. This was considered to be a safe Labour seat, and in the ensuing elections, she did indeed lose to Labour but succeeded in reducing their majority. At a dinner celebrating her nomination, she had met a wealthy, divorced local businessman ten years her senior, called Dennis Thatcher, and less than 12 months later, they were married. Dennis funded a career-switch for Margaret, who took the bar exams, and in 1953 she became a barrister specialized in tax law. In the same year, she gave birth to twins, who kept her out of the political arena until 1959, when she won the safe Conservative seat of Finchley. Her maiden speech was in support of a bill to make local council meetings open to the public, and her first opposition to the official policies of her own party came when she spoke in favor of the return of birching, the British version of flogging.

Margaret Thatcher, as she was now, stood out in her party and soon left the back-benches for a more prominent position, being selected at the end of 1961 by Prime Minister Harold McMillan as a junior minister. The following year she was selected by the American Embassy for a place in the Foreign Leader Program, being described as a potential future prime minister. She spent six weeks in America, meeting such prominent people as Nelson Rockefeller. This trip raised her profile, and shortly after her return, she received a coveted Shadow Cabinet position.

When Edward Heath won the election in 1970, Thatcher entered his cabinet as Secretary of State for Education and Science. One of her first actions was to cut costs by eliminating a program that gave free milk to school children. This unleashed a firestorm of attacks by the Labour Party and the media, almost leading her to leave politics. But she toughed it out and, despite her own grammar school background, played a major part in the conversion of many of them to more open schooling, called comprehensive schools. The 1973 oil embargo, subsequent inflation, and union battles for wage increases brought about the collapse of the Heath government, and in 1974 Labour returned to power. The Conservative Party looked for a replacement leader, and when Thatcher mounted a challenge to Ted Heath, she defeated him, and with the support of the right-wing of her party she became leader in February 1975.

Politically Thatcher was opposed to the welfare state introduced by Labour in the post-World War II period and was a tough political opponent, but she lacked the public appeal needed to win elections, so she underwent what we would today call a makeover, receiving voice coaching to remove her harsh Lincolnshire accent, and changing her hairstyle and clothing habits. She still retained her tough persona, and when a Soviet Russian newspaper dubbed her the 'Iron Lady,' she welcomed the nickname with pride.

The 1970s were a tough time in the UK, with very poor economic conditions, a series of major labor disputes and strikes, and high levels of both unemployment and inflation. When the Labour government lost a confidence vote and had to call an election in 1979, the Conservative Party won a majority, and Thatcher became the UK's first female Prime Minister. Much of the success of the party came from its adoption of some of the anti-immigration rhetoric of its major opponent on the right, the National Front, which collapsed when many of its voters switched to Thatcher. Once in power, she continued her opposition to unchecked immigration, limiting the number of Vietnamese boat-people entering the country to less than 10,000 of the 800,000 who fled their country at that time.

On the economic front, the Thatcher government was the first Western government to embrace neo-liberal policies, and she lowered direct taxes to stimulate demand while cutting government services in education and housing to cope with the resulting fall in government revenue. She famously said that there was no such thing as 'society,' only a group of individuals. Her approval rating quickly fell as the cuts took effect, and when tax revenue fell during the recession of the early 1980's she raised taxes again, going against her own policies and meeting strong opposition from many economists.

At this point, the military junta then in power in Argentina stepped in to unintentionally help. After a long-standing dispute over the ownership of the Falkland Islands, the junta misjudged, and in 1982 seized the islands, thinking that Britain would not intervene. After some hesitation, Thatcher responded with the full force of the British army and navy, quickly defeating Argentina and raised her status dramatically as a successful wartime leader. The victory also had an economic effect, ending the period of 'slumpflation' so that growth with reduced inflation returned, although manufacturing output had fallen 30% and unemployment stubbornly remained at over 3 million. With the opposition in disarray, a quick election was called in 1983, and the Conservatives were returned to power with an increased majority.

It took five more years and the huge revenue gained from the exploitation of the North Sea gas reserves before the economy fully recovered. Throughout her term, Thatcher had lower approval ratings than her party, and in both style and action, she was consistently divisive. A newly-revived Labour Party established a strong lead in the polls, and discontent with her leadership grew within her own party. Towards the end of 1990, the dramatic resignation of her Deputy Prime Minister, Geoffrey Howe, was immediately followed by a leadership challenge from the universally-popular Michael Heseltine, who polls showed could beat Labour. In the ensuing leadership ballot, Thatcher won the first round, but complex rules forced a second ballot, and when Thatcher found she lacked sufficient votes to win it, she resigned rather than face direct defeat. Feeling betrayed, she handed the Queen her resignation and left the official residence at 10 Downing Street in tears. Two years later, the Conservatives won another election under their new leader John Major.

Thatcher had resigned her seat by the time of that 1992 election, aged 66, and she retired to write her memoirs, lecture, and act as a highly-paid consultant to international corporations. She continued to make statements and give interviews challenging or supporting various UK and international policies, and she maintained a hawkish position in international affairs. In 2003 her husband Dennis died. The following year she attended the state funeral of her close friend President Reagan, and in 2005, she celebrated her 80th birthday in the company of the Queen and other establishment figures. However, in that same year, signs of the onset of dementia were apparent to her family, and although she continued to attend official functions at home and abroad - when her health permitted - life became more and more difficult for her. In 2012 she moved into a suite at the Ritz Hotel, and after a stroke, she died on the 8th of April, 2013.

Her Legacy

The many changes introduced by Thatcher during her time as Prime Minister had two purposes – to destroy the socialist welfare system introduced by the Labour Party after World War II and to re-establish Britain as a global power. Her policies quickly became described as Thatcherism and even converted much of the Labour Party, under Tony Blair, to a more moderate version of the same thing. She was highly divisive and still today has trenchant supporters and just as trenchant opponents. When the news of her death was released, there was mourning, but also public celebration.

The global position of Britain today, its relationship with the European Union, the decline of unions, the growth of corporate power, and even the housing bubble are all the direct result of policies introduced by her and continued in large part in the following years.

Sites to Visit

- There is a grave marker in the grounds of the Royal Hospital, Chelsea, where the ashes of her and Dennis are buried.

- There is a bronze statue inside the Houses of Parliament, Westminster.
- There are plans for a Margaret Thatcher Memorial Museum & Library, but construction has not yet begun.

Further Research

- The film The Iron Lady (2011) is a fictionalized account of her life, starring Meryl Streep.
- Season 4 of The Crown covered most of her premiership.
- Thatcher wrote two volumes of autobiography - The Downing Street Years (1993) and The Path to Power (1995). Also available as a single volume: Margaret Thatcher: The Autobiography (2013).

Biographies include:

- Margaret Thatcher: The Authorized Biography (2 volumes), by Charles Moore
- Margaret Thatcher: From Grantham to the Falklands, by Charles Moore
- The Iron Lady: Margaret Thatcher, from Grocer's Daughter to Prime Minister, by John Campbell and David Freeman
- Madam Prime Minister: A Biography of Margaret Thatcher, by Libby Hughes

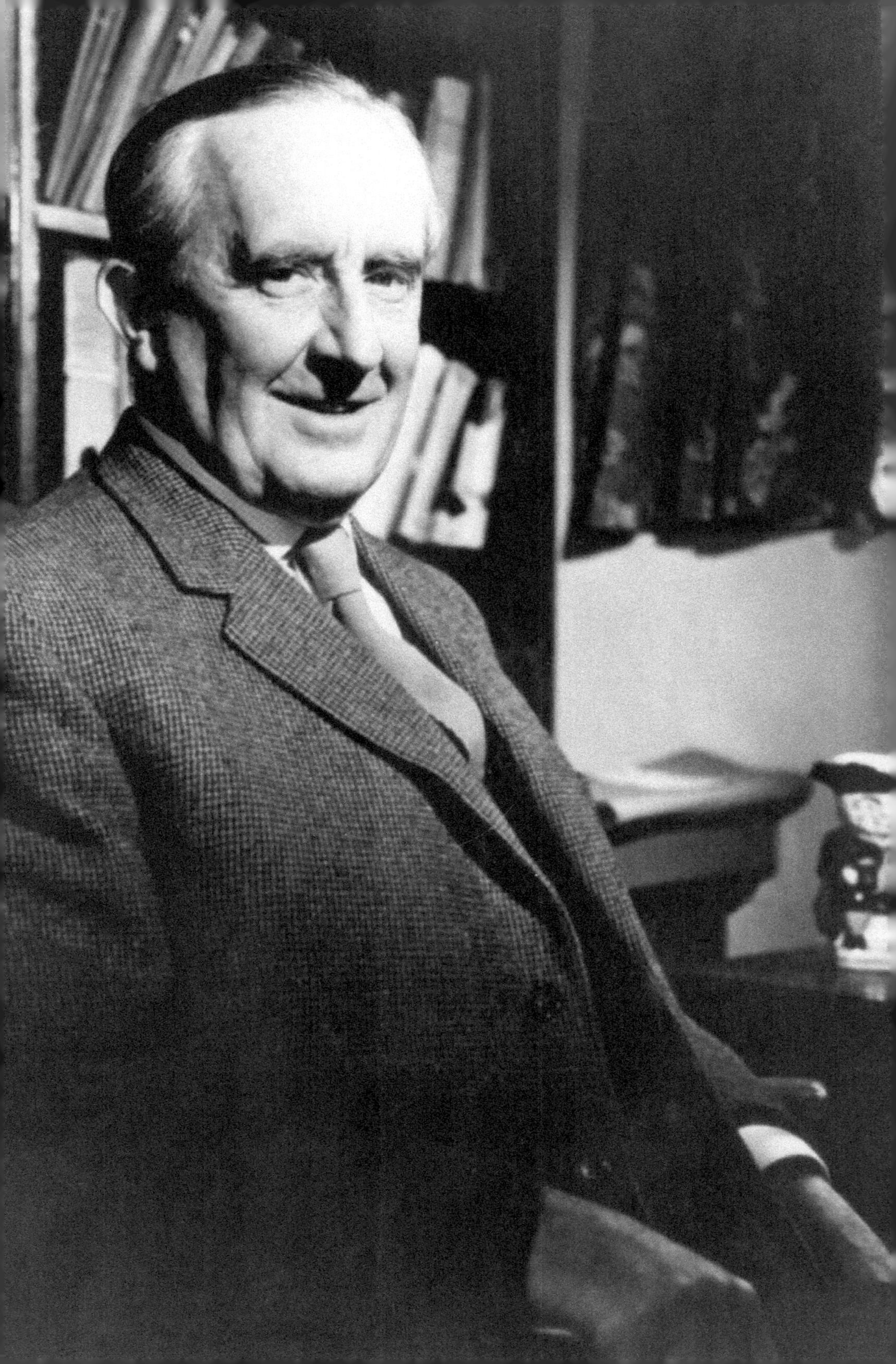

J. R. R. TOLKIEN
Builder of Middle Earth

Key Facts

- Born 1892 – died 1973
- Quiet Oxford don who created the modern fantasy fiction genre
- Wrote The Hobbit, Lord of the Rings, and other fantasy novels
- Lived a quiet life and avoided publicity, preferring to let his work speak for itself

Academic John Ronald Reuel Tolkien was the unlikely author of the most famous fantasy books of the last century, The Hobbit and Lord of the Rings. Born in South Africa and raised in Birmingham, he survived the Battle of the Somme in World War I and became a quietly married professor of English Language at Oxford, where he studied philology, Middle English, and mythology. From his teenage years, he simultaneously lived a parallel private fantasy life of immense proportions, captured in his novels, which created the whole genre of modern fantasy writing and appealed to a wide audience of children and adults. Since his death, an enormous industry has grown up around his work, although it is likely that Tolkien himself would have found much of it highly objectionable.

It was common practice during the days of the British Empire for people to spend time working in the colonies, and that was exactly what Arthur Reuel Tolkien did when he was promoted from clerk to manager of the Bank of Africa's branch in Bloemfontein in the Orange Free State. He was joined by his fiancée Mabel, and they were married in Cape Town. The following year, on the 3rd of January, 1892, their first son, John Ronald, was born, followed a year later by Hilary Arthur. In 1895, when John was three, Mabel took the children to England, but before her husband could join them, he died of complications following rheumatic fever, leaving Mabel alone and penniless in England with two small children.

Mabel was obliged to move back to Birmingham to live with her parents and soon after moved to a then-rural suburb of that city, called Sarehole at the time. She chose to educate her boys at home, and John, or Ronald, as he was called at home, had an almost idyllic childhood, exploring the countryside, drawing, and reading from an early age. He showed a keen interest in languages, and his mother began to teach him Latin, as well as botany and a love of plants. Her financial situation deteriorated further when she broke with her Protestant family by converting to Catholicism. She also suffered from diabetes in a period before the discovery of insulin, so she knew her life would be short. To protect her sons after her death, she made her friend and spiritual guide, Father Francis Xavier Morgan, their legal guardian, and as she had anticipated, when John was 12, she died at the age of just 34. Father Francis helped place Tolkien in the private King Edward's School, where he joined the cadets and took part in the Coronation Parade for King George V in 1910.

Tolkien already showed the active imagination and creativity that would mark his work and became interested in invented languages, poetry, and Pre-Raphaelite art, which was well represented in the Birmingham Museum and Art Gallery. Before going up to Oxford, he spent the summer hiking in Switzerland, a trip that, like many parts of his life, would be woven into his writing. At Oxford, he attended Exeter College, beginning in Classics but transferring to English Language and Literature, and graduating with a first in 1915.

When he was 16, Tolkien met the 19-year-old Edith Mary Bratt, also an orphan but a Protestant. When Father Francis discovered the romance, he insisted that Tolkien agree to break off all contact with her until he was 21. Besides the religious difference, Father Francis believed the romance interfered with Tolkien's studies. Remarkably, Tolkien agreed and scrupulously kept his word, with just one breach, but on the evening of his 21st birthday, he wrote to Edith and asked her to marry him. Despite having become engaged to someone else, she immediately broke it off and agreed to marry Tolkien. They were married three years later, but Tolkien remained a devout Catholic for all his life.

When World War I broke out, Tolkien was still at Oxford, and he violated the social convention of those nationalistic times by continuing at University and completing his degree. However, immediately upon graduation, family pressure forced him to enlist, and he joined the Lancashire Fusiliers and began military training. In 1916, less than three months after his wedding, he was sent to France, whereas a junior officer, he was placed in charge of a group of working-class men. Tolkien could not adapt to the role of commander and leader, having more sympathy for the plight of the men under him and contempt for those who relished giving orders. He and his men were sent to the Battle of the Somme, where 800,000 men were to die, but before he joined them, he was invalided back to England with Trench Fever, a very common bacterial disease transmitted by lice, which were rampant in the trenches.

Tolkien joined Edith in her cottage in the village of Little Haywood, Staffordshire, and it was there that he began to write. During the remaining years of the war, as his health returned, he resumed duties at his Regiment's base, rising to the rank of lieutenant. Demobbed at the end of the war, he worked for a time on the letter 'W' for the Oxford Dictionary before bypassing several ranks of junior professor to be appointed in 1920 as Reader in English Literature at the University of Leeds. There he became an authority on Middle English (the form spoken between 1066 and 1500). In 1925 he became a professor of Anglo-Saxon at Pembroke College, Oxford - a post he was to hold for the next 20 years. There he translated and became an authority on the Old English epic poem Beowulf, becoming famous among students for his dramatic performances of that poem as an integral part of his lectures on it. In 1945 he took another professorship at Merton College, still at Oxford, and he remained there until his retirement in 1959. Throughout those years, he and Edith lived quietly in Oxford, raising four children.

Tolkien loved entertaining his children with fantasy, and he also lived a rich internal fantasy life, playfully inventing his own languages.

He blended his academic knowledge with his fantasies to create his first book, written for children, called The Hobbit. It was published in 1937, and Tolkien never expected it to sell well. The sources and inspirations of his writing were immense, ranging from the adventure stories of his childhood; the fairy stories of the Scottish collector Andrew Lang; the writing of William Morris; the art of the Pre-Raphaelites; Old English and Germanic mythology; and the practices of Catholicism.

The book, in fact, sold well from the beginning and appealed to adults as well as children. Its steady sales led his publisher to ask for a sequel, which Tolkien finally produced for them in the three-volume work Lord of the Rings, published in 1954 and 1955. He had originally intended another children's book, but as he wrote, it became more complex and serious, speaking in the end to an adult audience. With the rise of the counter-culture in the 1960's the books became cult classics, widely read and discussed among the psychedelic generation, to the bemusement of the academic Tolkien, who had his phone-number de-listed to avoid the excessive attention of his many fans.

He would have preferred to have spent his retirement riding his bicycle through the lanes of the rural England he loved, but fame had more appeal for Edith, so they spent extended periods at the luxury Miramar Hotel in the coastal resort town of Bournemouth, where Edith could enjoy a full social life among genteel society. After her death in 1971, Tolkien returned to Oxford, where Merton College gave him rooms, and he could once again live the quiet academic life. Less than two years later, on the 2nd of September, 1973, he died.

After his death, his son Christopher helped complete and publish Quenta Silmarillion, a collection of fantasy legends that Tolkien had worked on for most of his life.

His Legacy

It is remarkable that a quiet academic of philology and extinct languages could have created the modern genre of fantasy novels, but that is exactly what Tolkien did with his novels. He tapped into a sense of loss for ancient ways and for an England whose last traces were rapidly disappearing under the industrial landscape of Britain. He shared with Carl Jung an ability to bring to life the archetypes of the unconscious, and his imaginary languages opened psychic doorways for him into the imaginary world of their speakers - which turned out to be worlds that millions wanted to inhabit by immersing themselves in the books, films and fandom surrounding Bilbo Baggins, Gandalf and the Dark Lord Sauron.

Sites to Visit

- Tolkien and Edith share a grave in Wolvercote Cemetery, Oxford.
- There is a blue plaque at 20 Northmoor Road in North Oxford, where he lived from 1930 to 1947, and at 76 Sandfield Road, Headington, Oxford, where he lived from 1953 to 1968.
- There are additional blue plaques at or near to locations where he lived in Birmingham, particularly 4 Highfield Road, Edgbaston, where he lived in 1910/11 and at the Hotel Miramar, East Overcliff Drive, Bournemouth, where he and Edith stayed in room 205 for long periods after his retirement.

Further Research

Despite Tolkien's opposition to dramatic versions of his works and his criticism of scripts sent to him while still alive, numerous film versions of his stories have been made, including an animated version of The Hobbit in 1977, an animated version of portions of Lord of the Rings in 1978 and most famously, Peter Jackson's live and computer-generated versions of both stories, filmed in New Zealand and released between 2001 and 2014. His early life and love story with Edith was also made into a film in 2019.

There are numerous biographies available, including:

- J.R.R. Tolkien: A Biography, by Humphrey Carpenter and J.R.R. Tolkien (1977)
- Tolkien: How an Obscure Oxford Professor Wrote The Hobbit and Became the Most Beloved Author of the Century, by Devin Brown (2014)
- Tolkien, by Raymond Edwards (2015)
- The Road to Middle-Earth: How J.R.R. Tolkien Created a New Mythology, by Tom Shippey (3rd edition 2003)

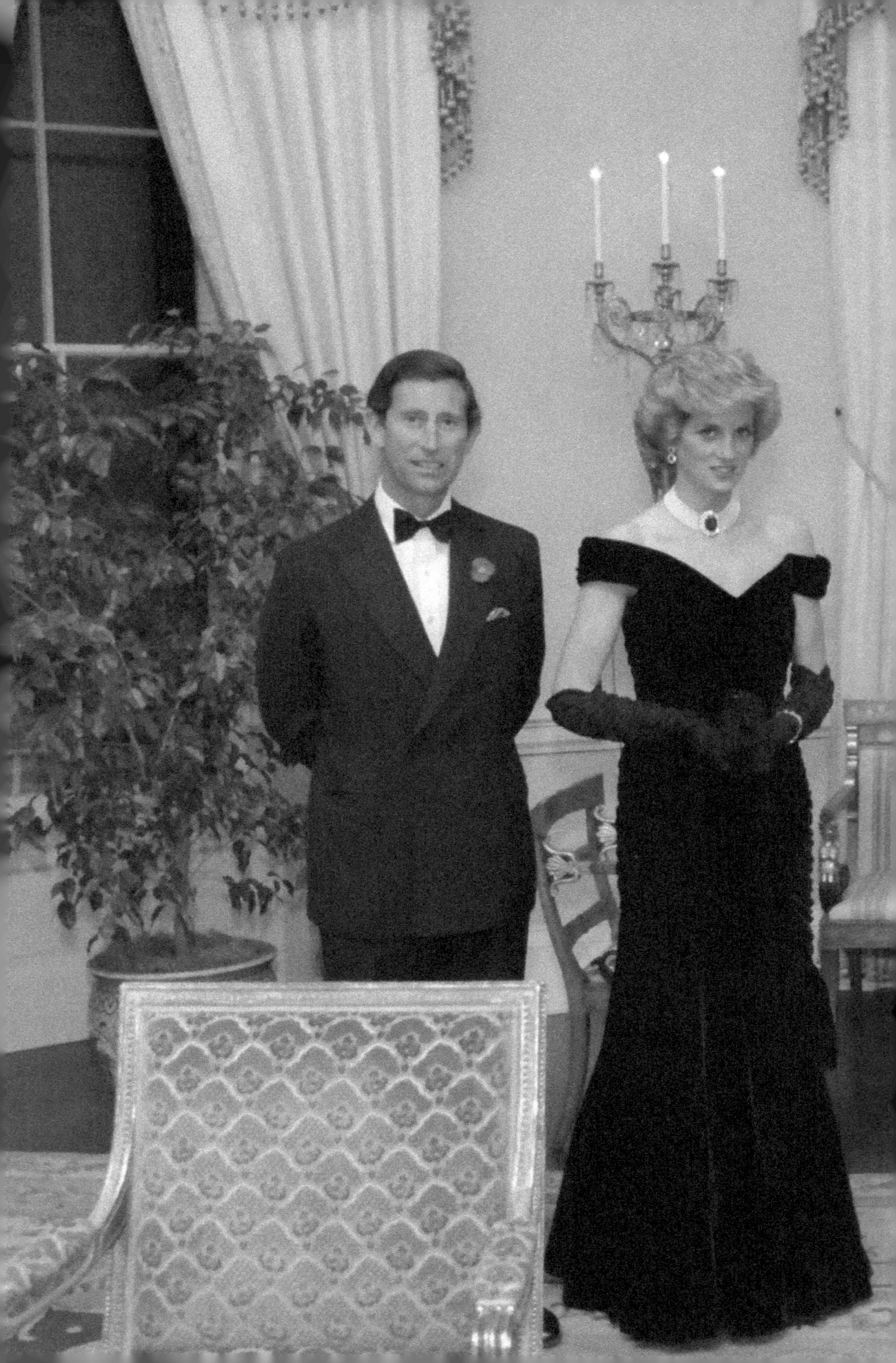

PRINCESS DIANA
The People's Princess

Key Facts

- Born 1961 – died 1997
- Married at 19 to Prince Charles, heir to the British throne
- Separated and divorced after a tumultuous marriage
- Died in a car crash in Paris

Known as the People's Princess, Diana Spencer was born into one of England's most prestigious families, and was brought up in a conventional aristocratic fashion, showing no particular aptitudes or talents. She was chosen as suitable to marry Charles, Prince of Wales, the heir to the British throne while still a teenager. The fairy-tale wedding received global attention, as did the marriage, and she gave birth to two sons, ensuring a stable future for the monarchy. Within a few years, the pressures of Palace life, marriage to an older man, intense media scrutiny, and the existence of Charles' mistress, Camilla Parker Bowles, led to a separation and later divorce. She became the most popular member of the Royal Family, and her sudden death in a car accident triggered an enormous outpouring of public grief. Her sons continued her modernization of the British monarchy, marrying genuine commoners.

The Spencer family is one of the most prestigious families in Britain, with strong historic associations to the various Royal Families going back centuries. Edward John Spencer had five children with his first wife, Frances, the daughter of an Irish Peer. Their daughter Diana Frances Spencer was born on the 1st of July 1961, in Park

House, Sandringham, Norfolk. Her grandmothers on both sides had been ladies-in-waiting to the Queen Mother, whose daughter Elizabeth sits on the British throne.

When Diana was seven, her parents separated, probably because Frances had been unable to produce the necessary male heir – their only boy child had died shortly after birth a year before Diana was born, and her gender was a disappointment to her father in particular. After the divorce, her father fought for full custody, which he won, with the support of his ex-wife's mother, Baroness Fermoy. Diana was raised by her father at Park House, and then in 1976, when he inherited the title 8th Earl Spencer, the family moved to the family seat, Althorp. The estate has been in the family for 500 years. The following year he married the daughter of Dame Barbara Cartland – Raine, Countess of Dartmouth.

Diana attended all-girl boarding schools from the age of nine, but she was not academic. Instead, she showed some talent in music, dance, and swimming. In 1978 she spent a year at a finishing school in Switzerland, l'Institut Alpin Videmanette, and when she returned to London, her mother installed her in a flat she owned, in the company of two school friends. With little need to be self-sufficient, she dabbled at cooking school, taught dancing, hosted parties, and worked as a pre-school playgroup assistant and then as a nursery school teacher's assistant. For her 18th birthday, her mother gave her a flat in the Earl's Court area of London, where she lived with flatmates.

Charles, Prince of Wales, is the heir-apparent to the British throne, as the oldest son of Elizabeth, the reigning queen. He was born in 1948 and became the Prince of Wales in 1958. Before taking the throne, it was expected that he would marry and produce an heir, preferably a male. However, breeding royal families is not unlike breeding thoroughbred horses. A suitable mate must be fertile and of good blood but not too closely related. In the late 20th century, the pool was small, and what European royalty remained was not likely to be welcome in a country that had introduced royalty from outside on several occasions. Breeding too close was not desirable, yet a good bloodline was essential. A great deal of speculation swirled around the Prince as he entered his twenties – and then approached thirty.

In the late seventies, the Prince was dating Diana's older sister, Sarah, when he first saw Diana, a schoolgirl of 16 to his 28 years. Already Lady Diana, and with impeccable credentials from the Spencer family, she seemed a suitable choice. The Queen Mother had made it known she wanted Charles to choose from the family of her close friend, Baroness Fermoy, Diana's grandmother. Invitations to polo weekends were followed by time on the Royal Yacht at Cowes. Then came the 'meet the folks' weekend at Balmoral Castle, the Queen's Scottish residence, in November of 1980. Diana was 19 years old, and no doubt her head was turned by the Royal attention, even if Charles was now 32. She passed muster with the Queen, Prince Phillip, and the Queen Mother, and a few months later, on the 6th of February 1981, Charles officially proposed and was accepted.

Diana left her nursery job and moved into Buckingham Palace. The couples' first public appearance was at a charity ball at Goldsmith's Hall (home of the Worshipful Company of Goldsmiths) in March of 1981. The media went wild. That summer, the perfect fairy-tale wedding took place in St Paul's Cathedral, with Diana in a £9,000 dress, before an international audience estimated at 750 million watching live on television. 600,000 people lined the streets to see an awkward, shy girl become Queen-to-be. The event was turned into Cinderella for the 20th century, the Prince who plucked a commoner from the crowd, but Diana was far from 'common.' In reality, she was from a powerful family of aristocrats and a member of the peerage. The hope was that the future king, seen as distant and aloof, would be humanized by the marriage, beyond its practical function in continuing the lineage.

The early years could hardly have been better. Their first child, Prince William, was born in 1982, and a second son, Prince Harry, in 1984. The royal lineage was assured, and it seemed that the fairy-tale had come true. The British and Commonwealth public adored their young Princess, and her warm, open style endeared her to them. British royalty enjoyed a period of enormous interest and popularity. Lady Diana was almost certainly in love with her Prince. The Prince, too, was in love – but not with Diana.

In 1971 Charles had met Camilla Shand, a minor aristocrat of his own age. Their relationship was never made public, and it is unclear if a serious attempt to marry took place at that time. It is, however, clear that it would have been, for numerous reasons, unacceptable inside the Palace. It remained an on-and-off relationship through the 1970s, and Camilla married, becoming Camilla Parker Bowles, but their relationship was almost certainly active before the wedding and certainly afterward. By 1985 the incompatibility between the naïve, fresh young Princess and the 'old-fogey' Prince was apparent. Charles had himself a full-blown royal mistress, a tradition as old as royalty itself.

But Diana was not a conventional Princess and not prepared to accept a sham marriage. She began an affair with a cavalry officer, Major James Hewitt. There were episodes of hysteria, bulimia, cutting, and even suicide attempts. The media moved in with exposés and secret interviews. There were attempts at reconciliation, but the tabloids were filled with revelation after revelation and tapes of intimate phone calls. In December 1992, John Major, the Prime Minister, read a statement to the House of Commons that the couple had reached an 'amicable separation.'

Diana had married before she had grown up, but she did grow up and took her life into her own hands. She took voice coaching to improve her public speaking, went to the gym to stay in shape, and raised her sons in a warm, modern way. Throughout the 1990s, she and the Prince provided endless fodder for the media and gossip columnists. The public fell into two camps – those who saw her as juvenile and possibly mentally ill and those who saw her as a victim of an arranged marriage with a cold man and a ruthless palace machine.

A divorce was finalized in August 1996. Diana received a lump sum settlement of £17 million and an annual income of £400,000. She was distressed when stripped of her title, Her Royal Highness, and became simply Diana, Princess of Wales. She continued to live in an apartment in Kensington Palace.

Throughout her marriage, Diana had been active as the patron of many charities. This is seen as an important function of modern royalty in Britain, and she became deeply involved in HIV/AIDS, cancer, and especially with landmines, where her involvement was instrumental in raising public awareness of this issue and creating an international ban on the use of anti-personnel landmines. As she matured, her public image strengthened, and her influence on style and fashion was considerable. At the same time, her life was an endless source of lurid media interest, with the invasive photographs and gossip that had dogged her marriage continuing after it.

Around the time of the divorce, Diana began a relationship with a British-Pakistani heart surgeon, Hasnat Khan. He was a private man, who wanted no publicity, but friends described him as the love of Diana's life. When they broke up in 1997, she almost immediately began dating Dodi Fayed, the son of Mohamed Al-Fayed, owner at the time of Harrods Department Store. They met when she was spending the summer with her sons at Al-Fayed's home in the south of France. Gossip and intimate photographs appeared in the press, with rumors of an engagement, but in August of 1997, while the couple was staying at the Ritz hotel in Paris, tragedy struck. Their driver was attempting to elude paparazzi and crashed into the wall of the Pont de l'Alma tunnel. Diana, Dodi, and the driver were all killed.

Dodi's grief-stricken father, and others, claimed the accident was a planned murder, but evidence of this was never found. Diana's funeral was a moment of public mourning on an epic scale. The hearse traveled from the service in Westminster Abbey to a private burial on the grounds of Althorp, on a carpet of flowers thrown by a public swept up in an orgy of grief.

In 2005 Charles and Camilla married. Diana's sons grew up to be the most ordinary of princes, following the path she had created for them. Both married true commoners and lived lives very different from the crushing formality their mother had fought against.

Sites to Visit

- Althorp, the Spencer family home in Northamptonshire, 75 miles northwest of London, is open to visitors during July and August. The memorial to Diana is not open to the public, and the reception center closed in 2013. Displays of memorabilia and clothing are created from time to time.

- Kensington Palace, where Diana lived, is today the home of Charles and Camilla. Situated in Kensington Palace Gardens, London W8, parts of the Palace and the gardens are open to the public.
- There is a Memorial Fountain in Hyde Park, London.

Further Research

- Diana: Princess of Wales, by Audrey Daly and Tim Graham
- Diana: Finally, the Complete Story, by Sarah Bradford
- Diana: Her True Story – in Her Own Words, by Andrew Morton
- Remembering Diana: A Life in Photographs
- Queen of People's Hearts: The Life and Mission of Diana, Princess of Wales, by Michael W. Simmons

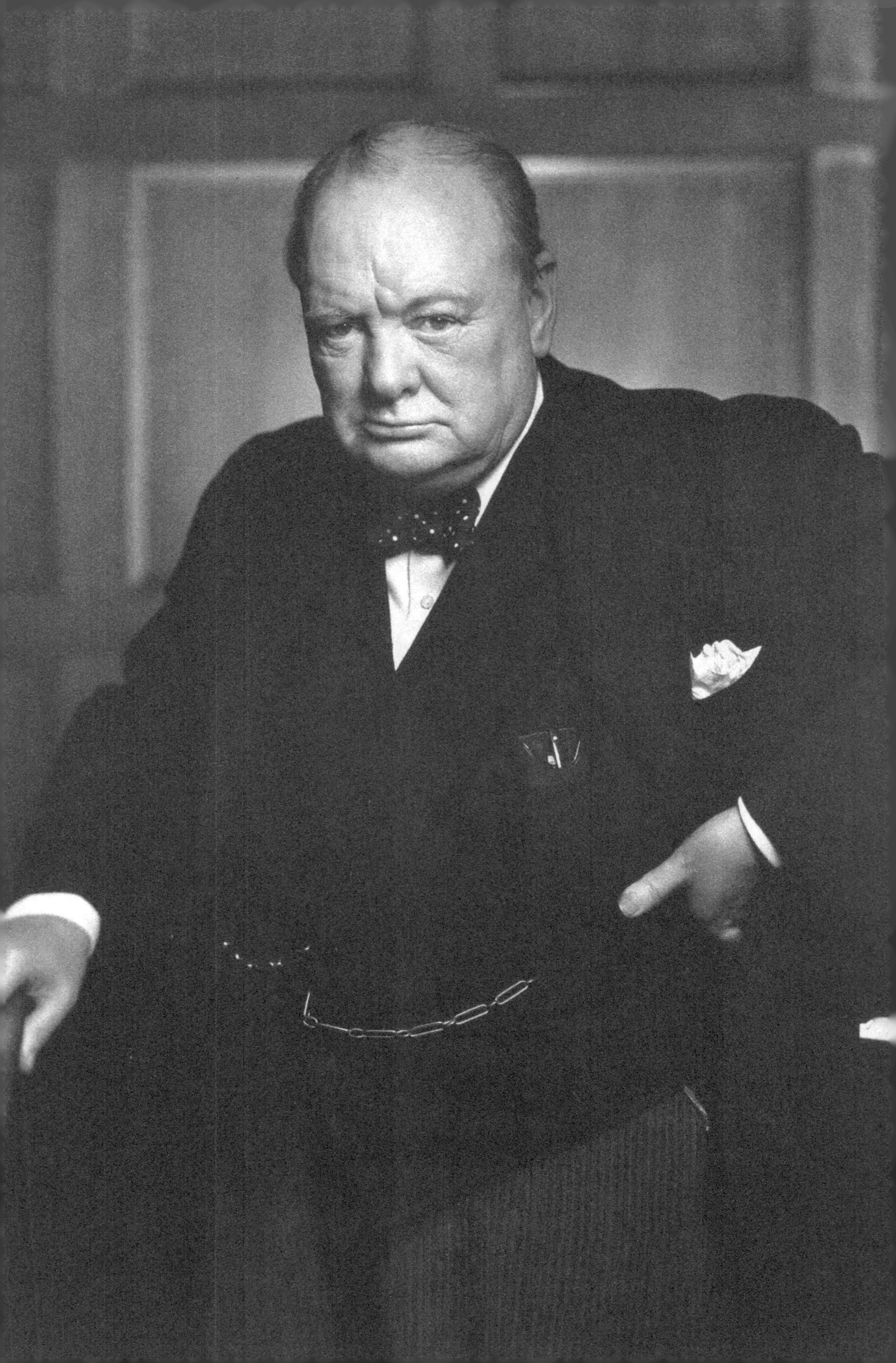

SIR WINSTON CHURCHILL
The Last English Lion

Key Facts

- Born November 30th, 1874 at Blenheim Palace, died January 24th 1965 in London
- From a long line of Churchill heroes dating back to the first Duke of Marlborough
- Member of Parliament for 55 Years
- Prime Minister twice, most famously during most of World War II (not all)
- Won Nobel Prize of Literature

We have saved the best, for last. In multiple surveys and in the eyes of many modern historians, the greatest 'Briton' who ever lived was Sir Winston Churchill, the Prime Minister to led Britain to victory through World War II. Churchill was a product of the late Victorian age and had an attitude and bearing to match. He was even out of place well into the 20th century. He was a man who was both full of his own self-regard - that he was destined for greatness - and also a gifted writer, politician, and family man. Looking at him through the lens of the 21st century, he's also become a controversial figure.

When Winston was born, he was not destined for any particular greatness. His father was the 'second son' of the Duke of Marlborough. So, while his older brother would inherit the title and Blenheim Palace, Churchill's father, Randolph Churchill, had to make his own way in life. Still, he managed to marry the glamorous Jennie Jerome and make a promising career in politics. But they were never rich, by British aristocracy standards. Winston was born at Blenheim Palace on November 30th, 1874, when Jennie and Randolph were visiting. It was a suitably grand birthplace for someone who was convinced of his own greatness his entire life.

Churchill's childhood was like that of most late-Victorian aristocrats. His parents ignored him mostly while they did other things, and he was raised by a nanny (whom he adored). When he was seven, he was shipped off to boarding school. He was a terrible student, and his father did not have high hopes for his prospects and just assumed he would join the military.

Which he eventually did. But this was the day when you had to buy your commission in the military. Still, Churchill attended Sandhurst but did not distinguish himself much (and his father complained that he was so terrible, he was shunted to the calvary, which cost him more to maintain).

Throughout his childhood and early adulthood, Winston craved positive attention from his father, whom he greatly admired (and thought a brilliant politician). But he never got it; Winston always seemed to be a disappointment to him.

Upon leaving Sandhurst, Churchill began his army career. As an officer at the height of Victorian Imperialism, he saw action in many key wars - like in India, Afghanistan, Sudan, South Africa. He gained a reputation as a 'medal chaser', someone who sought glory in battle to burnish his own reputation. While on his various missions abroad, Churchill began writing about his adventures, which eventually became extremely popular and more lucrative than his military career. By the time he went to South Africa to cover the Boer Wars, he had gone as a civilian covering it rather than a soldier fighting it.

Still, he was captured and became a prisoner of war. When he managed to escape and then traverse across several hundred miles of enemy territory undetected to the safety of the British lines, the eventual story he sold turned him into a sensation in the British Empire. This 'bright young thing,' returned to Britain a hero, and with the guidance of his mother, cannily turned his fame into getting elected into Parliament.

His father, always critical of him, was already dead by this point, dying rather young, most likely from syphilis. Churchill would try and measure up to his father's life for the rest of his days.

Political Career

After his maiden speech to Parliament, Churchill rose quickly in the political ranks. He was a capable politician, and while his political leanings had a tendency to change with the winds, he knew how to operate in the Westminster establishment.

In quick succession, he became a cabinet minister at 33 (the youngest is almost 100 years), then Home Secretary, then became First Lord of the Admiralty, responsible for essentially running Britain's navy - a position of enormous Imperial influence.

We're not going to go into great details of his various political stances and key votes - there's just too much to talk about there as he had such a long career as an MP. But essentially, Winston was occasionally on the right side (supporting Irish Home Rule, for example) of history and the wrong side of history (not supporting Indian Home Rule, for example). He was never particularly political consistent.

World War I interrupted his rapid rise. While he was a popular and competent First Lord of the Admiralty (the Navy loved him), he was a key planner of the Gallipoli disaster and took most of the public blame when it failed (the later inquiry somewhat exonerated him, but the public sentiment stuck).

Feeling defeated, he resigned from the government and signed up with the army and fought on the front lines of World War I as an officer. He is widely considered to have redeemed himself in his service at the front. So much that he was brought back into government as the munitions minister, finishing the war with his reputation largely restored.

The Poor Aristocrat

Winston spent the 1920s continuing his political rise, at one point becoming the Chancellor of the Exchequer, the second most powerful position in the British government (the Chancellor controls the purse strings). But before that, he spent a bit of time out of government and wrote his bestselling memoirs of World War I called The World Crisis. They were a bestseller.

Members of Parliament at this point in time were not paid, and maintaining an aristocratic life was expensive. The success of his journalism writing and his books became the bedrock of his expensive lifestyle (though he was always playing catchup - even after World War II). He also bought his beloved country home Chartwell in the 1920s, and this became a continual drain on his finances for the rest of his life.

The Wilderness Years 1929–1939

After the success of the 1920s, the 1930s are largely considered the 'Wilderness Years' of Churchill's career. While he remained an MP, many of his stances and causes became a public joke - he was more often on the wrong side of public opinion and was suitably ostracized by his party. He spent most of this decade out of government office. No longer the 'hot young' thing of the 1910s and 1920's, Churchill was a 'mature politician' who didn't really behave as such. Being an elder statesman didn't suit him.

So, while he continued to serve in Parliament, making unpopular speeches, he spent most of the 1930s writing an expansive biography of his illustrious ancestor, the 1st Duke of Marlborough. While writing this best-selling book (which kept his finances afloat), he began to warn of the specter of Hitler and Nazi Germany. He was widely considered a crank, as there was no public appetite to confront Germany on any matter of consequence. He made speech after speech showing that Germany was re-arming and had intentions of expanding.

They were ignored by the British government. He was vehemently opposed to appeasement and warned against it. War was unavoidable, and when it started, Churchill was asked to return to his old position of First Lord of the Admiralty, which he did with gusto (and the Navy was pleased sending a cable to the fleet that 'Winston was back'). He wasn't even in the position for a year when Neville Chamberlain's political capital collapsed, and Churchill was asked to form a national wartime government by King George VI. Churchill always thought he was destined for glory and to save the British Empire. This was his moment.

World War II Leadership

More books, documentaries and movies have been made about Churchill's World War II leadership than anything else. His wartime premiership started with a disaster. The British Army, the ENTIRE British Army, was corralled at the beaches in Dunkirk in France and was at risk of being completely destroyed unless they could be evacuated. They were a mere 20 miles from England's shores, but the English Channel separated them. While the Dunkirk evacuation was a massive defeat for British forces, the fact that most of the troops were successfully evacuated was a victory of sorts (though, as Churchill said at the time, we will not win the war by retreats). Churchill marshaled every ship available on the South Coast of England to evacuate almost every soldier it could.

This was when he made his famous 'fight them on the beaches speech.' And this is what really singled Churchill out for historical greatness. His gift for the written and spoken word is largely what is considered to have helped Britain get through the dark days of World War II. His stirring speeches kept Britain's morale up, and the people really thought that their 'bulldog' was doing everything he could to defeat the Nazis. Britain fought the war seemingly alone for the first few years of the war (if by 'alone' you also include its vast empire). This was through Dunkirk, through the Blitz and other military disasters, but his speeches kept morale higher than it deserved to be.

Of course, the story is much more complicated than that and out of the scope of this survey. Beyond his speeches, what set Churchill apart was his simple competence. He was a capable leader of his war cabinet, and while there were massive disagreements (and resignations), he successfully led a cross-party national government through a war. He inspired his people. He made key decisions that changed the course of the war. His relationship with American President Franklin D. Roosevelt helped cement the 'special relationship' and ensure that when America did enter the war, it used Britain as its launching ground to invade Europe (and treated Britain as an equal partner rather than a vanquished ally like France).

When writing history and going into details, the myth of the 'great man of history' usually falls apart. History is a team effort. But most historians agree that having a 'Churchill' was necessary to win the war, and if he hadn't been there, the war would have gone much differently. Winston led his people to victory.

They rewarded him by chucking him out of office at the first opportunity.

Post-War Premiership

While out of office after the war, Churchill began his post-premiership career as an elder statesman. He began touring the world, getting paid to give speeches. He began writing his firsthand account of World War II (which spans to 6 volumes and over 1 million words). He was really one of the first 'post-office' politicians to make a fortune on the world stage.

Only his political career wasn't over. He remained the leader of the Conservative party, and in a masterstroke of his political skills and popularity, he managed a second term as Prime Minister from 1951-1955. He was 77 when he entered office for this second act.

This period is less remembered than his illustrious World War II premiership. Britain's political landscape had changed. The Welfare State was firmly entrenched after the establishment of the National Health Service and massive state housing projects. This period was marked by the beginning of his long decline in health. At one point, he had a stroke and almost had to leave office early. When he did finally leave office in 1955, it was largely because he had stayed on long past his sell-by date and the deference his party paid to him due to his leadership in the war.

Retirement and Death

After leaving office in 1955, he stayed on as an MP but spent less and less time in the Commons while he wrote more books. He spent his final years being feted and getting awards - at one point getting Honorary US Citizenship. When he finally died of a stroke in

1965, he was given a state funeral, a rare honor for a non-royal (the last one being in 1898).

Legacy Today

Britain, in its current form, would not exist without Churchill. It is likely Britain would have lost the war without him or at least ended up surrendering like France, becoming some sort of German puppet state. While Churchill was adamant that Britain must win the war with the help of its Empire, after the war, Britain lost its Empire.

Born an Imperialist, he led his empire to enormous victory. But the age of Imperialism was over. Britain was no longer the global power it thought it was. Churchill himself has been glorified and over-analyzed more than any other British historical figure. It's rather easy to find things you agreed with and loved about him and just as easy to find things to hate about him and criticize him about. He was not a perfect man. But he was the perfect man for the job during Britain's darkest hour.

There's a movement nowadays to ascribe our modern views of things to a man such as Churchill, but this is rather unfair. He was a product of his time - an Imperialist, a militarist, a racist. That's the way most people in the British aristocracy were in the late-Victorian age when Britain's Imperial swagger was at its full height (not that any of that is a good thing by any means). We can continue to argue the details, but one thing is very certain: he was there when Britain needed him. Outsized figures in history like him are very rare and will be rare again.

Sites to Visit

- Blenheim Palace - The room he was born in is left as it was when he was born as a bit of a shrine; there's also a small exhibition on his life.
- Grave at Bladon - He's buried in the small churchyard at Bladon Church, down the road from Blenheim Palace.

- Houses of Parliament - He loved the Commons more than anything; there's a statue of him at the door and a big statue outside.
- Cabinet War Rooms - See the place where he led the war, left as it was when the war ended.
- Chartwell - Churchill's beloved house, on display largely as it was when he was alive. The landscape was designed by him, the brick walls built by him. Check out the artist studio, where you can see several hundred of his paintings.

Further Research

Churchill is probably one of the most written about historical figures after Hitler. Here's a rundown of a few very good books:

- Churchill: Walking with Destiny - A good single-volume biography.
- The Last Lion - An expansive three-volume biography started by William Manchester and finished by Paul Reid.

Churchill wrote millions of words himself during his lifetime. His most well-known works were:

- The World Crisis (World War I Memoirs)
- His World War II Memoirs
- A History of English Speaking Peoples
- Marlborough: His Life and Times

Movies about Churchill:

- Young Winston
- The Gathering Storm
- Into the Storm
- The Darkest Hour
- Churchill's Secret

About Anglotopia

Anglotopia.net is the world's largest website for people who love Britain. Founded in 2007, it has grown to be the biggest community of passionate Anglophiles all around the world. With daily updates covering British Culture, History, and Travel, Anglotopia is the place to get your British Fix and learn about all things British! Search for Anglotopia on the Apple App Store and Google Play Store to get daily British stuff on your smartphone.

https://anglotopia.net
https://londontopia.net